The Parables of Jesus

Strategic Stories that Change the Thoughts of Your Heart

John H. Voss

The Parables of Jesus: Strategic Stories that Change the Thoughts of Your Heart

ISBN: Softcover 978-1-955581-24-0

Copyright © 2021 by John H. Voss

All rights reserved. No part of this book may be reproduced or transmitted in any form or by any means, electronic or mechanical, including photocopying, recording, or by any information storage and retrieval system, without permission in writing from the publisher.

Parson's Porch Books is an imprint of Parson's Porch & Company (PP&C) in Cleveland, Tennessee. PP&C is an innovative organization which raises money by publishing books of noted authors, representing all genres. Its face and voice is **David Russell Tullock** (dtullock@parsonsporch.com).

Parson's Porch & Company *turns books into bread & milk* by sharing its profits with the poor.

www.parsonsporch.com

The Parables of Jesus

Contents

Preface 9
Introduction 11
Changing the Thoughts of the Heart 15
    My Personal Perspective 15
    The Strategic Purpose of the Parables 25
A New Concept of Evangelism 37
    The Parable of the Sower 37
The Concept of Faith: The Potential Growth of a Planted Seed ... 49
    The Parable of the Mustard Seed 49
    The Parable of Scattered Seed 52
A New Covenant Versus Old Religious Ritual 67
    The Parable of Unshrunk Cloth and an Old Garment 67
    The Parable of New Wine in Old Wineskins 80
A New Understanding of Grace 83
    The Parable of Workers in the Vineyard 83
A New Standard for Forgiveness 94
    The Parable of the Unforgiving Servant 100
    The Parable of the Pharisee and the Tax Collector 106
    The Parable of the Prodigal Son 111
A New Definition of Neighbor 119
    The Parable of the Good Samaritan 119
The Value of One 125
    The Parable of the Lost Sheep 125
    The Parable of the Lost Coin 132
The Value of All 135
    The Parable of the Great Supper 135

A New Level of Humility 146
    The Parable of the Lowest Seat at a Feast 146
The Priceless Value of the Kingdom 151
    The Parable of Treasure Hidden in a Field 151
    The Parable of the Pearl of Great Price 163
Spiritual Growth 173
    The Parable of the Leaven 173
Counting the Cost of Discipleship 185
    The Parable of the Tower Builder 185
    The Parable of the Warrior King 192
The Power of Persistence 195
    The Parable of a Friend at Midnight 195
    The Parable of the Persistent Widow 200
The Stewardship of Discipleship 206
    The Parable of Three Servants Given Talents 209
    The Parable of the Minas 221
    The Parable of the Unproductive Fig Tree 226
    The Parable of the Unjust Steward 230
A New Definition of Duty 236
    Parable of the Master and Servant 236
The Fallacy of Bigger is Better 242
    The Parable of the Rich Man and His Barns 242
The Fallacy of Riches versus Righteousness 247
    The Parable of the Rich Man and Lazarus 247
The Rewards of Preparation 253
    The Parable of the Wise and Watchful Servants 253
    The Parable of the Wise and Foolish Virgins 260

The Judgment Parables 268
    The Parable of the Weeds among Good Plants 269
    The Parable of the Fishing Net 275
    The Parable of Two Sons: One Obeys and One Does Not . 277
    The Parable of the Wicked Tenants 282
    The Parable of the Fig Tree 288
    The Parable of the Sheep Gate 295
    The Parable of the Sheep and Goats 302
Conclusion 315

Preface

"Repent, for the kingdom of heaven is at hand." These nine intriguing words are the key to a deeper understanding of the ministry of John the Baptist, the life and work of Jesus, and the theology of the New Testament. Yet, their importance is often unrecognized. When God sent His Son into the world to be the savior of mankind and establish a new covenant with believers through faith in Jesus, He used only these nine words to usher in this life-transforming divine revelation, spoken only by John the Baptist and Jesus. Of all the manifestations of divine power that could have been employed to herald this new covenant (which is the basis of the New Testament), God used only one short sentence consisting of nine simple words to accomplish His purpose. That is an amazing New Testament concept.

Repentance has long been understood as a fundamental turning in direction, mainly from bad conduct to more godly behavior. However, it involves far more than that, and a deeper understanding of Jesus' ministry hinges on one's deeper understanding of the spiritual power of repentance. This introductory quote from my earlier book is worthy of sharing here:

> "Repentance was not solely about ceasing prior bad behavior. Instead, its greater meaning involved turning away from self-righteousness under the ancient legal codes of Israel and turning to righteousness based on faith in the redemptive life and work of Jesus alone. In order to accomplish that, centuries of deeply entrenched religious legal standards, traditions of the elders, social standards and attitudes, and the very order of Jewish society would have to change. It would involve the greatest physical challenge and the greatest danger one could face, but the spiritual rewards would also be the greatest anyone could experience."

If entering into the kingdom of heaven depended on this magnitude of repentance, then Jesus would have woven His view of repentance into all of His words and works, and I began to study His methods of doing that. I first explored the depth of His views in a study of the Sermon on the Mount entitled "A Sermon on a Mountainside: Repentance and the Birth of Christianity." This book on the parables continues that study by examining how Jesus strategically used parables to foster a deeper understanding of personal spiritual change. A third book will explore the impact of Jesus' miracles and how they, too, revealed His belief in the need for spiritual repentance.

Hopefully, when this three-volume study is concluded, greater insight into the power and magnitude of spiritual repentance demanded by Jesus will emerge and provide an informative and inspiring examination of this important New Testament doctrine.

This work has been spiritually and physically challenging and required considerable time and effort. Yet, I have been greatly rewarded by a deeper understanding of the parables and a profound admiration of both Jesus' ability as a teacher and as a master strategist who skillfully used the simplest means to accomplish the greatest impact and change. The parables are not simple spiritual stories; rather, they are literary masterpieces that were carefully and strategically devised to encourage introspective thought about the need for change in one's personal attitudes and actions. They are spiritual seeds carefully planted by Jesus that matured into Christianity.

I am not a Bible scholar, nor am I adept with either Hebrew or Greek. Word resources that were used are available to any inquiring Bible student, and scripture references are from the New King James translation. I am especially grateful to Jeffery McClendon for his excellent work as a proofreader and editor and Joshua Lott for technical and computer assistance.

I did not intend to write a scholarly study of each parable, but rather a logical explanation of the parable's background, how Jesus strategically used it to encourage life-changing thought, and how each parable continues to challenge Christians today. I hope it is meaningful.

Introduction

I gently knocked on the door and quietly entered her room, having been told by the nurse what to expect. Although I was the hospital's staff attorney, on certain occasions I was asked to meet with a patient as a minister if the hospital chaplain were not available or the patient's pastor could not be contacted, and this was one of those moments. She was an elderly, frail, black lady in her final hours of life. She constantly moved around on her bed in obvious discomfort, mumbled incoherently, and seemed unaware of her surroundings. But, she had asked for a minister, and I now stood by her bedside.

I had no idea what to say. I did not know if she could even hear or understand me. I stood there for a moment looking at this helpless woman, sensing her pain and her fear. Suddenly, as if by divine inspiration, I leaned over and touched her forehead and began gently stroking her brow. Her weary eyes slowly focused on my face.

"Do you have a good imagination?" I softly asked. She looked at me, uncertain about my question, and slowly nodded her head.

"Good," I said, "because I want to tell you a story from the Bible, and I want you to imagine that this is happening to you right now." She slightly nodded her head in agreement.

"Imagine that you are a little lamb, and you are alone, frightened, and do not know what will happen to you. But off in the distance you see someone, and He is coming toward you. You look closer, and you realize that it is your shepherd—the one you have been following—and He is a good shepherd, and He cares for you. He has left all his other sheep just to look for you."

I have no idea what she saw in her imagination, but I remember the intense look on her face and the firm tone of her voice. "I see Him," she slowly mumbled. "I sure do...I see Him." As I continued to stroke her brow, she stopped moving around in the bed and seemed to relax and breathe easier.

"He sees you now, and He is here with you. He is bending down and picking you up in His arms to take you with Him."

Her eyes became fixed and focused, as if looking past me at something distant, and she exclaimed, "I feel His arms. I surely do. He is holding me tight and safe."

I continued, "Your Shepherd is Jesus, and He is taking you to a green pasture beside still water, and He is going to personally make sure you are safe and cared for. You have no reason to fear. Your Good Shepherd is holding you."

With supreme serenity, she said, "I see Him, I feel Him with me, holding me in His arms, and I'm not afraid." She lay there motionless with her eyes closed, and then she quietly went to sleep. About four hours later, she died peacefully.

Without knowing what I was doing, the Holy Spirit used me to provide this dear lady with a priceless gift in the final moments of her life. Through this parable, I showed her a new way to think about Jesus, and she found rest in His eternal peace. For her, the parable of the shepherd who would leave ninety-nine other sheep and go look for one little lost lamb became real.

It did so for me, also. Pain shows no partiality and neither does the grace and peace of God. If one ponders that truth, the eternal beauty and transforming power of a simple parable can forever change his understanding of the love and mercy of God, and that was Jesus' intent.

Jesus came into this world in order to reveal a dynamic new spiritual realm. It is unlike anything one has ever known and can transform not just an individual believer's life, but also the life of mankind as a whole. In order to enter this spiritual kingdom, one must first experience a change in their emotional and spiritual attitudes toward God, their fellowman, and life in general. Jesus, as had John the Baptist before Him, envisioned that change occurring through repentance.

But what is repentance? Traditionally, repentance is viewed as discontinuing sinful behavior, professing Jesus as savior, joining the church through baptism, and then attending church regularly. But repentance is much more than that. Repentance involves a fundamental redirection of a person's beliefs, values, and the overall direction of life. The new life that one turns to is far more consequential than the life he turned from.

Consider this analogy: While driving, an individual realizes he is headed in the wrong direction and makes a complete turnaround. The direction and intent of the journey are no longer the same. But, after a change of direction, what if no effort is made to proceed in the new direction that has been chosen? Granted, the wrong direction is no longer being pursued, and that is good, but neither is the new direction, and that is not good. Repentance is both turning from the wrong direction away from God, in every facet of life, and instead making a complete turnaround toward God and going the distance in the new direction that one's life is now headed. The full meaning of repentance is found in the good experiences of the new direction, which will far outweigh the bad experiences of the old.

But not everyone sees repentance in that manner, and that is unfortunate. Many Christians live a spiritually unfulfilled and frustrating life because they are like the automobile driver. They may have turned around and are no longer headed in the wrong direction, but they are just sitting still with no new and meaningful spiritual direction or purpose in their life. That is not the meaning of repentance. Repentance is directly connected to the covenant relationship that one enters into with Jesus. It is a life transforming commitment to Him in which His life, His work, and His blessings become those of the believer.

Repentance produces a new form and capacity of life—a life lived in the image and likeness of Jesus—because it is His nature in the believer through a covenant of faith. It encompasses new values, new attitudes, a new relationship with God, a new attitude toward one's fellowman, and new redeeming love and appreciation for all people of different races, creeds, and colors. It involves a new direction and purpose for life manifested in new relationships, new desires, and new activities. It is life with a new spiritual passion, new energy, and new goals. It is impossible to experience repentance of this nature while sitting still and doing nothing. Repentance means becoming both a "new creature in Christ" (II Cor. 5:17) and a "doer of the word" and will of God and not just a hearer only (Matt. 7:21). According to Jesus, the kingdom of heaven is given only to those with this kind of spiritual desire and purpose for life.

That is what Jesus wanted the entire nation of Israel to consider. In terms of fulfilling their divine purpose as God's nation of priests and representing His redeeming love to the world, where was life under the rigid, unyielding, religious law of Israel taking them? All that the law had produced was coldness of heart, exclusion of others, obsession with earthly riches, self-righteousness through fanatical obedience to impersonal law, and none of that was good in Jesus' opinion. Repentance would mean a total transformation of all those attitudes and a completely new direction and purpose in a personal covenant with Him of redeeming love for all others.

But how could He get people to re-think religious concepts and beliefs that were centuries old? He could not destroy the law, and He could not compel them to view life differently through divine force. However, He could introduce them to a new way of thinking about themselves, their mission, their relationship with God and others, and their spiritual values in life. He would do that through carefully chosen parables that would simply make them think differently.

Biblical writers have differing opinions regarding the exact number of parables due to differing views about the criteria for a parable. It is not my intent to engage in an exegetical examination of them, but rather to look at these stories as unique, masterful, literary gems that were used to transform the thoughts of God's covenant people. I hope this book will draw the reader closer to the heart and mind of Jesus and will enhance the understanding of repentance.

Changing the Thoughts of the Heart

My Personal Perspective

Regarding the impact of an individual's deepest thoughts, the Bible states, "For as he thinks in his heart, so is he" (Prov. 23:7). Thoughts are ordinarily associated with the mind, not necessarily the heart. But, in a broad sense, the mind deals with analytical ideas and determines our actions. The heart, figuratively speaking, is the seat of our emotions and determines our feelings and attitudes toward both life and others. Thoughts of the mind are often immediate, changing, and occasionally of short duration. Thoughts of the heart are deep-seated, long-term, and form the basis of character and personality. They are also the basis of our most personal thoughts about others. Thoughts of the mind can change rather quickly based on new facts, whereas thoughts of the heart can take years to change, or even a lifetime. Indeed, as a man thinks about life, God, and his fellowman within the secret confines of his heart, so he is for a considerable portion of his life. A person can change their mind fairly easily and quickly. But, changing the thoughts of their heart is something, quite often, that only God can do.

Although the parables are fascinating topics of biblical study, they are as relevant today as when first spoken. Jesus' parables are literary gems that are ageless in their application and unmatched in their ability to challenge and change human thought. A modest comparison between the attitudes of Jesus' time and those of today reveal their eternal relevancy.

For example, there were three characteristics that were generally viewed as attributes of a righteous life in Jewish society: the regularity and sincerity of one's prayers, the generosity of one's charitable deeds for others, and the obvious financial success and blessings that one enjoyed. In many ways, each of these became an obsession with many people, especially the Pharisees and even prominent rabbis. As a result, prayers were often prayed openly and publicly in order to be heard by others and to enhance one's personal self-righteous image. The same was true of charitable deeds, which were often done openly in order to be seen and admired by others. It was all very hypocritical, according to Jesus.

The obsession with money was perhaps even greater, and it fueled a widespread belief that God especially blessed those who were wealthy and condemned those who were not. Consequently, a general belief emerged that only the rich were considered as righteous, and they were widely admired and respected for their wealth and status with God. The poor, however, were condemned and shunned.

Jesus told a parable about a rich man and a beggar named Lazarus, who lay at the rich man's gate pleading for crumbs of food from the rich man's table but was contemptuously ignored. However, it was the poor beggar who ended up in paradise while the rich man was in torment—the exact opposite of accepted beliefs. Is that parable relevant today, or is it just a vivid and sobering picture of human need existing then?

A church member where I served as pastor had an obvious admiration for those who were blessed financially, and he openly sought them for membership. He had a quaint expression that he often used to describe their wealth and financial status: "He always carries the correct change," he would admiringly say of those with noticeable wealth. I have no recollection of him ever speaking equally as positively about someone less financially fortunate. The Gospel of Luke refers to the Pharisees, who viewed possessions as evidence of their righteousness, as "lovers of money" (Luke 16:14). Does this trait still plague the church? Yes. Is the parable of Jesus still relevant? Yes.

A man actively attended another church I served as pastor. He was successful and had accumulated modest wealth through his hard work. A bit eccentric at times, he had a peculiar habit of easing up beside me and opening his wallet in order to reveal the amount of money he was carrying. His ego was obviously stroked by my comments about his wealth and success.

I once preached a sermon about the parable of the laborers hired to work in the vineyard, and I noted with emphasis that Christians and the church are represented by those who were hired last and worked only a short time but received a full day's pay. It portrays the magnitude of God's grace, as opposed to works, in bestowing the fullness of His kingdom on those who have not earned it.

This gentleman was unable to comprehend the parable, and he vocally rejected its meaning, in effect calling it meaningless. He could not comprehend grace, for indeed he focused only on what he had earned. Whatever material blessings he possessed had been obtained by his own effort, and he viewed his spiritual blessings no differently. He had been a faithful believer for many years, seldom missed church, tithed faithfully, and performed whatever work within the church he was asked to do. To him, it was nonsense to pay someone a full day's wage for only an hour of work, and he had equal trouble believing that God's blessings were also given to those who had not earned them through faithful service. As long as I knew him, he never changed his view. In the language of the parable about the prodigal son, he was identical to the older son who had remained at home and resented the mercy and grace his father bestowed upon his brother.

There is no greater example of the continuing relevancy of the parables than in the area of human relations. The people of Israel were inculcated by generations of religious ritual to believe that they were the exclusive recipients of God's love though His covenant with them, even though they never fulfilled the covenant purpose of being God's nation of priests. As a result, other people and nations were contemptuously viewed in the most scathing way. Those labeled as sinners—anyone who did not steadfastly follow the law and religious ritual—were condemned. The diseased and infirmed, such as lepers, were unmercifully abandoned. Anyone not Jewish, which was the entire Gentile world, was viewed as inferior, and it even became unlawful to have any association with them.

But, special hatred and bitterness was meted out to the Samaritans, who lived in the central area of Israel between Judea to the south and Galilee to the north. These people were descendants of foreigners brought into Israel by the Assyrians following the conquest of northern Israel in 722 B.C. and were generally regarded as "half-breeds." Most devout Jews would have no relationships with Samaritans, referred to them as dogs, and would not journey through Samaria.

Jesus, however, specifically traveled through the region, revealed some of the greatest truths about Himself to a Samaritan woman at a well near Sychar, and used a Samaritan in His iconic parable of the "Good Samaritan." He well knew that if repentance was to be real and life changing, it must challenge and change how God's covenant people thought about others.

I have seen the parables' impact in my own life in many ways, perhaps none greater than my changed attitudes toward other people and other races. Did I read the parables and suddenly start thinking and considering situations and people differently? Not exactly. But I did read the parables early in my Christian life, and they slowly began impacting my thoughts and attitudes. I have always been intrigued by the Good Samaritan and find his willingness to go to such great personal effort and expense for another to be truly inspirational. That became magnified even more when I learned the depth of hatred that most Jews felt toward Samaritans and how the Samaritan resisted feeling that same bitterness, resorting instead to love and kindness for those who despised him.

I grew up on a farm outside of a small town in South Mississippi, and I attended public school prior to racial integration. During my first few weeks in college, I went to my first college football game and, along with other students, was in a designated-seating section shouting for my favorite team. At halftime the opposing team's band came onto the field. The band had one black member, and since this was only three years after the integration of public colleges in my state, the student section began chanting an insulting phrase about the band having a black member, using a derogatory racial epithet. Amidst all the noise, I looked behind me and saw a middle-aged black couple quietly sitting several rows back. Each of them was weeping and had tears streaming down their face.

I was almost sickened with guilt. I did not really think much about the game during the second half; I just had this deep desire to go to them and apologize. For nearly fifty years, I have wished that I had done that. I have never forgotten them. The mustard seed of personally understanding the pain of racism was planted, and it has continued to grow throughout my life. The thoughts of my heart were changing.

This was also an especially painful experience for me as a pastor. Early on I began to see the incongruity between the efforts of my denomination to annually raise funds through special offerings to support foreign missions and our own attitudes within the church about the same race of people we were sending missionaries to evangelize. I knew they would not be readily accepted as brothers and sisters in Christ and welcomed into the fellowship of the church. I became deeply troubled by that. The whole mission purpose seemed to be annually reaching some arbitrary monetary goal and not examining the attitude of our hearts about others.

It is sad, but this clash of attitudes ended my ministry as a pastor. I was blessed to serve a growing church in a thriving community where the membership had significantly increased and several new facilities had been added, including a beautiful new sanctuary. But underneath all this outward appearance of unity and growth lay a simmering problem—the attitudes of several members about people of different races and ethnic backgrounds.

The sobering reality of this first appeared when a young Filipino woman joined the church. She was married to a church member, and they both regularly attended. After she requested membership, and before she was baptized, a well-respected church member quietly asked me if I was certain about her nationality and also certain that her darker skin color was not due to another racial background. Literally, coldness swept over me. No one had to explain the intent of his question. When I answered yes, he said, "Good. I just wanted to make sure about that."

Sometime later, a young black college student started attending the church. He was a very pleasant, quiet, dignified young man and well-liked by all his college friends. I was excited to have him attending and showing interest in our church.

After he had attended a couple of weeks, an elderly man, who seldom missed attendance each Sunday, came directly to me after the morning service was dismissed, took me by my arm and physically turned me toward where the young man was standing, and pointedly asked me, "What are we going to do about him?" There are times when even preachers lose their temper, and I spun the man back around, looked him in the face, and said, "How dare you ask me a question like that at the end of a beautiful service! Let's turn and face God's pulpit, and you ask God that question!" We stared at each other, and he turned and walked away. I knew then that our joyous, happy ship of gospel truth had struck a large, cold, hidden, destructive iceberg of racial bitterness. Events would later prove the sinking feeling I felt was justified.

A few days later, one of the church's volunteer leaders asked to meet with me. Ironically, he was involved with teaching other church members the meaning of Christian discipleship. He did not mince words. Coming straight to the point, he expressed concern about the negative impact this young black student was having on the congregation. I told him that I was not aware of any negative impact, and he became very upset. He heatedly said, "I may have to work with them, and my kids may have to go to school with them, but I do not have to go to church with them!"

I quietly responded in what I thought was a sensible, reasoned manner. "I am a son of the South," I said. "I was born and raised here. My great-great-grandfather died fighting for the Confederacy in the Civil War. I have heard every racial attitude known in the South, and I have been exposed to that all of my life. But, when I became a Christian, and especially when I became a pastor, I experienced the full meaning of God's love for all people of every color. As the pastor of this church, here is what I have to ask myself: Is the gospel of Jesus Christ open to all people who quietly and reverently come here to worship? If it is not, then you are asking me to stand in the pulpit and preach a lie, and I absolutely will not do that."

Raising his voice, he said, "Well, let him go to his own church." "That is not the issue," I said. "The real issue that we must face is whether the gospel of Jesus Christ is open to him here, in this church, and in this family of believers. I will not proclaim it any other way." He left my office without saying another word.

The following Sunday, after the sermon, I invited the church family to come by the offering table as they departed and voluntarily sign a resolution clearly stating that our church welcomed all who came sincerely desiring to worship and be a part of the church fellowship. Most families signed, but others did not. Some expressed sincere appreciation that we had taken such a positive approach as a church family; others were less enthusiastic.

As I returned to my office with the resolution in hand, a young deacon quickly approached me with an obvious look of concern on his face. He said, "Please explain to me what we just did." Again, I stressed that it was a positive statement by our church family that all who truly desired to worship were welcome. He shocked me with his response. "Well, that's not what I was just told. What I heard was that all we did was throw open the church doors to Blacks and gays." I was speechless and simply wanted to weep over the gross distortion. In only a matter of minutes, the spirit of peace and unity that should be the hallmark of a church was broken by the ugliness of prejudice and racism.

Not long after those events, a situation arose that required a meeting with two families. We gathered in a conference room and, as the discussion ended, the situation of the young black visitor again arose. One of the men became very vocal. "He is tearing this church apart by coming here. People are leaving left and right." I quietly disagreed with him and again stated my point that I had made earlier to the other church leader.

This man had a more temperamental response. Jumping to his feet, he exploded in the angriest outburst I have ever seen in a church setting. Yelling at me, he said, "I'll have you know my grandfather laid the foundation of this church, and I am not going to watch it destroyed!" And I responded, "Your grandfather is not the foundation of this church. Jesus Christ is its foundation, and I will not preach the gospel any other way." He furiously left the room.

Within a few weeks, I was presented an ultimatum from the deacons asking me to resign. I could have refused, and many said I should have. I spent a lot of time in thought and prayer about the best decision that would keep me within God's will, allow me to continue to share the gospel, and keep peace within the church. My last sermon focused on the faith of Abram to leave behind the surroundings to which he had grown accustomed and journey to a new land, a new experience, and new blessings that God would show him (Gen. 12:1-3). I left behind the ministry of preaching, and I began writing. I may no longer serve an individual church congregation, but I will always serve as a pastor to the covenant church of Jesus Christ, for that is what He called me and gifted me to do. I pray that I will not fail Him.

Does the parable of the Good Samaritan still apply to current attitudes about other people and other races? If one substituted "a young black man" for "Samaritan," would it apply to the circumstances in this situation? Would it make Christians think about their attitudes toward others? Would it hopefully lead to a greater attitude of repentance in their thought process? Yes.

Jesus did not place a caveat on His parables and say that they were limited to the time and circumstances in which they were spoken. They are eternal, and they apply just as powerfully to human attitudes today as they did when He spoke to them. Jesus' ability to challenge and change the thought process of man for all time with a simple story is truly amazing.

The parables have a unique capacity to redefine the meaning of life, and I have experienced that personally in other ways. Growing up on an impoverished dairy farm, my parents divorced when I was ten years old, and from that time on I worked on the farm with my two brothers and mother as if I were an adult.

Early on, I developed an interest in law and government that became even greater as I attended college and law school. I became employed in a position with the Mississippi Hospital Association that required me to have frequent contact with members of the Mississippi Legislature and other top state leaders. I became deeply interested in entering Mississippi politics with a personal goal of becoming governor of Mississippi.

But, one Sunday morning in June 1975, during the closing of the service at First Baptist Church in Jackson, Mississippi, something happened that profoundly changed my life. I experienced an overwhelming affirmation of God's call and claim on my life to enter the ministry. It was so powerful, sudden, and dynamic that I almost collapsed onto the pew. I began preaching sermons in my mind, and that did not leave me for days. Preaching became the focus of my life. In the language of Jesus' parable, I discovered a treasure buried in a field that required me to be willing to sacrifice everything else in order to acquire that treasure. I later enrolled in New Orleans Baptist Theological Seminary and served as pastor of three different churches over the next twenty years, while also having the opportunity to continue legal work.

How shall I define the treasure I discovered? Perhaps what I found personally valuable and meaningful is the best way. I eventually became legal counsel for a large public hospital in Hattiesburg, Mississippi and then the Mississippi Baptist Convention for a short time. That was followed by serving several years as Vice-President and General Counsel of Mississippi Baptist Health Systems in Jackson, Mississippi, one of the largest hospital systems in Mississippi. One would expect that such professional roles would produce great personal satisfaction and fulfillment. Actually, and surprisingly, they did not.

Nothing I have ever done equaled the sense of purpose I experienced in the pulpit preaching the gospel. It is difficult to explain, but from the moment I stepped behind the pulpit, I truly experienced a perceptible sense of emotional, spiritual, and physical power unknown to me in any other setting. I spoke differently, thought differently, used verbal skills that I did not normally use, experienced insight and shared truths spontaneously that were completely new to me. Preaching was an experience unequaled by any other thing that I have ever known in life. It was how I worshipped and served God. Nothing else ever came close to that in meaning and importance to me. I have seldom been able to discuss and describe my call into the ministry without becoming emotional and teary-eyed. Was it a priceless treasure to me? Yes.

But the parables later took on an even more personal meaning. Because of certain financial success, I was able to buy an old farm that had been a childhood dream, and I envisioned the various things I could build there to make it more beautiful and enjoyable. But, after spending an excruciating night grasping my chest and left arm in order to reduce the throbbing pain, spending a period of time battling heart issues, and having my heart surgeon ominously tell me that I was one lucky man to still be alive, my perspective on life changed.

The parable of the rich man who boastfully assessed his holdings and declared that he would tear down his barns and build bigger ones really does have meaning, especially the part about having his life taken from him. That parable has the power to change priorities. The farm has now been sold, and I moved into my grandfather's old home, which is one hundred years old. I lease it from other family members, and I personally own no part of it. I just get to live here for the duration of my earthly days. The glitter of worldly treasure is gone, and life is remarkably more peaceful. Treasures laid up in heaven have acquired a far greater meaning. More and more, I have less reason to be attracted to the things of this world. Did the parable of the rich man with all his earthly dreams who lost his life one night influence this change? Yes.

It is often easy to say to someone whose opinion has changed, "I see that you have changed your mind." That comment is often casually, perhaps even humorously, made. But, saying to someone "I see you have had a change of heart" is much deeper in meaning and is made in response to a noticeable change of moral and emotional attitudes about something or someone. Changing one's mind often does not alter the course of their life too greatly; changes in the thoughts of their heart often make them into a different person. Changes of the mind may not have that great of an impact on others, whereas changes of the heart can alter the course of an individual, a family, a church, or even an entire nation.

The parables of Jesus remain relevant today because the problems confronting people are the same today as when He first spoke to them. Many Christians remain locked in a legalistic attitude about religion while feeling that regular, routine worship is all that is required and disregarding deep spiritual change. People making up Jesus' covenant church, who are to be holy and distinct, act no differently than the world around them. They are, as I have observed, chameleon Christians who easily and effortlessly blend in with the changing situations and settings of life around them.

Attitudes among Christians toward others can still be prejudicial, cold, and judgmental. The love of Jesus for sinners, for people who have experienced some moral collapse in their life, and for people who deeply struggle with different views and orientations about life often is not revealed through the understanding, mercy, and acceptance of other Christians. If a person or family fits the social, economic, and moral mold and measurement, they can find acceptance and happiness within most churches. But, if they do not, if they are different—look different, speak differently, have a different skin color, or have different social values—many churches can be a painful place to visit, and that is sad. It should not be that way.

During my legal career, I had the opportunity to work with a wide range of people—lawyers, doctors, business people, board members of corporations and government agencies, and even a few crooks and con men along the way. Many were driven to succeed; some were short tempered and sharp-tongued who would quickly voice their opinion in very demanding and often demeaning ways. Some treated others as if they were objects to be used for their own enrichment, and some would fire employees for no justifiable reason out of anger with no concern whatever for the resulting personal damage. I formed a lot of opinions about people in general during that time.

But the worst treatment I have ever personally experienced, the greatest emotional and spiritual pain I have ever endured, and the greatest humiliation I have ever known have been inflicted by fellow Christian church members. That may sound like an angry, resentful statement, but it is the truth. I never cried over my experiences as a lawyer, but I have wept more than once over things said and done by church members, often those in leadership positions. I am not the only pastor who can say that. And, again, that is sad, and it should not be that way.

Christians today not only need to change their minds about certain actions and attitudes in the church, but more importantly they profoundly need a change of heart—a change of heart about whether they truly are in a covenant with Jesus Christ, a change of heart about God and His love and mercy for all people, and a change of heart about whether they love their neighbor and are willing to accept others into the fellowship of believers.

The parables can help them experience that change through repentance. The parables of Jesus really do have the power to change thoughts of the heart.

The Strategic Purpose of the Parables

Some of Jesus' parables are plain and simple, while others are obscure, enigmatic, and mysterious, yet all of them are enormously important to the development of Christian theology. Can quaint little stories told over two thousand years ago during a three-year period by a man in his early thirties, who was widely considered by the religious leaders of His country to be the half-crazed, demon-possessed, illegitimate son of a peasant girl, actually change our thoughts about God, humanity, and life itself? That is the challenge of understanding the parables.

That description of Jesus may sound extreme, but it is part of the parables' mystery. Regardless of how He is viewed now, Jesus was not widely accepted as the son of God and savior of the world. Even for those who believed Him, it was hoped that He would restore a political kingdom in Israel similar in power and stability to the ancient political rule of King David, and many referred to Him as "the son of David" (Matthew 12:22-23). Others followed Him for the miraculous healing He could provide or the possibility of food. Although multitudes crowded around Him, in the end He was rejected by those same admiring throngs, who demanded His crucifixion, and His own disciples abandoned Him and denied knowing Him.

One must envision Jesus' emotional and spiritual struggle in order to better understand how He sought the most effective way to explain Himself and the kingdom of heaven. He could not deny the negative misconception many people had about Him, or the reality that He was considered by some to be mentally unstable because of His assertions, including members of His own family. Thus, He had to formulate an approach that would adequately capture the spiritual essence of His teaching, yet be within the comprehension level of multiple cultures, ethnic divisions, and intellectual levels. Creating parables with the power to change human thought from that mixture of doubt, uncertainty, misunderstanding, and diversity was divine genius.

Compared to His contemporaries, Jesus' theological views of God and His fellowman were radical and revolutionary, and even His own close followers had difficulty understanding His teaching. Jesus understood that, and He often used metaphor, hyperbole, and other verbal tools to emphasize or enhance a thought. But, frequently, He employed the ancient technique of a parable to create lasting impact with His teaching. He was a master teacher, and His use of this thought-provoking process was brilliant.

Parables are a fascinating and powerful tool. Based on the idea of parallel lines, a parable positions an unknown spiritual truth alongside a known physical truth thus allowing the listener to form conclusions regarding the meaning of the unknown based on his understanding of the known fact. It allows that which is imponderable to be compared to an understandable truth, thus leaving a lasting impression that stimulates greater understanding of the unknown.

Parables are fascinating because they actually do not reveal a known fact, and they are not intended to, for that is not their purpose. They are designed for mental stimulation. Factual statements are often made on face value and credibility with no deeper thought being required. Parables are purposefully designed and intended to stimulate prolonged thinking, and once that begins there is no limit to the depth and duration of the mental and spiritual process.

For example, how would Jesus have completed the following if He were communicating truth about the kingdom of heaven only in a physical, factual statement: "Heaven is like..."? One is at a loss to complete the sentence because it is impossible to accurately describe a spiritual truth in physical terms. For example, poets since the beginning of time have been trying to describe love, and even if one reads the sonnets of Shakespeare, the Apostle Paul's letter to the church at Corinth, or counts the poetic ways that Elizabeth Barrett Browning tried to capture love's definition, the emotion still cannot be adequately described physically. The same is true for the kingdom of heaven.

But it is possible to lead one into a deeper spiritual thought process about the spiritual kingdom by comparing it in parallel terms to a known everyday fact or experience. Without using physical description, it makes one think and better enables him to visualize and imagine the nature of the indescribable with his own spiritual capacity. That is the purpose of a parable. Thus, Jesus never attempted to describe heaven in physical terms. Rather, He told parables about the kingdom of heaven, such as comparing it to a mustard seed or to a pearl of great price in a manner that stimulated thought—thought that was personal, private, spiritual, questioning, and beyond the control of religious ritual, tradition, and the law.

Jesus could have chosen any means of communication. He could have made any statement and proclaimed these new spiritual ideas in several different ways, yet He chose to use parables as His most effective teaching tool. Based on various examples around Him and covering multiple aspects of the truths He taught, clearly the parables hold enormous spiritual meaning not fully explored and understood. They were not chosen at random and were not verbalized as spontaneous little stories on the spur of the moment in order to make a point.

The parables were carefully crafted by a master communicator to convey new truths in an environment hostile to critical thinking in which thought outside of the regimented religious framework was condemned and suppressed. They were strategic masterpieces guised as harmless stories with a lasting and unforgettable impact that generated deep introspective spiritual self-examination. The parables were chosen through a careful calculation of their potential impact to change popular understanding and prepare people for life within the kingdom of heaven. Each of them was strategically created by the genius and divine mind of the Son of God to make people think differently and to understand both the meaning and necessity of repentance.

What truths did Jesus want to communicate? What was the significance of the sequence in which they were told? What was their intended impact? The strategy behind the formulation and use of the parables as the means of establishing a deeper understanding of the kingdom of heaven and also creating an understanding of the need for repentance to enter that divine realm is truly amazing.

Jesus is revered and worshipped by Christians as the Son of God and Savior of all who believe in Him by faith. His parables remain ageless and just as challenging, relevant, and inspiring today as when first spoken. Their potential to change human thought has not diminished. But their real purpose is seldom considered. The parables were part of Jesus' broad-based plan to bring about repentance in the life of God's covenant people so they could truly function as a nation of priests and be His divine ambassadors and witnesses in the world. That is what God originally called Israel to do, but she woefully failed in that divine purpose.

Jesus echoed the earlier prophetic call of John the Baptist and premised His teaching and His redemptive work on one concept—repentance. Jesus masterfully wove repentance into all of His words and works as He taught new truths throughout Israel. These are especially evident in His Sermon on the Mount, His unique views on joy in serving God, His redeeming love for others, His efforts to change the meaning of prayer, charitable deeds, and fasting, and His proclamation of a new basis of righteousness with God.

Jesus proclaimed repentance as encompassing the deep, spiritual transformation of every believer in whom the eternal law of God is no longer chiseled in stone on a legalistic list of commandments, but rather is written on their heart and becomes the spiritual basis of their life within the kingdom of heaven. If those called into a covenant relation with God were to truly understand the meaning and purpose of that divine union and experience a dynamic new spiritual life within the kingdom of heaven which both Jesus and John said was "at hand" (Matt. 3:1, 4:17), they would have to fundamentally change their actions, attitudes, and thoughts about God, their fellowman, and the purpose of life in general.

The ministry of Jesus reveals a four-fold plan to create a broad desire for repentance in the heart of His disciples, and that includes all who believe in Him and profess him as Lord. His overall teaching provided the basis for understanding the need for personal repentance, His miracles provided evidence of His power to change and redeem life, and His great prayer for the church, recorded in John 17:1-26, reveals the ultimate power and purpose of His eternal covenant with believers. But it was parables that He strategically chose to transform the thoughts of His followers, consistent with His desire for repentance, that eternally challenge and change the attitudes of Christians toward God, each other, and life.

The challenge Jesus faced was revealing understandable truth about spiritual concepts to a people who historically considered those truths only in physical terms. For example, consider the idea of the kingdom of heaven. Surprisingly, it was essentially an unknown concept to Jesus' Jewish listeners. When asked about the coming of the kingdom, Jesus responded, "The kingdom of God does not come with observation; nor will they say, 'See here!' or 'See there!' For indeed, the kingdom of God is within you" (Luke 17:20-21). But, that idea was totally opposite to what Jews had historically believed.

Every new and unusual development was met with the question of whether the beginning of the messianic age and the physical appearance of the messiah was about to occur. That is why John the Baptist attracted such wide attention. Indeed, his preaching was powerful, but many believed that he was heralding the appearance of the long-awaited messiah, who would transform Israel economically, politically, and militarily, and multitudes came to not only hear his message but also to see the political spectacle. There was a long-standing belief that the prophet Elijah would reappear prior to the manifestation of the messiah, and many believed that John the Baptist was in fact the reincarnation of Elijah. Many Christians fail to grasp the drama and suspense of that moment when reading about the preaching of John the Baptist.

But Jesus consistently spoke of the unseen spiritual values of His heavenly realm and clearly said, "My kingdom is not of this world" (Jn.18:36). How could He explain and describe in clear, understandable terms the nature of something that was not visible and not understandable to a mind that traditionally and habitually thought only in physical terms—a mind that was forbidden by religion, culture, tradition, and even the religious law to think otherwise? It would be extremely difficult, and so He utilized a different strategy to project a new way of thinking about and visualizing His truths—parables.

Jesus confronted a wide range of both religious and intellectual challenges, including the following:

- Can an entire nation be taught a new thought process? Can religious beliefs that are chiseled in the rock of unquestioned obedience and ritualistic practice be moderated in order to change attitudes as well? Can a religious and social culture that is based on the physical practice of revered religious traditions be taught that those traditions instead have a higher and holier spiritual interpretation?

- Can the spiritual bond of righteousness that has bound a people to God for centuries—a bond that is manifested in individual physical obedience to thousands of laws—be modified so that the basis of the spiritual bond with God becomes faith in the righteousness of one man? If so, how?
- Can the reality that this effort will result in Jesus' death be overcome by a promise to His followers that His death will not be a defeat, but instead will be God's final atonement for sin and will be followed by His resurrection from the dead, which will usher in the most powerful spiritual experience ever known to God's covenant people?
- Would people truly listen to the promises of a thirty-year-old carpenter who professed to be the Son of God and Messiah of Israel yet who had no army, eschewed violence, and spoke of loving one's enemies, even though His words were captivating, and He performed miracles to validate His claims about Himself? Surely that would require a noble man of great power with the obvious ability to guarantee those promises, and outwardly Jesus possessed neither. He owned no property, had no formal education and training in the religious law, and only had a handful of followers.
- If the religious laws of the nation prohibited anyone from espousing and teaching any doctrine contrary to the centuries-old traditional views and practices, and labeled anyone who voiced any different view as an infidel and heretic, would anyone listen to a man who respected religious leaders described as demon possessed?
- If the people had been taught to close their ears and their minds to any new interpretation of the ancient law—even if it required placing their hands over their ears in order not to hear—how could that barrier be broken so that they would at least consider, if only in the privacy of their own thoughts, the truth He was teaching? How could that mental barrier be effectively penetrated?

- Could all people throughout the world who were steeped in their own cultures and traditions be taught that the ancient beliefs of one small, remote nation equally impacted them and therefore override their own beliefs and ideas about God and heaven?
- Could the meaning of the ancient religious practices of one people be transformed by a new thought process and understanding in such a way that the entire world and all of its multitude of religious beliefs and practices be transformed by those practicing these new religious concepts? How could such a transforming level of spiritual and religious understanding be attained?
- Could a small group of followers be personally instructed and inspired to go into all other nations and introduce this new covenant of faith so that people of all cultures, nationalities, and ethnic origins would become disciples of Jesus? How could a thought process be devised that would have that kind of worldwide application and acceptance?
- Could the parables be stated in a way that allowed those with an open mind to understand and ponder their meaning, while those whose minds were closed and darkened to the light of new truth remained mystified about the parables' meanings?

When the parables are viewed retrospectively, they are usually considered as a collection of meaningful, albeit puzzling and somewhat challenging, short stories that help expand one's understanding of spiritual truths regarding Christian life and the kingdom of heaven. But, when the parables are examined prospectively, as if one were looking at the challenge confronting Jesus and viewing the parables as a strategic means of communicating new truths, they take on a vastly different purpose.

Their greatest meaning is found in considering them from Jesus' perspective, as if one were visualizing Him devise a mental assault on closed minds locked in the trap of religious ritual in order to free them to think. He had declared that the kingdom of heaven was at hand, and He was traveling around Israel teaching new truths that were not only challenging the status quo but also upsetting the entrenched power structure. It was essential that He formulate a method of teaching and communication that would lead His listeners into deeper thought, leave a lasting impression, and inspire them to better understand their need for repentance, in spite of resistance from the entrenched religious establishment.

The disciples once specifically asked Jesus, "Why do You speak to them in parables?" (Matt. 13:10). His answer reveals the narrow line He walked in conveying spiritual truths understandable to those who were sensitive to His teaching, yet puzzling to those disinterested and opposed:

> *"Because it has been given to you to know the mysteries of the kingdom of heaven, but to them it has not been given. For whoever has, to him more will be given, and he will have abundance; but whoever does not have, even what he has will be taken away from him. Therefore I speak to them in parables, because seeing they do not see, and hearing they do not hear, nor do they understand. And in them the prophesy of Isaiah is fulfilled, which says, 'Hearing you will hear and shall not understand, and seeing you will see and not perceive; for the heart of this people has grown dull. Their ears are hard of hearing, and their eyes they have closed, lest they should see with their eyes and hear with their ears, lest they should understand with their hearts and turn so that I should heal them.' But blessed are your eyes for they see, and your ears for they hear; for assuredly, I say to you that any prophets and righteous men desired to see what you see, and did not see it, and to hear what you hear, and did not hear it"* (Matt. 13: 11-7).

Jesus faced the challenge of formulating thought that was totally outside the traditional mold of Jewish understanding. Consider the following:

- There were no real concepts of the meaning of repentance and no understanding of the need for any other methodology of thought.
- There was no immediate reason within the existing social and religious structure to change existing rituals and traditions.
- There was no concept that the messiah would establish anything other than an earthly political kingdom that would propel Israel to new heights of economic and military power and remove her detested conquerors.

- There was no belief that the messianic kingdom was spiritual and not physical in nature.
- There was no thought that the kingdom was an internal, spiritual experience versus an observable physical, external kingdom.
- There was no belief that the kingdom involved transforming inner feelings toward others.
- There was no understanding of salvation through faith and grace as opposed to obtaining righteousness by keeping the law.
- There was no comprehension that the meaning of the law was found in its spiritual purpose and not in its physical implementation.
- There was no idea that the messiah would die as a sacrifice for believers as compared to dynamically living and ruling over the nation.
- There was no idea that believers could personally enter and experience the kingdom of heaven.
- There was no belief that the kingdom of heaven was near and at hand compared to the kingdom being a past memory, such as King David's rule, or a future golden age to be ushered in by the messiah.

Formulating a plan that would not force and compel thought but would instead encourage and stimulate deeper private understanding of the new truths that Jesus was revealing was an indescribable challenge. The spiritual impact of these strategically chosen parables would lead believers into the desire for repentance as a result of commitment, rather than compelling them to act through religious law, thus enabling every Christian to more fully understand and experience the life-changing nature of the kingdom of heaven.

Interestingly, one can glimpse the spiritual mindset of Israel in two separate New Testament verses. In the Sermon on the Mount, Jesus said to His disciples, "Do not think that I came to destroy the Law or the Prophets. I did not come to destroy but to fulfill" (Matt. 5:17). The Greek word *nomizo* provides interesting insight into the meaning of His statement because it describes something that one habitually and automatically thinks. Consequently, Jesus well knew that the disciples were accustomed to closing their minds to any new idea that potentially modified the law and would automatically refuse to listen. Jesus urged them not to automatically assume this, but rather to listen to and consider the truth of His words.

When Stephen, one of the first deacons and a devoted follower of Jesus, passionately defended his faith and accused the leaders of Israel of being Jesus' betrayers and murderers, members of the Sanhedrin, who were listening with growing anger and resentment, "…gnashed at him with their teeth" (Acts 7:54). But when Stephen spoke of seeing the Son of Man standing at the right hand of God, "…they cried out with a loud voice, stopped their ears, and ran at him with one accord" (Acts 7: 57). Stephen was thrown out of the city and stoned to death. Rather than hear the truth, these religious leaders grimaced, clasp their hands over their ears, and did all they could to prevent his words from even entering their minds. By killing Stephen, these defiant zealots assumed the truth of his words would be silenced, but they were wrong.

In some countries today, the proclamation of Christian ideas and truths is punishable by imprisonment or death. It was no different in Israel when Jesus preached and when the first disciples began to proclaim the truth about His crucifixion and resurrection. The crucifixion of Jesus, and the subsequent imprisonment of the disciples, is proof of this hostile attitude toward new thought and new ideas. If one is to understand the parables' purpose, each of them must be viewed as a strategic literary tool Jesus used to break the lock of the law on Jewish minds and free them to think independently.

Further, in a broader sense, the parables are Jesus' chosen means to loosen the grip of religious attitudes, social custom, racial and ethnic prejudice, and individual and family traditions on the minds of all Christians throughout history. Most people follow traditional lines of thought they have been taught by family, friends, and their immediate society, and most will not get outside those confines and comfortably view new truths. Just as members of the Jewish Council did, some even have a way of mentally clasping their hands over their ears and refusing to listen to divine truth that challenges their beliefs and opinions and causes them to think differently.

Human action is essentially divided into voluntary and involuntary acts. For example, we have no control over our heart beating or our eyes blinking because those are involuntary actions. We do, however, have control over how we act and what we say. Interestingly, the process of how one thinks is often trapped somewhere between voluntary and involuntary actions. Thoughts that immediately enter one's mind are not easily controlled and are the result of a lifetime of processing mental and emotional reactions to ideas, attitudes, beliefs, traditions, prejudices, family and social customs, and hundreds of other mental stimuli. Those essentially cannot be helped, nor can they be easily controlled or prevented, but they can be gradually changed through repentance. Every Christian can indeed learn to think differently if they truly desire to change more into the likeness of Jesus.

That is the essence of the mental process of repentance. All human action, if it is not truly involuntary, is of a premeditated and intentional nature. We voluntarily choose to act as we do, and we voluntarily choose to think as we do, and we certainly choose to close our mind and refuse to consider new truth and ideas that may foster spiritual change. Spiritual responsibility is much like criminal guilt. The key distinction between murder and involuntary manslaughter is intent and premeditation. A person never voluntarily acts unless he has first thought, if only for a fleeting second, about his actions, except in those cases where his actions are uncontrollable and involuntary. Thus, action is controlled by thought, and in order to change action, thought must change first. Jesus realized that, and one of His greatest priorities was changing the manner in which His disciples thought.

Repentance, therefore, is a fundamental redirection of an individual's thoughts, attitudes, and actions. In religious terms, it is the reorientation of one's life toward God as opposed to a life that is sinful and contrary to God's will and purpose. For Jesus, repentance was much broader in scope than merely changing bad behavior to good and godly behavior. It involved changing the manner in which the covenant people of God perceived themselves in the world, and, as a result, dramatically changing their thoughts and actions toward others. Repentance would involve a fundamental reorientation away from self-glorifying obedience to law that excluded most other people to an all-inclusive attitude toward others motivated by a deep, heart-felt sense of redeeming love for them. It would be a love that would propel them out into the world as God's priestly emissaries and ambassadors in a manner that would alter human history. In order to accomplish that, Jesus had to teach them a new way to think about God, about His heavenly kingdom, and about the world around them. His most effective method for accomplishing that was the parables.

It is interesting to note that the Gospel of John concludes with this statement:

> *"And there are also many other things that Jesus did, which if they were written one by one, I suppose that even the world itself could not contain the books that would be written. Amen"* (John 21:25).

Bible historians generally believe the gospels were written several years after Jesus' death and resurrection. The historical record of what Jesus actually did and said was initially orally transmitted to His followers. Logically, even when an account was written later, such as the Gospel of Mark, it would not have been widely circulated for many years. According to John, Jesus did many things that were not recorded for history. However, it is interesting to note the number of parables remembered by His disciples and told to other early Christians who continued sharing them with new believers until they became part of the written gospel record. The parables made them think differently, just as Jesus intended.

A New Concept of Evangelism

The Parable of the Sower

"Listen! Behold, a sower went out to sow. And it happened, as he sowed that some seed fell by the wayside; and the birds of the air came and devoured it. Some fell on stony ground, where it did not have much earth; and immediately it sprang up because it had no depth of earth. But when the sun was up it was scorched, and because it had no root it withered away. And some seed fell among thorns; and the thorns grew up and choked it, and it yielded no crop. But other seed fell on good ground and yielded a crop that sprang up, increased, and produced: some thirtyfold, some sixty, and some a hundred" (Mark 4:3-8).

Does a painter paint in order to see his finished masterpiece or solely for the joy of putting brushstrokes on canvas? Does a musician write music in order to hear a symphony or for the joy of arranging notes on paper? Does a farmer sow seed in anticipation of a good harvest or for the joy and reward of sowing? In these examples, logic focuses on the joy of the finished product that results from dedicated labor. But Jesus taught His disciples a totally different concept about their task. He personally knew the work of sharing the gospel would be physically tiring, emotionally draining, and spiritually challenging, often producing no immediate results, and a new basis of reward would be needed to inspire continued commitment.

Therefore, Jesus had to plant the understanding in His disciples' minds that effort alone is rewarding, persecution and rejection can become joyous and blessed, and the harvest derived from spiritual seeds that are planted today may not be seen in a disciple's lifetime. The joy of the sower must come through planting, and not through the harvest. That is the opposite of human logic and behavior, but that is the reality and challenge of Christian discipleship. For centuries, Israel had celebrated the providential blessings of God on the nation through various harvest festivals. Jesus radically changed that celebration to the joy of planting. He did that through an ingenious parable known as the "Parable of the Sower."

Jesus faced a unique challenge as a teacher. In order to reveal the magnitude of the kingdom of heaven, He needed to change the thought process of one group—Gentiles—who could not easily comprehend His teaching and another group—Jews—who would not readily consider and accept His truths. Jesus fully knew that He could not get the vast majority of them to listen and understand. For example, John records that after Jesus had spoken about His blood and His flesh, many of those who professed to be His disciples said, "This is a hard saying; who can understand it?" Challenged by the depth of His statements, "From that time many of His disciples went back and walked with Him no more" (John 6:53-66). Though He preached and taught extensively throughout the nation of Israel, in truth, Jesus mainly focused on twelve men in order to get them to understand, hoping this small group would later produce the great harvest He desired through the seed of truth he was implanting in them.

Jesus well knew that His own ministry foreshadowed the ministry of His disciples as they went throughout the world, both then and in future generations. He knew that the work would be hard, the hours long, and the earthly rewards few. Only a small percentage of people would understand and respond, and He sought a way to prepare His disciples for this reality. Unlike ordinary human activity in which effort and results are related, Jesus had to devise a means whereby effort itself became the reward, and the results were left to be enjoyed by others. He could not have faced a greater challenge.

The religious law of Israel rewarded self-righteous behavior with immediate results. The Pharisees, scribes, and other devout adherents enjoyed the admiration, praise, and respect of others who viewed them as righteous stalwarts of society. Thus, they paraded around performing charitable acts, praying, and fasting "that they may be seen by men" (Matt. 6:5), and they hypocritically gloated in this public perception, desiring to be called "Rabbi" and receiving the praise of others (Matt. 23:7).

But the opposite would be true for the disciples. In their service to Jesus, they would incur rejection, ridicule, hostility, persecution and even torture and death. None would be praised, and most would be hated and reviled—even as Jesus was. They would receive no earthly reward. All they had was Jesus' promise that the spiritual reward awaiting them in the kingdom of heaven would be greater than any possible earthly reward (Matt. 5:10-12). Therefore, Jesus had to instill in His disciples a concept of reward for labor that was contrary to ordinary expectation, and that principle remains true today.

The parable primarily focuses on four types of soil and the response of seed planted in that soil. As Jesus told this parable to the multitudes, perhaps a nearby sower was visible to them. Because the gathered crowd was large, Jesus got into a boat and sat while the people on the shore listened to His description of the sower and the seed (Matt.13:3-9). As the sower cast the valuable seed, consider what happened:

(1). Some seed fell by the wayside. This described soil in a pathway that had been trampled and packed. In a dry and arid region, it would no doubt be extremely hard, almost like concrete. Having no cover, the seed were soon eaten by birds.

(2). Some seed fell on stony places. The tillable land was filled with stones, and these were often piled or used for construction. When they had not been cleared from the field, what might appear as fertile soil was misleading because hidden underneath were rocks that would prevent the seed from growing. The seed might immediately germinate, as if it were good soil, but the plants would soon begin to wither because the soil was very shallow, and underneath was impenetrable stone.

(3). Some seed fell among thorns. Along the edges of the fields, and in untillable crevices and ravines, thorns and other prickly type plants often grew. The common thorn plant was a nuisance, and its rapid growth had a disastrous choking effect on seedling plants.

(4). Other seed fell on good ground and produced an abundant crop. The results of the good soil are an interesting study. Some areas produced a hundred times greater than what was planted, whereas other areas were less productive, some producing sixty times greater and others only thirty.

However, applying simple multiplication to the volume of the seed that was planted yields an illuminating result. Using a grain of corn as an example, one grain produces a plant that has two or three ears of corn, each containing a few hundred individual grains of corn. So, one seed would ultimately produce hundreds of other seeds. If the sower planted one pound of seed in good soil, he would get hundreds of pounds of seed in his harvest, and that would overcome all of the seed that was lost by falling in the wayside, the rocky places, and the thorns.

After Jesus had spoken the parable, His disciples asked Him to explain, and He opened their minds to its obvious meaning:

> *"When anyone hears the word of the kingdom, and does not understand it, then the wicked one comes and snatches away what was sown in his heart. This is he who received seed by the wayside. But he who received the seed on stony places, this is he who hears the word and immediately receives it with joy, yet he has no root in himself, but endures only for a while. For when tribulation or persecution arises because of the word, immediately he stumbles. Now he who received seed among the thorns is he who hears the word, and the cares of this world and the deceitfulness of riches choke the word, and he becomes unfruitful. But he who received the seed on the good ground is he who hears the word and understands it, who indeed bears fruit and produces, some a hundredfold, some sixty, some thirty"* (Matt. 13:19-23).

It is one of the best summations of human response to divine truth found in scripture. It is also an accurate portrayal of the kinds of cultures that the disciples would encounter as they journeyed into the world teaching and preaching the gospel. Its truths are well stated and undeniable.

However, the unstated genius of this parable is the subtle yet powerful portrayal of the attitude of the sower. Sowing seed was a well-known agricultural act that Jesus had often seen, and He used that as the parable's foundation. But the sower's approach to his work is so different, illogical, and unusual that his actions are difficult to comprehend.

First, consider the seed. A certain amount was always saved from the harvest and held in reserve for future planting. Unlike the grain that was used for food or animal feed, seed grain was usually the best so that it would germinate, produce healthy plants, and yield a bountiful harvest. Every farmer protected his seed grain with great care because his future success depended on it. It was never wasted and was always sown in the most fertile and productive soil available.

Soil preparation for planting was also critical. Seed will germinate and grow best in soft, moist soil, and every good farmer takes great care in preparing a good seedbed. It is a waste of time to plant in hard, dry soil because the seed will not normally germinate, and if it does, the seedling plant will quickly turn yellow, rather than a vibrant green, and will wither and die. A good sower only plants good seed in good soil. That basic practice is fundamental and is never altered. The idea of casting precious seed grain onto a hardened pathway, into briars, or among stones would have been totally foolish.

Most planting today is done with well-designed agricultural planters that precisely plant seed at a pre-determined rate and depth. It is all calculated to minimize seed loss and maximize yield. However, in older agricultural practices, planting was done by hand, usually in one of two ways. The first involved carefully dropping seed into a small furrow, or in small individual holes, at an appropriate depth and with adequate space between the plants to allow growth. Under no circumstance would a farmer have dug a furrow or seed holes and planted his choice seed in a hardened path, among stones, or in briars.

The second planting method was called "broadcasting" and, as the word implies, involved taking a handful of seed and broadly casting them in front of the sower as he walked and moved his hand rapidly from side to side. The seed were then covered with soil using a harrow and allowed to germinate. Again, the seed grain was carefully sown to avoid waste and was cast only in good soil that allowed the best germination and growth. Seed was always planted with careful and calculated anticipation of the harvest in mind. In fact, although sowing was critically important, it was of secondary importance to the size of the harvest. If his sowing produced a harvest that fed a sower's family, his animals, and provided enough seed grain for the next planting, he would have considered it a bountiful harvest. Whether on a small plot or in a large field, these methods of sowing and reaping are basic and timeless.

Any farmer who intentionally broadcast seed onto a pathway, into briars, or among stones knowing they would not produce would have been considered foolish and wasteful, yet the sower did exactly that in violation of every known planting guideline. Any good farmer who heard Jesus' parable would have wondered about the sower's skill and probably scornfully laughed at his sowing method.

But Jesus was a master teacher who inspired His disciples to find deeper truth and meaning, and this parable is a masterpiece of motivation. Its greatest truth is found in what is unsaid but is discovered through experience. Jesus motivated His disciples to share the gospel in a wide variety of areas and among people of diverse backgrounds and interests. He knew from personal experience that His disciples' message would be rejected by many people, ignored by some, and others would initially follow only to fall away through indifference. Their reaction is described by the four soil types: outright hardness and rejection, shallow commitment, cluttered lives, and personal agendas, and some who would believe and make enormous spiritual commitments for Christ. Therefore, in order to encourage and sustain them in their ministry endeavors, Jesus created a new concept of labor reward by describing the mindset of a sower whose attitude and actions so differed from all standards of traditional sowing that he obviously found great joy in casting seed everywhere he went, rather than solely focusing on the eventual reward of his harvest.

The sower in the parable refused to be bound by traditions of the past, or disillusioned by the laughter, ridicule, and negative attitude of others, and he devised a method for producing a bountiful harvest through untried methods that many deemed radical. He was unlike any sower that anyone had seen before.

The sower's actions are described in an interesting manner: "Behold, a sower went out to sow, and as he sowed, some seed fell..." (vv. 3-4). Unlike an ordinary farmer who would carefully plant in order to conserve his seed, this sower sowed with abandonment. His focus was not on the ultimate harvest; rather, it was on widespread sowing. His sowing method was innovative, indiscriminate and unprecedented. He cast seed anywhere and everywhere. Where the seed fell was secondary to the act of sowing. Sowing was his motivation and passion, and the fact that seed fell in unproductive locations was of little concern to him. His thought was not on the harvest, but rather on the sowing.

By sowing in the pathways, among the rocks, and in the briars, the sower knew that the vast majority of his seed would never produce any meaningful harvest, but he sowed anyway. He sowed equally, and the same amount of seed and the same effort were applied to all areas. He was nonjudgmental, he showed no preference, and He gave his best effort to all areas. He was not irresponsible, nor was he a poor steward of his seed. He had to overcome the ageless sowing traditions of his elders that would have dictated and controlled his efforts. A sower who focused only on the harvest would have sown only in the best soil and would have neglected and shunned other areas. But this sower was determined not to do that.

He was not a foolish farmer, and he knew the value of the seed he cast as he sowed. He knew full-well that seed sown on hard soil, rocky soil, and on soil cluttered with other growth would produce little or no harvest, but still he sowed indiscriminately, unconditionally, equally, and passionately in all areas. Avoiding no area considered useless, he showed equal commitment to all. He never complained and asked God to move him to another field, nor jealously looked at another sower who he thought had better soil and fewer stones and briars. The sower simply took the seed with which he had been entrusted, and he sowed them the best he knew how in every area that he had been given to sow. He did not falter under the load, nor was he discouraged and disillusioned by others who said he was foolishly wasting his time and seed on unproductive soil. He was focused on his mission and unfazed by the disappointing results. His reward was watching the growth of the seed cast in the good soil and the varying results it produced.

The genius of this parable is how Jesus planted the seed of evangelism in the hearts of His disciples and narrowed their focus to the joy of sowing rather than the joy of the harvest. Jesus planted that seed of truth and never told them; He let them discover it. The joy of sharing the gospel comes from sowing seed, not totally from the resulting harvest. That sounds illogical and contrary to human motivation, but it is true.

Realistically, much of one's Christian effort falls on hard hearts, disinterested minds, cluttered calendars of life, and short, half-hearted commitments. But a small percentage of people produce a harvest that is many times greater than the efforts of the sower to plant the seed of the gospel. The great unknown is who will actually become the productive good soil. Sometimes it is an amazing discovery and a total surprise to see the least expected soil become spiritually fertile and produce a great servant for the Lord, and therein is the joy of sowing. The sower's passion must simply be lovingly, unconditionally, and equally sowing the seed of the gospel in every type of human soil—the hardest heart, the shallowest soul, the most disinterested mind—and, yes, in the good soil of new disciples with open hearts and attentive minds.

Jesus' disciples faced the challenge of going into the world teaching and making disciples in multiple nations, among numerous and varied ethnic groups, and among people with strong beliefs and opinions uninfluenced by Jewish religious traditions. In fact, many would find the tenets of Judaism and Christianity foolish. It would be an enormous physical, emotional, and spiritual challenge that could be achieved only through repentance and a profound personal transformation in attitude about other people.

In order to accomplish this global mission, the early church had to adopt an entirely new vision and a radically different attitude about the rewards of godly service. No longer would that reward focus on the occasional convert, but rather the spiritual reward for service would be found in personally sharing the gospel with people of all cultures, classes, nationalities, and ethnic backgrounds, regardless of their immediate response.

Judaism did not emphasize evangelism in the way Christianity does. Regardless of the stringent demands of the law, the nature of Jewish belief in an exclusive covenant between God and Israel did not readily allow the inclusion of non-Jews into the faith. The covenant focused on blood kinship with the patriarchal fathers of Israel, notably Abraham, and being Jewish by birth. Consider, for example, Paul's description of himself: "…of the stock of Israel, of the tribe of Benjamin, a Hebrew of the Hebrews…" (Phil. 3:5). Allowing a Gentile into this bond was not easily done and was not actively sought out. In fact, relationships with Gentiles were considered unlawful (Acts 10:28). The idea of going into other nations and cultures with the intent of converting numerous new followers to Judaism did not exist. For Jesus' disciples, this reticence was dramatically altered by the emergence of one word—evangelism.

Evangelism stems from a concept denoting one who proclaimed good news. Historically, in Judaism only recognized prophets spoke for God, and no person would have assumed this role without a divine calling and commission. Now, however, these men, chosen to be disciples of Jesus, would become messengers of God, and their message would be the gospel of Jesus. The transition from revering one who spoke for God to His covenant people to personally becoming one who shared good news from God with all people of every nation was a major spiritual transformation for the disciples that is largely overlooked today by most Christians.

Therefore, Jesus' disciples had to change from a religious view that occasionally permitted conversion to Judaism to a religious view that openly, aggressively, and tirelessly sought new believers among people of any nation. That is the evangelistic message that the church and every Christian is responsible for sharing throughout the world. That good news is the clarion call of the church in every corner of the world. The gospel has not lost its power, just some of its faithful proclaimers.

Even though "gospel" literally means good news, it has a more significant meaning as "God's good news." The concept not only denotes a good tiding or good news but also the reward for the bearer of the good news who becomes God's chosen messenger. The gospel is nothing less than God's joyous message to the world.

But the real meaning is more personal. Indeed, the good news is more than just chit-chat good news. It describes news that is so important and produces such immense joy and immediate response that it requires a special messenger to proclaim it. When that concept is applied to God, gospel means a divine proclamation that is so overwhelming and important that God sends His chosen messenger bearing His specific commission to proclaim this news. As a result, a close bond is formed between God, the messenger, and the message, and they are inseparably related in meaning and purpose and are viewed as one.

When Jesus was born, God sent angels bearing this good news, which was declared as "good tidings of great joy which will be to all people. For there is born to you this day in the city of David a Savior, who is Christ the Lord" (Luke 2:10-11). Jesus the Savior then became the messenger of the good news as He preached the gospel. God, Jesus, and the good-news message of salvation through faith in Him were all inseparable. Jesus then commissioned His disciples to go into all the nations preaching the gospel and making other disciples.

Although the good news of the gospel is evangelism, the message is not limited to an evangelist, even though God calls certain individuals to preach the gospel. As disciples of Jesus, all Christians are personally empowered by Christ to proclaim this divine good news. Every Christian is Jesus' special messenger through how we live, love, and share this divine news with others, and we are inseparably related to Jesus and His message of salvation. Just as it was in the beginning, so should it be now: Christ, His message of salvation, and the redeeming love of His messengers, all viewed as one. In the original Bible language, the words for messenger, message, and proclaiming the message inseparably stem from the same word. Neither can exist without the others. That is one reason Jesus said, "I am the vine, you are the branches...without Me you can do nothing" (John 15:5).

Many Christians today have lost sight of the transforming meaning of the word "gospel," and it has become a common part of our Christian vernacular. We refer to the first four books of the New Testament as "the four gospels," and the entire message of Jesus is generally referred to as "the gospel message," but few Christians can explain the meaning of "gospel." That is tragic because a personal understanding of the word is both a personal commitment to and a personal empowerment of its message.

Where did the English word "gospel" originate? That, too, is fascinating and inspiring. The Old English translation used the word *spellian*, which means "to announce or declare a word or message." It is the basis of our word "spell" and the phrase "spell it out," or the act of declaring something clearly and emphatically.

However, there is a further aspect of the word's meaning that is even more powerful. This message that one spells out and declares to another can be so overwhelming that it leaves the listener stunned, speechless, and in something of a trance. To use an everyday expression, it puts him under a "spell." Grasp the full meaning of this: This news from God is so good, exciting, powerful, and overwhelming that those hearing it for the first time are left in a "god-spell."

Jesus' teaching must be examined in this light in order to grasp its importance and impact. It was truth that had never been heard nor contemplated by anyone in the world. It was so fresh, powerful, and personal that any serious listener would have been left in something of a trance. For example, following the Sermon on the Mount, those listening were astonished. Literally, they were so startled it was as if they had been hit on their head and left senseless. They did not know what to think or what to do because nothing of that magnitude had been spoken in Israel. The power of the gospel can be so spiritually electrifying, joyous, and liberating that people fall into a god-spell of praise and thanksgiving to God for such good news. That amazing concept is the Gospel of Jesus Christ!

Good news is shared because it is new, life changing, and is inherently good, producing unrestrained joy and excitement. Good news is not determined by the reaction to it. A hearer may scoff at it, reject it, or laugh at its perceived foolishness, but it is still good news. The joy of the bearer of this news is determined by the magnitude of his message and not the response. So, he joyfully shares in all kinds of responses and reactions without despair or disillusionment. The opportunity to share is the reward—not the measurement of who believes, responds, or reacts. That was the transition that Jesus was encouraging in His disciples. Their reward would be found in being the messenger of this exciting, transforming good news from God. That concept has not changed. Every Christian is God's messenger bearing divine good news to others that is so powerful it casts a "godspell" on its hearers. Unfortunately, we have lost sight of this historic meaning.

Today, evangelism is viewed most often as the organized outreach of the church to others. It has become a well-defined and usually well-financed aspect of many denominations. That is not what it is biblically intended to be. Christian evangelism should focus on the basic responsibility of sharing the good news through teaching, preaching, and personal sharing. It is about living one's beliefs in Jesus with such personal commitment and integrity that one's words and work leave a lasting impact on others.

Jesus knew the heart and mind of men, and He knew also that His disciples would need motivation that would triumph over rejection, hostility, indifference, and the attitude of those who responded enthusiastically and then waned away. The reaction of a majority of people would be very disappointing and produce disillusionment and even despair. But there would be a minority who would hear and respond with unwavering commitment and discipleship. The good soil represented by their life and devotion would eventually produce a harvest that would more than compensate for the people and the soils that produced nothing.

Jesus also knew that His joy must become the joy of the disciples (John 15:11) in order for them to keep sowing and planting in every kind of soil, in every category of humanity, and in every nation of the world. In explaining this parable to His disciples, Jesus said, "Do you not understand this parable? How then will you understand all the parables?" (Mark 4:13). In effect, He said, "If you don't understand the joy of sharing the good news of the gospel to all mankind, then none of the other truths will be meaningful." That remains true for the church and for every Christian today.

Over the years, I have observed the seed of the gospel falling on all four kinds of the soil of human reaction. I have watched people reject it outright because of the hardness of their heart, even curse God in the process. I have watched many people, especially younger individuals, react with enthusiasm and then drift away as their commitment waned under the choking entanglements in life's many pleasures and pursuits. I have watched as some committed themselves to the Lord, only to sadly observe them later react with anger and rejection of the gospel's demands when the seed of divine truth fell on the rocky hardness of buried hatred and bitterness.

I have watched specific individuals demonstrate spiritual reactions that were identical to the types of soil identified in this parable. For some individuals, there are spiritual ideas that are never accepted, some grow for a while and wither, and some are choked out by other interests. But in every person, there is some dimension of their life for the potential of the good soil where the seed of the gospel can take hold and grow. They may not be perfect in all areas, but the harvest of the good soil compensates.

The joy of sowing the seed comes from not knowing. It is worth the effort to cast the seed of the gospel on a heart of stone, the barren sand of spiritual indifference, and in a briar patch mind choked by other interests. Somewhere in all of that, the seed of the gospel may fall in some good soil in which the gospel grows and matures into a fruitful disciple of Christ. That is a joyous reality that makes the labor worthwhile. The joy of evangelical Christianity is found in the joy of sowing the seed. The harvest is in the hands of God.

The Concept of Faith
The Potential Growth of a Planted Seed

The Parable of the Mustard Seed

> *"...To what shall we liken the kingdom of God? Or with what parable shall we picture it? It is like a mustard seed which, when it is sown on the ground, is smaller than all the seeds on earth; but when it is sown, it grows up and becomes greater than all herbs, and shoots out large branches, so that the birds of the air may nest under its shade"* (Mark 4:30-32).

The parable of the mustard seed is one of the best known of Jesus' parables. It portrays the potential for growth from a small seed to a large, vibrant plant, thus symbolizing the potential for spiritual growth within the kingdom of heaven from a small act of faith to maturity as a dynamic disciple of Jesus. Yet, in reality, the parable's truth is much broader and deeper.

The transition from the Old Testament covenant to the New Testament covenant involved far more than two different views of God. For the disciples, the spiritual and emotional change from righteousness based on compliance with religious law and ritual to a concept of righteousness based on faith in Jesus could not have been greater. Although the Apostle Paul was not one of the twelve disciples, his description of his previous devotion to the law and his subsequent commitment to the new covenant in Christ is telling:

> *"...If anyone else thinks he may have confidence in the flesh, I more so: circumcised the eighth day, of the stock of Israel, of the tribe of Benjamin, a Hebrew of the Hebrews; concerning the law, a Pharisee, concerning zeal, persecuting the church; concerning the righteousness which is in the law, blameless. But what things were gain to me, these I count as loss for the excellence of the knowledge of Christ Jesus my Lord, for whom I have suffered the loss of all things, and count them as rubbish, that I may gain Christ and be found in Him, not having my own righteousness, which is from the law, but that which is through faith in Christ, the righteousness which is from God by faith"* (Phil. 3:4-9).

The cornerstone verse of New Testament theology is John 3:16: "For God so loved the world that He gave His only begotten Son, that whoever believes in Him should not perish but have everlasting life." This one statement changed the entire covenant relationship with God from self-righteous works under the religious law to personal faith in Jesus. The fundamental question in the mind of every person who considers this statement is "how much belief is required?"

Under the law, a person's religious actions were measurable. One could tabulate how often he prayed, how much he tithed, how often he worshipped, and how extensive were his acts of charity. But faith is entirely different. It can neither be seen nor measured, and there is no way for one to become comfortable that he has sufficient faith to be saved if he is attempting to apply some physical measurement. Thus it is quite understandable that anyone moving from a tradition of legal compliance to a relationship with God based on faith in Jesus would have found the uncertainty somewhat unnerving.

Jesus realized that uncertainty, and He addressed the spiritual concerns about the necessary amount of faith with a parable so startling in its simplicity that it bordered on unbelievable. The Parable of the Mustard Seed portrays the growth of virtually the smallest thing one could imagine to the largest thing one could visualize. A mustard seed is exceedingly small, about two millimeters in diameter, yet it has the potential to grow into a very large plant, and that is how Jesus wanted His followers to envision the level of faith initially needed to experience the spiritual growth of the kingdom of heaven within them. So, in answer to the question, "how much faith is needed?" Jesus said any amount faith, however small, will begin the growth process. Such profound simplicity is amazing.

There is, however, a broader application of this parable. In Jewish society, a person of great intellect and accomplishment was often referred to as a "mover of mountains." But a mover of mountains under the law and traditions of Israel was profoundly different to one described by Jesus. In Judaism, one became a mover of mountains through mastery of the religious law and all of its complex requirements, both through intellectual knowledge and understanding and in the personal practice and performance of the law's myriad requirements.

Interestingly, there was no concept that such growth and attainment could be accomplished in an individual by the Holy Spirit as a result of faith. Frankly, that would have seemed preposterous. The focus of Judaism was on righteousness through personal performance of the law, not through faith in a crucified carpenter who promised a powerful inner spiritual transformation by an unseen and virtually unknown Holy Spirit.

Yet, Jesus said that was exactly what would happen. Answering His disciples' questions about their inability to cure an epileptic boy, Jesus said to them:

> *"Because of your unbelief; for assuredly I say to you, if you have faith as a mustard seed, you will say to this mountain, 'Move from here to there,' and it will move; and nothing will be impossible for you"* (Matt. 17:20).

From Jesus' perspective, the ability to become a mover of mountains was directly related to faith and not personal works of legalistic righteousness. It was not great and mighty works, but rather the smallest seed of unseen faith in Jesus that would enable one to grow and mature into a mover of mountains.

Thus, the parable of the mustard seed portrays the difference between a seed of faith planted in the law and a seed of faith planted in the Lord. The former requires all of one's self-righteous effort and work to become a mover of mountains, whereas the latter requires faith no greater than the smallest mustard seed to mature into a towering spiritual giant. The former shuns and shames all who do not comply with the law's countless requirements for righteousness, whereas the latter beckons all who believe in Jesus into the comfort of its wide-open branches. The former is limited in potential to the physical ability of man to comply, whereas the latter is unlimited due to the unrestricted power of the Holy Spirit to bless a believer for the glory of Christ. Compliance has limits; consecration does not.

Peter could have rejected Jesus' invitation to discipleship and remained shackled by the burden and bitterness of the law, and nothing more would have been heard about him. Instead, he allowed the seed of faith to be planted, and he followed Jesus into the unlimited future of divine destiny. When the Apostle Peter left his fishing net to follow Christ, the mustard seed implanted by faith began to grow. These strategic stories of repentance made him realize that the kingdom of heaven and the messiah were unlike anything he had been taught. Through pondering these truths, Peter was slowly transformed by the Holy Spirit from a frustrated fisherman into a founding father of the Christian church. Two thousand years later, the harvest produced in Peter's life by the Holy Spirit continues to grow, and the mustard plant, symbolizing the kingdom of heaven, will not stop growing until the end of time.

The amazing truth portrayed by the parable of the mustard seed is that the same great harvest is potentially true in the life of every Christian who allows the seed of faith to be implanted in their life. The growth of the kingdom of God in His people never ends and will not end until Christ returns. Only then will the final harvest be known. The mustard plant continues to grow!

The Parable of Scattered Seed

> *"...The kingdom of God is as if a man should scatter seed on the ground, and should sleep by night and rise by day, and the seed should sprout and grow, he himself does not know how. For the earth yields crops by itself: first the blade, then the head, and after that the full grain in the head. But when the grain ripens, immediately he puts in the sickle, because the harvest has come"* (Mark 4:26-29).

Jesus sought to transform the desire for political revolution into the reality of religious evolution. The people of Israel wanted change, but they could conceive no other way to obtain their objective than revolt against Rome and restore the old kingdom of David under messianic leadership. Jesus, on the other hand, consistently said the kingdom of heaven was a slow and steady spiritual transformation from the constraints of Jewish religious law to the freedom of love and grace.

The concept of a kingdom is vitally important to this parable's meaning and merits initial discussion. The longstanding Jewish dream was for the messiah to appear and usher in the golden age of Jewish life. The messiah would rid the country of its enemies, establish unrivaled economic prosperity, create, and command an undefeatable army, and govern the country under the guidelines of established religious law and tradition. This messianic kingdom would mirror the ancient kingdom ruled by King David, and it would establish Israel as the dominant nation in the region, ensuring peace and prosperity free from any external threat. The kingdom would be physical and visible, and its boundaries and beliefs were widely known and discussed, especially among Israel's respected elders and religious leaders. However, no one knew when this political kingdom would be established because no one knew when the messiah would appear. Creation of this physical messianic kingdom was a national hope and dream.

In direct contrast, Jesus spoke about a spiritual kingdom that was "not of this world" but was so readily available that He described it as being "at hand." It would not be experienced through any physical means, but rather through personal repentance that would spiritually transform every believer.

The political kingdom would be established by the sudden acts of the messiah and would be immediate and overwhelming. However, the spiritual kingdom would be unseen, gradual, and hardly recognizable immediately. The political kingdom would transform the nation; whereas the spiritual kingdom would transform each individual believer. The political kingdom was well understood by most people; whereas, the spiritual kingdom was understood only by Jesus, who slowly tried to reveal it to His disciples and others. Almost every resident of Israel had heard about the coming messianic political kingdom; however, the spiritual kingdom of heaven was unheard of.

Jesus faced the challenge of shifting the commitment of His disciples and others from an unwavering belief and hope in the creation of a future messianic political kingdom to an equally unwavering commitment to the present experience of a spiritual kingdom. To accomplish this, Jesus challenged them to change their beliefs from following the teachings of the most respected religious leaders in Israel to believing and following the teaching of a thirty-year-old carpenter who these same respected religious leaders laughingly and scornfully dismissed as being mentally unstable.

In order to overcome this deeply imbedded view of the messianic kingdom, Jesus had to transform traditional Jewish understanding and beliefs in at least three major areas: (1) the well-established view of the revelation and role of the messiah; (2) the absence of understanding regarding the person, power, and purpose of the Holy Spirit; and (3) the meaning and spiritual definition of the "word of God." The challenge of changing the engrained mindset of

Israel in these critical areas could not have been greater, and in order to further His goal, Jesus strategically employed the parable of scattered seed.

(1). The Messiah of Israel: How He would appear and what He would do

During the first century B.C., the Roman Empire steadily expanded militarily until it conquered most of the known world. Greek control, which had been established under Alexander the Great, receded into history, leaving behind the beauty and felicity of the Greek language and the brilliance of Greek philosophy. Israel was greatly influenced by both, as was the early Christian church.

The control over Israel, which had been established under the Hasmonean Dynasty, was replaced by Roman control. In the early years of Roman occupation, Israel was allowed to retain a level of self-governance and the freedom to maintain her traditional religious practices. Essentially, Rome was content with allowing Jewish autonomy as long as Roman tax assessments were paid and there was no rebellion against overall Roman control.

However, many in Israel refused to recognize this pact of peaceful coexistence and became increasingly rebellious. Roman authorities became intolerant of this defiance and began exerting increased military and administrative control, in effect ending Israel's ability to manage her own internal affairs. Rome finally asserted total control around 40 B.C. with the designation of Herod the Great as King of the Jews and his appointment to serve as governor over the Roman province of Judea, which encompassed the geographical area of Israel.

Although Herod the Great did much to gain Jewish acceptance, such as rebuilding the Temple, his administrative control was never fully accepted. In his final years of life, Herod's health deteriorated both physically and mentally. Having been told by the three wise men that a child had been born who would be "King of the Jews," Herod ordered the murder of all male children two years of age or less who were in Jerusalem and surrounding districts in order to eliminate this future potential rival (Matt. 2:16). The "Massacre of the Innocents," as it is known in Christian history, forced Joseph to take

Mary and the newborn Jesus into Egypt for safety until Herod died (Matt. 2:13-15).

Following Herod's death in 4 B.C., Judea was subdivided into four regions, with each of Herod the Great's three sons and his sister given one of the regions to administer for Rome, and this administrative and political division was known as the Herodian Tetrarchy. Herod Archelaus was given Judea, the largest region that encompassed Judea, Samaria, and Idumaea. In year 6 A.D., Rome restructured Judea, abolished the rule of Herod Archelaus, and formed the Province of Judea out of the region, which brought it under direct Roman control. Thereafter, Judea was ruled by a series of Roman governors. Of particular significance to Christian history was the rule of Pontius Pilate, the fifth Roman governor, who ruled from 26-36 A.D. and presided over the trial and crucifixion of Jesus.

It is noteworthy that Herod the Great's son, Herod Antipas, was given the territory encompassing Galilee and Perea. Although an able administrator, Herod Antipas appears in Christian history as the King Herod (although he technically did not have the title of king) who ordered the execution of John the Baptist and who was involved in the events of Jesus' trial and crucifixion. Following His arrest, Jesus was first brought to Pontius Pilate, who upon learning that much of Jesus' ministry had occurred in Galilee, sent Jesus to King Herod, who he knew was in Jerusalem at the time. Herod and his soldiers mocked Jesus and unmercifully heaped abuse and scorn on Him with their actions and contemptuous questions. Herod then returned Jesus to Pilate for final adjudication. Although the gospels refer to King Herod in both Jesus' birth and death narratives, it was two different men who were father and son and known by the same name.

Israel was locked in political intrigue and uncertainty for the duration of Jesus' earthly life, with minor revolts and threats of rebellion occurring frequently, and often Herod the Great's descendants were directly involved in the political uncertainty. The ongoing unrest produced numerous groups with nationalistic ideals advocating rebellion against Roman rule, and the Zealots were one of the most aggressive and outspoken. Interestingly, Jesus chose one of the Zealots, Simon, as a disciple.

Coupled with this background of political turmoil, Israel was beset with a long-standing belief that God would eventually send the messiah of Israel, who would usher in the golden age of messianic rule.

Through divine, supernatural power and skill, the messiah would restore Israel's military and economic power, unite various factions into one cohesive brotherhood, banish Israel's enemies, and establish unprecedented peace and prosperity.

There was universal belief throughout Israel that the true messiah would reveal himself to the nation through spectacular displays of power transcending human ability and undeniably establish himself as God's divine messenger. Major natural phenomena, such as unexplainable heavenly and cosmic displays, were also anticipated. There was no doubt that the appearance of the messiah would be sudden and amazing, transforming the nation from a subservient, vassal state of Rome into a powerful, dominant nation that would completely destroy all vestiges of Roman rule. It was like a dream world of hope and anticipation.

For generations, "the day of the Lord" was predicted as a colossal upheaval of existing norms, validated by natural phenomena and cosmic manifestations in which it would seem that all of the social and natural order of life had been transformed (Zeph. 1:18). Thus, it was assumed that messianic change would be a sudden, visible, glorious, and awe-inspiring manifestation of divine power physically occurring around them.

But Jesus described the kingdom of heaven in an entirely different way. For example, a group of Pharisees once specifically asked Jesus when the kingdom of God would come, and He shocked them with His answer:

> *"The kingdom of God does not come with observation; nor will they say, 'See here!' or 'See there!' For indeed, the kingdom of God is within you"* (Luke 17:20-21).

Nothing in their religious understanding either prepared them for His answer or taught them that messianic change would initially be small, invisible, unknown, and occurring spiritually within them. Anyone who espoused such an idea would have been quickly labeled by religious authorities as insane and demon possessed, and those were indeed allegations leveled at Jesus. The concept of inner individual spiritual change occurring as a result of personally turning from commitment to the law to commitment to an attitude of redeeming love for others, which would eventually change their nation and the world, was not understood. In order for the kingdom of heaven to become an earthy reality, these entrenched beliefs would have to slowly change, and the use of parables to facilitate a new thought process became a major teaching tool for Jesus.

Thus, Jesus had to devise a teaching method that would not only subtly bypass the entrenched refusal to consider new religious thoughts but also generate a change in understanding about how God gradually reveals the nature of the kingdom of heaven. He created a parable about the growth of scattered seed in order to do that.

The people of Israel obsessively looked for signs of impending change. The appearance of a new leader with unusual ability or intellect prompted widespread speculation regarding whether this was the messiah, and demands were often made for the individual to perform some sign in order to prove the authenticity of his claims. Jesus was treated no differently. Even John the Baptist sent messengers to Jesus asking, "Are You the Coming One, or do we look for another?" (Matt. 11:3), and the Pharisees asked "…What sign will you perform then, that we may see it and believe You? What work will You do?" (John 6:30).

Jesus' initial popularity must be understood in the context of this historic messianic expectation. Those who followed Him, including His own disciples, anticipated the establishment of an earthly kingdom, and the disciples often argued about what position each of them would have and who would be greatest in this new kingdom (Luke 22:24). This expectation continued until shortly before Jesus' ascension into heaven when the disciples asked Him, "Lord, will You at this time restore the kingdom to Israel?" (Acts 1:6). There was never any real understanding that the kingdom of heaven which Jesus proclaimed was a slow, internal, spiritual growth process.

The challenge Jesus faced in changing this ancient, entrenched thoughts was greater than any modern-day Christian can readily understand. Jesus had to teach His disciples another way of thinking about and understanding the kingdom of heaven, as well as the time process involved in its revelation. He had to break through the historic mindset locked into their belief system and show them that the kingdom of heaven would be revealed in a manner totally opposite to their most basic beliefs.

In order to accomplish this, Jesus crafted a parable about the growth of scattered seed in order to help people think differently about how God's kingdom is revealed on earth. Through this parable, Jesus taught that the revelation of the kingdom to an individual would be through a slow process of growth toward spiritual maturity and not through some sudden and powerful transformation. Thus, He walked a narrow path of fostering spiritual evolution without inciting political revolution.

(2). The person, power, and purpose of the Holy Spirit

One of the pivotal considerations in the scattered seed parable is the work of the Holy Spirit. Although the Holy Spirit is a part of the triune Christian concept of God, His role in the Old Testament is not as pronounced as it is in the New Testament. The immediate challenges facing Jesus in explaining the work of the Holy Spirit included the following:

- How to explain the person, purpose, power, and work of the Spirit to a people who had no real understanding of the Spirit's existence.
- How to explain the spiritual transformative work of the Holy Spirit within the heart and mind of a person when their only concept of divine power focused on external, physical power manifested and displayed by the anticipated messiah.
- How to modify expected sudden change to an understanding of slow, gradual, incremental change over a long period of time.
- How to help close-minded people understand that the dynamic qualities and characteristics of the messianic kingdom of heaven will be brought forth in our life by the unseen person and power of the Holy Spirit and not our personal visible, measurable, self-righteous efforts under religious law.
- How to get God's covenant people to realize that the great spiritual harvest envisioned in the reign of the messiah would result from the growth of spiritual truth and not from the rigid enforcement of religious law.

- How to encourage God's covenant people to stop waiting on a religious revolution and begin experiencing the God-wrought evolution of spiritual growth enabled by the Holy Spirit within them, a process of growth that would spiritually transform them into witnesses for Christ and His ambassadors to the world?

The spiritual transformation inherent in the answers is important in understanding the magnitude of repentance demanded by Jesus.

The absence of understanding about the role and work of the Holy Spirit was indeed troubling for many early Christians, and Nicodemus is a prime example. Although Nicodemus was a Jewish ruler (John 3:1), he was nevertheless mystified by Jesus' teaching and went to Him for clarification, his mission being concealed under the cover of nighttime darkness.

Jewish religious belief held that, if a person unreservedly committed themselves to the law of Israel, they might be baptized as a symbol of washing away any other religious thought, and it would be as if they were born again as one wholly devoted to the law. However, it was all physical, as if the baptismal water washed their entire body just as the ceremonial washing of one's hands was thought to symbolize religious cleanliness. But in the ritual of physical baptism, there was very little thought about cleansing the heart and mind. Yet, Jesus specifically said the thoughts of the heart were what defiled a person, not the cleanliness of his hands or body (Mark 7:20-23).

Therefore, Jesus shocked Nicodemus by telling him that "unless one is born of water and the Spirit, he cannot enter the kingdom of God" (John 3:5). Being "born of water" was a Jewish idiom regarding natural birth, but Nicodemus had no understanding of what it meant to be "born of the Spirit." Sensing Nicodemus' confusion, Jesus explained, "That which is born of the flesh is flesh, and that which is born of the Spirit is spirit" (v. 6). Judaism had no concept of spiritual regeneration. The primary focus was both a true Jewish heritage and obedience to the religious law of Israel. In effect, being naturally born into this heritage and complying with its religious requirements was believed sufficient to enter the kingdom of God. There were no other requirements for experiencing a more spiritually oriented life.

Being a natural born Jew—or even a converted, baptized Jew—and complying with the law might make one born of the water, but it did not make him spiritually reborn. One can only imagine Nicodemus, a scholar of the law, trying to understand the necessity of also being "born of the Spirit" in order to enter the kingdom of God, because Nicodemus had no concept about the person, power, and purpose of the Holy Spirit despite his status as a religious scholar and teacher. Because of his Jewish heritage and obedience to the law, he would truly have thought that he was already a part of the kingdom. His struggle to understand the words of Jesus should be studied with fascination, compassion, and understanding.

Noting Nicodemus' consternation, Jesus responded, "Do not marvel that I said to you, 'You must be born again'" (v.7). Nicodemus must have quietly looked at Jesus in speechless amazement, as if he were dumb-struck, and one can picture the blank stare of shock, uncertainty, and concern on Nicodemus' face. Jesus then taught Nicodemus a truth that is a vital part of understanding these parables. Comparing the Holy Spirit to the unseen wind, Jesus said, "The wind blows where it wishes, and you hear the sound of it, but cannot tell where it comes from or where it goes. So is everyone who is born of the Spirit" (John 3:8). Jesus told Nicodemus that true spiritual change necessary for entering the kingdom is an unseen work of the Spirit, versus the visible physical acts expected of the messiah, and the Spirit moves independently of human control and direction. Thus, in this parable, the scattered seed germinate and begin to grow even while the sower sleeps and goes about the routine activities of life, because the growth is a work of the Spirit and not of human effort.

Only the Spirit can bring about such spiritual change in a person, but Jesus' followers possessed no understanding of the spiritual work that the Holy Spirit would perform. Therefore, Jesus specifically explained the purpose and power of the Holy Spirit in the spiritual transformation that would occur within them through repentance:

> *"However, when He, the Spirit of truth, has come, He will guide you into all truth; for He will not speak on His own authority, but whatever He hears He will speak, and He will tell you things to come. He will glorify Me, for He will take of what is Mine and declare it to you.*

All things that the Father has are Mine. Therefore I said that He will take of Mine and declare it to you" (John 16:13-15).

Jesus' statement contains a word that is critically important in understanding the concept of these two seed parables and the work of the Holy Spirit in Christian growth and discipleship. Jesus stated that the primary work of the Spirit is to take "what is Mine and declare it to you." Declare means making a report, uttering a declaration, or making an important announcement. However, its importance lies within the nature of the declaration because it does not mean a preliminary report, but rather something that has gone through all essential stages of completion and clarification so that the declared truth is fully mature and final.

Therein is the work of the Holy Spirit in growing a new Christian into a mature disciple of Christ. The Spirit completes the words and work of Jesus in His covenant disciples, spiritually maturing them and enabling them to function as effective witnesses and ambassadors for Jesus in the world. The ability to love one's enemies, turn the other cheek, and go the extra mile is a manifestation of the harvest of spiritual maturity and is a visible fruit of the unseen Spirit at work. The potential priestly impact of this maturity is incalculable. Jesus challenged His disciples to "Let your light so shine before men, that they may see your good works and glorify your Father in heaven" (Matt. 5:16). That is the mystery and the great spiritual truth that Jesus sought to explain, or to at least cause people to consider, through this parable.

(3). The nature of the seed and the Word of God

One of the fascinating concepts involved in this parable is the meaning of the seed that is planted. In the parable of the sower (Matt. 13:1-9), Jesus identifies the seed as the "word of the kingdom," which is the "word of God." That concept, too, is included in the transformative meaning of this parable.

In the Old Testament, the "word" of God is significant, particularly in the Psalms. For example, the Psalmist stated, "Your word have I hidden in my heart, that I might not sin against You" (Psalm 119:11) and "Your word is a lamp to my feet and a light to my path" (Psalm 119:105). The "word of God" denotes the law of God and the multiple requirements of the law.

But there is an enormous truth that must be considered: Law neither grows nor expands spiritual understanding, but remains an unyielding, static, and stifling requirement for action alone. Law does not change any attitude, nor does religious law grow one more into the spiritual likeness of God and nurture them into spiritual maturity and fulfillment as His adopted children. Under the law, the seed would have been planted in the rock-hard soil of legal tradition where any growth would have been quickly stomped out by the repetitive, mindless, lifeless weight of legalistic religious ritual.

However, Israel considered herself yoked to the law and its burdensome requirements as an ox would be yoked to a plow. In contrast, Jesus proclaimed that "... My yoke is easy, and My burden is light" (Matt. 11:30). Through grace, Jesus removed the burden of personal righteousness under the law and introduced a radical concept that the "word" of God was in fact the spiritual nature of God implanted in believers through faith and given to them as an act of grace. It was a gift from God, not a righteous relationship with Him earned through personal works under the law.

The New Testament most often defines "word" as *logos*. It generally means the word of a person that grows from and reveals their inner nature. More specifically, it is the reason or logic behind one's words and actions. Thus, John wrote that "In the beginning was the Word, and the Word was with God, and the Word was God" (John 1:1). John then declared that "...the Word became flesh and dwelt among us..." (v. 14). That is a truly powerful concept. In the beginning was the reason for God's creation, the reason for redemption, the reason and logic for the Cross of Christ, the reason and logic underlying the work of the Holy Spirit, and the reason for the church to be God's new covenant people, those who live by faith in His word and commit themselves to the logic of His work. Jesus' eternal life is the rationale for the resurrection and the promise of everlasting life to all believers.

God's reason for loving us, His logic behind saving us, and His purpose for empowering us with the Holy Spirit took on human form and became one of us, promising to live and work within us through a new covenant. The work of the Holy Spirit is to take the totality of God's reason and logic for sending Christ into this world and powerfully declare that in our redeemed life so that we become a new spiritual creation in Jesus. Through our personal declaration of that divine truth, we each serve as witnesses for Christ, validating the eternal truth of God's purpose and logic for His life to the world around us.

Surely, one must understand that, when the spiritual nature and purpose of God is received into the life of a believer by faith, it has the power to significantly change him spiritually, even when the soil of his life is full of stones and briars. When implanted in the good soil of life, the spiritual word of God grows exponentially, enabling and empowering spiritual works greater than imagined possible. But how long does that change take? It does not occur immediately, and, in fact, it continues for the duration of life.

One should ponder what Jesus said to the inquisitive Nicodemus about the mysterious, unseen, wonder-working power of the Holy Spirit. In effect, Jesus said that the Holy Spirit's power was beyond human understanding. In comparing His nature, influences, and power to the unseen wind, Jesus described to Nicodemus how the Holy Spirit moves independently from human restraints imposed by religious ritual and tradition. He moves unseen in whatever direction He desires in order to accomplish God's will and glorify the redemptive work of Jesus.

The ability of the Holy Spirit to take the dynamic, living word of God—as opposed to the static tradition of religious ritual and law—and miraculously transform a person or a nation in a manner known only to God is unquestioned. It is imperative to understand that this spiritual growth and transformation does not occur suddenly or spontaneously. It involves long-term maturation and discipleship brought about by sincere repentance. The dynamic, powerful spiritual change brought about by the Holy Spirit would not be sudden, cataclysmic, and physically transforming, according to the demands and dictates of the law and in conformity with centuries-old religious tradition. Conversely, it would be spiritual, internal, and gradual according to the desires of God, and would be mysteriously brought about by the unseen power of the Holy Spirit.

This concept of physical versus spiritual change was one of the great challenges facing Jesus in helping people understand the true meaning of Christianity, and Christians still struggle with understanding this truth today. Religious change that is brought about through compliance with law is limited only to the demands of the law. There is neither reason nor motivation to go beyond compliance. Conversely, change brought about by the Spirit is unlimited, boundless, and is motivated by a spiritual desire to grow into the image and likeness of Christ. The two could not be more opposite in nature and long-term consequences.

For example, under the law, if one is required to love his neighbor, then logically he seeks to define "who is my neighbor?" (Luke 10:29). Once he has met the minimum requirement, the law neither compels nor inspires him to care for those who are not his neighbor. In fact, he is perfectly free under the law to hate anyone not a neighbor. Law doesn't inspire change of those attitudes, whereas redeeming love does. That is precisely how Israel viewed religious compliance, and that is precisely what Jesus sought to change through repentance.

But repentance is a spiritual growth process occurring over time. It may indeed begin with a singular decision, but the fundamental change, growth, and maturation into a spiritually different person with different beliefs, ideas, and attitudes does not occur automatically and spontaneously. It is foolish to think of a freshly planted grain of seed suddenly and miraculously popping from the ground as ripened grain ready for harvest. That does not happen. Neither does true Christian discipleship happen spontaneously. It is a lengthy growth process involving different phases of commitment, understanding, and service. In truth, it never ends. But there is one fundamental reality: Regardless of the final harvest, it begins with the planting of the seed of the word of God, and that is the basic truth of these two seed parables.

When the Psalmist stated that he had hidden the word of God in his heart, he accurately described the image of sowing the seed and implanting the word of God in our heart and in our life. It means to store, treasure up, and secure something within the unseen and hidden confines of one's innermost thoughts and values. In the parable of the sower, Jesus clearly identified the word of God as the seed that was being sowed. The concept is not physical and should not be envisioned as putting a seed into the ground. Rather, it should be understood as the implanting of a divine spiritual truth in the physical life and circumstances of a believer.

However, there is a great truth that must be explored here: It is the nature of what is hidden and the reason why it is hidden. If one is a legalist, then the word of God is essentially viewed as written, and it is memorized and internalized solely in order to comply. That is how Israel viewed religious law. As the rich young ruler stated to Jesus, "All these things I have kept from my youth…" (Matt.19:20). He had memorized the law in order that he might perform each aspect of it, yet he saw it only as a standard controlling his actions, but not his attitudes. Even though he could say "all these things I have done," he could not say "all these things I have felt in my heart" or "all these things I have spiritually experienced and have spiritually grown."

Far too many Christians similarly view the word of God as an obligation to act physically in compliance with its demands and not as an opportunity to grow spiritually and mature into a dynamic disciple of Christ and a living witness of God's redeeming love for others. Indeed, if that is how one views the word of God, then the seed is planted in rocky soil where it will soon wither because it has no spiritual depth.

But, if the word of God is viewed as a standard of spiritual commitment transforming emotions and attitudes, it will ultimately change the actions of an individual. In this manner, the word becomes implanted in the heart—the figurative seat of control for our emotions and attitudes. This is one of the major contrasts that Jesus portrayed about the law. Jesus specifically stated that it is from within one's heart that evil and sinful desires arise (Matt. 15:19), and the uncleanliness of the heart is not corrected by the ritualistic washing of one's hands. Thus, David, the Psalmist, rightly asked God to create a clean heart within him (Psalm 51:10), and that spiritual transformation for every Christian is a work of the Holy Spirit sealing the life of Christ into a believer's heart as a result of repentance and faith in Jesus as Lord and Savior.

The law, even when perfectly complied with, does not have the capacity to change attitudes such as hatred, prejudice, and bitterness. One may boast that he has been obedient to the legalistic word and never killed another, while being unburdened by the bitter attitudes toward others that boil within his heart. That is precisely why Jesus taught a new thought process that first addressed underlying motivational attitudes of the heart. It would take time, repentance, and spiritual growth, but the word of God implanted as a spiritual standard of attitude would eventually transform human actions also, thus providing a complete transformation into the image of Christ. This transformation and spiritual maturity does not happen immediately, but as a result of steady spiritual growth and maturity. It begins with repentance and blossoms into dynamic Christian growth and matures into the harvest of discipleship and living as a witness for Christ and being His ambassador to the world (II Cor. 5:20).

The parable of the scattered seed is not intended to convey mysterious steps of meaning, such as trying to attach separate and specific meaning to the blade, head, and harvest. One can attempt to attach some interpretation to each but doing so misses the greater meaning. It is akin to the wise admonition of not seeing the beauty of the forest because of one's obsessive focus on each tree. It is an overall process of growth that is different in each believer's life.

No individual Christian is a mature disciple the moment he commits his life to Christ. Instead, he continues to grow and mature throughout life. Can any Christian truly say at any point in life that they are fully mature spiritually and have nothing more to learn about Jesus or nothing more to do for Him? No. Can any church say that they are fully mature as a body of believers and have no more work to do or no more people to reach for Christ? Of course they cannot.

The growth of Christian discipleship is a mystery. The actions of discipleship are something that one does; but the attitudes of discipleship are mysteriously given to him by the Holy Spirit. Once the seed of faith in Jesus is planted in his heart, the Holy Spirit begins working quietly within to bring about spiritual change. The growth of attitudes befitting a disciple of Jesus occurs at all times of the day and night, even while one sleeps or goes about the affairs of daily life. The Holy Spirit slowly replaces old attitudes with new ones that glorify Christ. Jesus described this process perfectly through this parable of scattered seed—once the seed is planted, then the first evidence of new life emerges in the blade as it is slowly nurtured by the soil in which it is planted, then a grain head of potential maturity gradually appears, and finally the fully ripened grain is ready for an abundant harvest.

The process is no different in the life of a Christian. The great joy of evangelism is watching that growth process occur in the life of one in whom you have planted the seed of the word of God

A New Covenant Versus Old Religious Ritual

The Parable of Unshrunk Cloth and an Old Garment

"No one sews a piece of unshrunk cloth on an old garment; or else the new piece pulls away from the old, and the tear is made worse" (Mark 2:21).

Truth may be stated in a parable either in a short story or even in a few sentences, but the imagery portrayed must be vivid and detailed, creating a lasting impression. The most effective parables are drawn from everyday experiences to which almost everyone can relate. Although relatively short in length, Jesus' parables regarding unshrunk fabric on an old garment and the corresponding parable about new wine being put into old wineskins are great examples of common experiences that evoke meaningful imagery in the listener's mind, for each was drawn from the wisdom of everyday life and yet convey a profound and lasting eternal truth.

Jesus sought a transformative change in the spiritual mindset of Israel through repentance, as well as creating a visionary new approach to understanding a covenant relationship with God for all believers. Thus, He was confronted with the challenge of breaking His followers away from the ancient way of thinking about God and man's righteous relationship with Him. Centuries of established religious law and traditional worship would have to yield to Jesus' new spiritual interpretations, and very little of Jesus' teaching fit the mold and method of traditional Jewish worship.

Consequently, Jesus had to impart an understanding that new thought about old religious laws did not mean their rejection and destruction, but rather the fulfillment of their inherent spiritual purpose (Matt. 5:17). He sought a simple yet meaningful way to help His followers realize that the proverbial stream of divine truth can find a new streambed of spiritual consciousness in which to flow, never again returning to the old physical form and path from which it departed. Jesus sought a meaningful way to establish that new wisdom does not always mesh with the mindset of old methods, and that a new covenant of faith is not the same as an ancient covenant of law.

He sincerely wanted all Christians to know that allowing the Holy Spirit to cleanse one's heart is not the same as trying to cleanse one's hands, and that the daily sanctification of a believer is not comparable to the annual sacrifice of a lamb. Regarding old attitudes toward others, Jesus taught His followers that the outstretched hand of redeeming love for all will not fit into the glove of scorn and rejection of Gentiles and sinners; that proclaiming redeeming love by compelling obedience to religious law is hypocrisy; and that attempting to experience unmerited grace through the practice of religious ritual gains nothing.

How could Jesus say all of this without appearing to reject the law and prophets which He came to fulfill? He could have just said it as a matter of fact, but instead He chose to make people think about these truths for themselves through two parables about unshrunk cloth on old fabric and new wine in old wineskins. We still ponder their meaning today.

The challenge of formulating a parable is first envisioning the social and spiritual issue that is to be considered and then finding a simple, commonly understood truth from everyday life which will capture the essence of the desired change. When there are multiple social, spiritual, and religious issues that need consideration, the ability to articulate that need within a single parable framework becomes even more challenging.

Once stated and accepted, a parable's truth is obvious. But deciding the basis that best enables the parable to convey the greatest truth with the most lasting impact is enormously challenging. As an example, envision the multiple issues that Jesus wanted His disciples to reconsider. In order to appreciate the brilliance of this parable, the religious and cultural issues that Jesus considered as "an old garment" should be compared to the new covenant promises that He viewed as "unshrunk cloth." The contrast is both spiritually enlightening and personally challenging. As one examines the myriad social and religious changes needed through repentance in order to best prepare a disciple to understand new truths about the kingdom of heaven, what examples from everyday life could Jesus have chosen that would best capture the transformation from the old covenant of law (the old garment) to the new covenant of grace (the unshrunk cloth)?

He strategically chose an everyday example that remains a familiar issue with new clothing even today. A new piece of fabric will usually shrink in size when it is washed the first time. Consequently, if one patches a tear in a piece of old cloth already shrunk by age and multiple washings with new, unshrunk cloth, the threads binding the new to the old will often endure great stress and break as the new shrinks and pulls away from the old. In a stroke of divine genius, Jesus used this well-known example to describe the spiritual struggle of trying to fit concepts of faith under the new covenant to the legalistic fabric of the old covenant.

Nothing is more fundamental to Judaism than the b*erith*. This ancient covenant with God historically defines Israel as a special nation divinely chosen by God from all the nations on earth and uniquely blessed by Him. A covenant is an exclusive agreement between two individuals, or nations, or between God and man. It may be viewed as an unbreakable promise, an eternal testament and personal commitment, a solemn oath, and a blood covenant backed by the sworn dedication of the life and possessions of one to the other.

A covenant was signified physically by a cut on the body, and the word also historically means "to cut." The cut mark used in Judaism to identify the covenant commitment is the circumcision of all Jewish males, which has been practiced since the days of Abraham (Gen. 17:10-11). However, the Apostle Paul gave this ancient practice a new interpretation when he wrote to the church at Rome, "…he is a Jew who is one inwardly; and circumcision is that of the heart, in the Spirit, not in the letter; whose praise is not from men but from God" (Rom. 2:29).

In addition, a covenant was also often symbolized by the parties passing between the dismembered parts of a sacrificial animal denoting the commitment of life through the covenant and the penalty of death for breaking the solemn pledge. The death penalty for a broken covenant would later add great meaning to the cross of Christ.

Thus, when God entered into a covenant with Abraham, He instructed Abraham to bring sacrificial animals and cut them into halves and lay the parts opposite each other. Later, Abraham saw "a smoking oven and a burning torch that passed between the pieces." Symbolizing the presence of God, this oven and torch was God's covenant promise to fulfill His divine promise to Abraham. Knowing man's foibles and that Abraham's descendants would not live up to the covenant, it is significant that God alone passed between the parts of the sacrificial animals, in effect declaring an unbreakable, divine pledge to fulfill the covenant to those who faithfully believe Him (Gen. 15:17).

God's covenant promise appears several times in the Old Testament, with it being first made to Noah and his descendants, and the sign of the covenant for perpetual generations was the rainbow. Each time a rainbow formed; it would be a reminder of God's promise never again to destroy all life through a flood (Gen. 9:9-17). Most significant was God's covenant with the Israelites made on Mount Sinai during the exodus from Egyptian captivity (Exod. 19:3-6). As a means of identifying the Israelites as God's covenant people, God gave them the Ten Commandments defining their relationship with God and their fellowman. By following and living by these precepts, Israel would be divinely set apart among the nations of the earth as "a special treasure to Me above all people…and you shall be to Me a kingdom of priests and a holy nation" (Exod. 19:5-6).

These Ten Commandments and the other laws and religious codes recorded in the first five books of the Old Testament are known as the Torah, the law of Israel. Over the centuries, their interpretation produced volumes of laws controlling every facet of Jewish life during Jesus' earthly life and ministry. These laws and the writings of the major and minor prophets form the basis of "the law and the prophets" and were the most revered aspects of ancient Judaism (Matt. 5:17). In the Jewish mindset of Jesus' day, having great respect and reverence for the writings of the prophets and dutifully keeping every aspect of the law was the basis of the covenant.

However, as one looks at these parables, it is critically important to understand that the Old Testament covenants were primarily with groups of individuals, such as Noah and his descendants, Abraham and his descendants, or the Israelites as a whole. The legalistic covenant led to an intense inclusive attitude, particularly among the most ardent adherents to the law, such as the scribes and Pharisees, who viewed only those who steadfastly kept the law as being within the covenant relationship with God, and all others were excluded.

A bitter dislike and condemnation of Gentiles developed, and a cold, unmerciful, and unloving attitude toward others became deeply engrained in Jewish religious attitudes. In fact, the law stipulated that one was to love only their neighbor and hate their enemy, which was essentially every Gentile (Matt. 5:43). A covenant with God that lovingly and graciously included Gentiles was simply inconceivable.

However, that is exactly what Jesus proclaimed, and that is one reason He was so hated and rejected by Jewish religious leaders. Immediately prior to His betrayal and arrest, Jesus shared a final Passover meal with His disciples, known in Christian tradition as the Last Supper. During the meal, Jesus spoke of the bread as a symbol of "My body which is given for you." But He took the wine and declared a new covenant with God, which radically altered the historic covenant concept, by stating, "This cup is the new covenant in My blood, which is shed for you" (Luke 22:20). It is one of the most amazing and powerful statements in Christian history.

In describing the work of Christ as God's true High Priest, the writer of Hebrews stated that Jesus "has become a surety of a better covenant" (Heb. 7:22). What an incredible statement! In legal terms, a surety guarantees, at his own personal risk and expense, the performance of an act or of an agreement, and if there is a breach of the contract or a default in the performance of an obligation, the surety will cover any losses incurred by the other party. Applying this legal concept, Jesus personally guarantees and assures all who trust in the new covenant that it is divine truth which will be fulfilled, and no believer will suffer loss as a result of his faith.

Continuing the description of Jesus' priestly ministry, the author of Hebrews describes Him as the "Mediator of a better covenant, which was established on better promises" (Heb. 8:6). Mediator is a legal term denoting one who stands in between divergent parties, reconciles their differences, and produces an agreement, or a covenant of peace. He then uses his power and influence to assure performance of the covenant agreement. The essential work of a mediator is to produce peace, reconciliation, and mutual commitment to the covenant terms. That is the work of Jesus as the eternal priestly intermediary between God and man. Thus, no one can truly come to the Father in peace and reconciliation except through the covenant established and guaranteed by Jesus.

Why is this covenant better than the old one that had existed for centuries? The Hebrews author explains:

> *"For if that first covenant has been faultless, then no place would have been sought for a second. Because finding fault with them, He says 'Behold,*

the days are coming, says the Lord, when I will make a new covenant with the house of Israel and with the house of Judah—not according to the covenant that I made with their fathers in the day when I took them by the hand to lead them out of the land of Egypt; because they did not continue in My covenant, and I disregarded them', says the Lord. 'For this is the covenant that I will make with the house of Israel after those days', says the Lord: 'I will put My laws in their mind and write them on their hearts, and I will be their God, and they shall be My people. None of them shall teach his neighbor, and none his brother, saying, 'Know the Lord,' for all shall know Me, from the least of them to the greatest of them. For I will be merciful to their unrighteousness, and their sins and their lawless deeds I will remember no more.' In that He says, 'A new covenant,' He has made the first obsolete. Now what is becoming obsolete and growing old is ready to vanish away" (Heb. 8:7-13).

Under the old covenant, the High Priest annually went into the holiest part of the tabernacle and offered the proper sacrifices for the sins of the people. But, according to Hebrews:

"...if the blood of bulls and goats and the ashes of a heifer, sprinkling the unclean, sanctifies for the purifying of the flesh, how much more shall the blood of Christ, who through the eternal Spirit offered Himself without spot to God, cleanse your conscience from dead works to serve the living God? And for this reason He is the Mediator of the new covenant, by means of death..." (Heb. 9:13-15).

Why are these old and new covenants (testaments) important and what is their relevance in our modern tech-savvy, information-packed, highly mobile society? Despite all of man's technological advances and the massive increase in our intellectual capabilities, every person's personal relationship with God still remains a key issue in the meaning and purpose of life. If one believes in biblical truth, then the only way to have a life-changing relationship with God is through a covenant with Him. One may immediately think that a right relationship with God is through faith in Jesus, and that is correct. But, God's eternal promises of redemption and salvation, in which every believer has faith, are all encompassed in the new covenant made with mankind through faith in Christ.

It is that important. Christianity is not just a faith or a religious belief among many others. Uniquely, it is an eternal, unbroken relationship with God premised entirely on the life and work of Jesus. A covenant is a personal relationship in which two separate lives are joined together. All that one has, is, or hopes to be is based on the life of the other covenant party. As that relates to Jesus, His life becomes our own and our life—with all its sin and failures—that is given to Him to be entirely cleansed by the power of His blood. That is the meaning of the cross of Christ: He took all of our sins into His own life and bore the penalty of death for our broken covenant with God.

Ponder this personal question: How can I be in a relationship with God in which I know He accepts me, forgives me, and gives me His eternal life so that I can live in His presence? The eternal promise of the New Testament is that it is through a personal covenant in which Jesus takes my old life and replaces it with His so that, when I stand in the presence of God, He sees Christ, not me, and blesses me as if I were Jesus. That is so amazing it borders on unbelievable, but Jesus is the guarantor of its truth!

Why is the new covenant so much better than the old covenant? Consider the following: In our modern politically correct society, a "blood covenant" evokes images of animal sacrifices and an unpleasant connotation emerges. But its real importance is found in the life sustained by the blood. So, a blood covenant is really a life covenant in which one's blood becomes a vivid and graphic symbol for one's life. Therefore, the ancient cut denoting a covenant meant that one was giving up his life to, and for the benefit of, the other.

Thus, blood symbolized the covenant life itself, and it also represented the penalty for breaking the covenant. If one pledges his life in a blood covenant, just as he gives his life, he also faces the penalty of losing his life for violating the blood (life) covenant. Therein is the picture of man's relationship with God, for throughout history, mankind has failed to faithfully live in a covenant with God—except Jesus.

Therefore, we are all under the penalty of death, and that goes all the way back to Adam and Eve. That is why the Bible states, "all have sinned and fall short of the glory of God" and the consequence of this failure is death (Rom. 3:23, 6:23). But, what if God, as an expression of His mercy, wanted to forgive man's breaking of the life covenant and somehow pay the penalty of death for breaking the covenant Himself? How could God do that? What if He provided a substitute for a sinful man that would shed its blood—give up its life—as penalty for the broken covenant in place of the sinful covenant breaker? Who or what would be an acceptable substitute, and how often would a substitute have to shed their blood and give their life?

Consider the answer on a personal level: If God found you guilty of violating the covenant of life with Him and imposed the death penalty, to what or who would you turn to stand in as a substitute for you and bear your penalty? An animal—a lamb or a goat? Would you truly have confidence in the adequacy of the life of an animal substitute in your place? Would the blood of a lamb fully compensate for your sins against God? What if Jesus offered to be your substitute rather than a lamb? Would you accept that covenant offer? That is one of the fundamental differences between the old covenant and the new covenant.

The issue of atonement is at the heart of the question. Atonement essentially describes a covering, or something that covers over and blots out the record of prior bad actions. For every Christian, the question becomes personal: "What is the one thing that will wipe the slate clean and position one before God guiltless, blameless, and without any record of prior sinful deeds—just as if he had never sinned at all?" The blood—the life—of Jesus standing in God's presence as one's substitute and asking God to accept His perfect, sinless life in substitution is the answer. That is what the new covenant is about. The amazing truth is that God accepts that for all believers, regardless of the nature or magnitude of the prior sinful acts that broke the covenant with Him.

The old covenant provided for the annual atonement of the sins of the nation through the sacrifice of a perfect lamb by the High Priest on the Day of Atonement. However, despite its significant meaning, the process became an institutionalized ritual with little value for many. Even God became weary with the peoples' indifference toward the covenant of life and the meaningless slaughter of sacrificial animals with no repentance or change in attitudes toward God and their fellowman. It was a shallow, superficial, heartless effort at atonement. Two Old Testament prophets specifically denounced the whole meaningless process:

> *"'To what purpose is the multitude of your sacrifices to Me?' says the Lord. 'I have had enough of burnt offerings of rams and the fat of cattle. I do not delight in the blood of bulls, or of lambs or goats...bring no more futile sacrifices'"* (Isaiah 1:11, 13).

> *"I hate, I despise your feast days, and I do not savor your sacred assemblies. Though you offer Me burnt offerings and your grain offerings, I will not accept them, nor will I regard your fattened peace offerings"* (Amos 5:21-22).

Despite offering thousands of sacrificial animals over hundreds of years, the people never changed their attitude toward God. The entire sacrificial system under the law never made them more loving, kind, merciful, or caring about others. It just made them mean-spirited and cold-hearted, especially the scribes and Pharisees. Jesus said they were as spiritually dead as a tomb full of bones (Matt. 23:27).

Instead of all the noise of sacrificial festivals, Amos declared, "...let justice run down like water, and righteousness like a mighty stream" (Amos 5:24). In like manner, Jesus, quoting the prophet Hosea, told the Pharisees, "...go and learn what this means, 'I desire mercy and not sacrifice'" (Matt. 9:13). However, even with the revered prophets, who were a respected part of the "law and prophets," denouncing the meaningless sacrifices, the system continued because Judaism knew no other alternative for atonement.

Against this ancient ritual of animal sacrifice to cover the sins of man, the writer of Hebrews penned these words:

> *"Therefore, when He came into the world, He said: 'Sacrifice and offering You did not desire, but a body you have prepared for Me. In burnt offerings and sacrifices for sin You had no pleasure.' Then I said, 'Behold I have come—In the volume of the book it is written of Me—To do Your will, Oh God.' Previously saying, 'Sacrifice and offering, burnt offerings, and offerings for sin You did not desire, nor had pleasure in them' (which are offered according to the law)', then He said, 'Behold, I have come to do Your will, O God.' He takes away the first that He may establish the second. By that will we have been sanctified through the offering of the body of Jesus Christ once for all"* (Heb. 10:5-10).

Thus, God, through Jesus, took away the first covenant under the law so that He could establish the second covenant (the new covenant) through the blood of Jesus "once for all."

These three words—once for all—are enormously important in understanding both the meaning of the new covenant work of Christ and Christianity in general. The new covenant is premised on the death of Jesus on the cross as a "once for all time" sacrifice of His life as the penalty for the sinful broken covenant with God in substitution for all who believe, both Jew and Gentile. Thus, the new covenant must be viewed from two aspects: the meaning of Jesus death and the meaning of His covenant resurrected life given to all Christian believers.

Jesus' death marked a radical change from the ancient sacrificial system of Israel. By offering His perfect, sinless life (the ultimate perfect sacrifice without spot or blemish) once for all, He eliminated the need for any other sacrifice as atonement for man's sins. Through faith and God's grace, the meaning of His death is appropriated to every believer as a full and final atonement for the sins of believers. The atoning power of His blood shed on the cross extends to any person in the world who believes in Him. This covenant transcends both the boundaries of Israel and the constraints of the religious laws of Judaism.

This new covenant shifts from a national to an individual focus. On a personal level, considering the nature of one's sinful actions and attitudes, how often would an animal need to be sacrificed to atone for sin and place one back in a righteous relationship with God? Daily? Weekly? Would one annual sacrifice be sufficient? And what would the adequate sacrifice be? A lamb, bull, goat, or some other creature specified in a religious law? What sacrificial ritual would give one total confidence in the adequacy of the sacrifice for the atonement of sin and produce a deep spiritual peace that one was right with God?

The search for an answer leads to the amazing truth and grace of the new covenant in Christ. Jesus gave His life once for all sin of all people who place their faith in the adequacy of the atoning power of His blood, and He assures and guarantees all believers that it is acceptable to God. His blood is the final and ultimate substitute for all who believe—once for all!

Not only are we guaranteed the forgiveness of our sins under the new covenant, but we are also guaranteed eternal life through His resurrection, for, under the covenant, our sinful life becomes His, and

His sinless, everlasting life becomes ours. Nothing in the old covenant compared to this divinely assured promise of life. Through the new covenant in His blood—a covenant of life—there are several amazing aspects of grace that are part of the covenant life:

(1). The gift of everlasting life

Unlike the old covenant, the new covenant in the blood and life of Jesus assures a believer the gift of eternal life through the power of His resurrection. Speaking to heartbroken Martha, grieving over the death of her brother, Lazarus, Jesus said, "I am the resurrection and the life. He who believes in Me, though he may die, he shall live. And whoever lives and believes in Me shall never die" (John 11:25-26). Describing Himself as the Good Shepherd, Jesus said, "My sheep hear My voice, and I know them, and they follow Me. And I give them eternal life, and they shall never perish; neither shall anyone snatch them out of My hand" (John 10:27-28). The old covenant knew no concept of eternal life, and instead mentions Sheol, the abode of the dead, as a place into which one descended, and it was perceived as a dark, shadowy, mysterious place of uncertainty.

(2). The status of adoption

In the covenant life of Jesus, a Christian becomes an adopted spiritual child of God and a joint heir with Jesus to all the blessings of the kingdom of heaven. As an adopted child, every Christian receives the Spirit of adoption enabling them to "cry out, 'Abba, Father'" (Rom. 8:14-17). "Abba" is a tender, highly personal Aramaic word for "father" denoting the closest affinity and intimacy. However, under the old covenant, referring to God as "father" was a blasphemous crime worthy of death (John 5:17-18).

(3). The position of grace

Through the life of Christ, every Christian stands before God fully knowing that Jesus assures and guarantees us that we are forgiven, redeemed, sanctified, and justified—which may be seen as "just as if I'd" never sinned. Our record is clean, and God promises that He will remember our sins no more. All this is because Jesus died "once for all."

But there is an amazing aspect of grace that positions the church—and every Christian—in a position with God seldom considered by most Christians. The New Testament states that Jesus is now at the "right hand of the God" (Acts 2:33). That is an ancient expression denoting the greatest position of honor, trust, and fidelity. To the one at His right hand, God grants power and authority to represent Him and act for Him.

Through the covenant life with Jesus, we are in Him, and He is in us, and that bond is unbreakable. Thus, we are where He is. The Apostle Paul, writing to the Colossian church, said that Jesus is "head of the body, the church" (Col. 1:18), and, therefore, where the head is, the body is also. Thus, in Christ, every Christian, and the church body as a whole, sits at the right hand of God in the same position as Jesus. It is the highest position of honor in the kingdom of heaven, and we are empowered to act on His behalf in the world as ambassadors for Christ through whom God pleads for man to be reconciled to Him (II Cor. 5:20).

Under the old covenant, it was inconceivable that any individual would be viewed as sitting at the right hand of God.

(4). Fruits of the Spirit

Through the power of the Holy Spirit declaring the living Word of God through us, the redeemed life of each Christian becomes a public declaration of the truth of the new covenant. This is manifested through the "fruits of the Spirit," which may also be seen as the "fruits of repentance" we are to bear, making every believer in Christ more loving, joyous, peaceful, longsuffering, kind, good, faithful, gentle, and able to maintain self-control (Gal. 5:22). Life under the new covenant is so dramatically different to life under the old covenant, and so spiritually focused, it is as if one has been born again and has become a new creature within the covenant life of Christ. In comparison, there were no "fruits of the Spirit" specified under the old covenant.

(5). Personal relationships

Relationships with others under the new covenant drastically change also. Rather than the hatred of enemies and the old covenant sanctioned condemnation of Gentiles, the new covenant is manifested by redeeming love, tolerance, concern for all others, and humility in personal relationships demonstrated by "turning the other cheek" and "going the extra mile" (Matt. 5:39-41). One prays for all others, even one's enemies, and realizes that all believers—of every race, creed, and color anywhere in the world—are spiritual brothers or sisters through the new covenant with Jesus. The covenant established by Jesus is the worldwide basis for the brotherhood of believers and the Fatherhood of God for all Christians, compared with the old covenant which excluded everyone but Jews. The blessings of the new covenant are given by God to believers through His amazing, unmerited grace, because of their faith, and not because of their self-righteous works under the law.

(6). Worship

The method of worship also significantly changes. The full meaning of "Emmanuel" (God with us) is not only revealed, but it is also taken even farther. Through the new covenant, Christ lives in us, and we are sealed into that life covenant through the power of the Holy Spirit (Eph. 4:30). Therefore, the testimony of every Christian becomes "Christ in me, my hope of glory" (Col. 1:27). The worship of God moved from a tabernacle or temple ritual to joyous gatherings in the homes of Christians (Rom. 16:3-5; Philemon 1:1-2), and other places, where believers were "admonishing one another in psalms and hymns and spiritual songs" (Col. 3:16), enabling worship to become an expression of joyous praise and thanksgiving.

How could all of these profound differences between the old covenant of law and the new covenant of grace, and their inherent incompatibility, be summarized in an easily understood comparison? How could Jesus tell His disciples that the powerful proclamation of the gospel's good news would not fit into the rigid framework of old legalistic, religious ritual? By telling them that the effect of trying to merge the new with the old is just like sewing a piece of new, unshrunk cloth onto an old piece of cloth. The inherent tension between the two will eventually pull them apart. The simple brilliance of the parable of unshrunk cloth is ageless.

The Parable of New Wine in Old Wineskins

"And no one puts new wine into old wineskins; or else the new wine bursts the wineskins, the wine is spilled, and the wineskins are ruined. But new wine must be put into new wineskins" (Mark 2:22).

Considering all the social and religious issues that needed changing, and given all the options Jesus had to stimulate thought about the new covenant, why did He strategically choose parables about putting unshrunk cloth on an old garment and putting new wine in old wineskins? Perhaps the answer is found in Jesus' first miracle where, at a wedding feast in Cana, He turned water into wine (John 2:1-10). The well-known miracle represents one of the best comparisons of the old and new covenants in the New Testament.

One of the basic requirements of Judaism was the ritualistic washing not only of one's hands, but also various household utensils, such as cups, pitchers, and other items (Mark 7:3-4). Failure to follow the prescribed routine was a grievous violation of the law and the traditions of Israel. Thus, prior to the wedding feast, the host had gathered six large, stone pots of water, each holding twenty to thirty gallons, in order to have a sufficient supply of water for ritualistic washing during the feast "according to the manner of purification of the Jews" (v. 6). For the purpose of understanding the miracle, these water pots symbolize the law and life under the old covenant.

However, a terrible thing happened: The wedding party host ran out of wine, and not only was this embarrassing, but the assembled guests likely considered it a social faux pas. Jesus seized the opportunity to perform a startling miracle immensely important in understanding the difference between the two covenants.

At the insistence of Mary, His mother, Jesus turned the water in the pots into wine—exceptional wine of the highest quality. If one calculates the volume of the pots filled with water, it became one hundred twenty to one hundred eighty gallons of the best wine the guests had tasted. The host was startled and said to the bridegroom, "Every man at the beginning sets out the good wine, and when the guests have well drunk, then the inferior. You have kept the good wine until now!" (v.10).

Wine is a well-known symbol for life in biblical literature, and its use and meaning in the miracle represents covenant life. Thus, the water that had been designated for a meaningless ritual of cleansing under the law was transformed by Jesus into an abundant source of joyous celebration of the covenant life symbolized by the marriage festival. And once the new wine had been made, there was no more water for ritualistic washing. The new had totally replaced the old. Indeed, the best had been saved until the last!

Why does the admonition not to put new wine into old wineskins so fittingly portray the contrast between the old covenant and this joyous new covenant life? Wineskins were usually made from goat skin, and they became brittle with usage and age. Old wineskins are hardened, inflexible, unyielding to change, and they become constricted and unable to respond to the expansive character of new wine placed within them. Old wineskins simply are not capable of containing the effervescent bubbling pressure of the new wine. The old wineskin refuses to relinquish its set ways, its inherent form, its traditional shape, and the constraints that bind it together. The residue of age will also tarnish the fresh taste of the new wine placed in it.

Old wineskins and new wine are fundamentally incompatible, and the new wine cannot be contained within the old skin. Thus, the new wine of the new covenant can only be placed in the new vessel of a new wineskin. In the strategic reasoning of the parable, the new wineskin is the resurrected life of Jesus and the covenant of life given to all Christians through faith and God's amazing grace.

Old wineskins have no capacity to grow and accommodate anything new, and neither did the law of Israel. The law forbade thinking anything outside of the confines and restraints of the ancient religious law and the traditions of the elders. Newness was not tolerated. Following the Sermon on the Mount, the people were shocked and dumbfounded over the power and freshness of Jesus' new teaching. The sermon's content, when contrasted to the traditional doctrines of the Jewish faith, was so startling and overwhelming that the peoples' reaction could hardly be contained (Matt. 7:28). It is simply the same as placing effervescent, new wine as it ferments into a rigid old wineskin. The old can neither contain nor restrain the new.

The difference between the unyielding religious legalism of the old wineskin and the unlimited grace of the new wineskin is like the difference between night and day. It is impossible to fit boundless grace into the confines of law; it is impossible to express redeeming love for others through cold, legalistic indifference and exclusion; and it is impossible to both experience and express the joyous, abundant spiritual life of the new covenant through continuation of the meaningless, regimented, religious ritual of the old covenant. It is as impossible to fit the new into the old as it is to successfully sew a piece of unshrunk cloth on an old garment or to put new wine into an old wineskin.

Through these simple parables, Jesus redirected the mindset of His followers away from their rigid past and toward a dynamic and spiritually expansive new relationship with God and each other. The parables of Jesus do have the power to change the thoughts of one's heart, and that is the essence of repentance.

A New Understanding of Grace

The Parable of Workers in the Vineyard

"For the kingdom of heaven is like a landowner who went out early in the morning to hire laborers for his vineyard. Now when he had agreed with the laborers for a denarius a day, he sent them into his vineyard. And he went out about the third hour and saw others standing idle in the marketplace, and said to them, 'You also go into the vineyard, and whatever is right I will give you.' So they went. Again he went out about the sixth and the ninth hour and did likewise. And about the eleventh hour he went out and found others standing idle, and said to them, 'Why have you been standing here idle all day?' They said to him, 'Because no one hired us.' He said to them, 'You also go into the vineyard, and whatever is right you will receive.' So when evening had come, the owner of the vineyard said to his steward, 'Call the laborers and give them their wages, beginning with the last to the first.' And when those came who were hired about the eleventh hour, they each received a denarius. But when the first came, they supposed that they would receive more; and they likewise received each a denarius. And when they had received it, they complained against the landowner, saying, 'These last men have worked only one hour, and you made them equal to us who have borne the burden and the heat of the day.' But he answered one of them and said, 'Friend, I am doing you no wrong. Did you not agree with me for a denarius? Take what is yours and go your way. I wish to give to this last man the same as to you. Is it not lawful for me to do what I wish with my own things? Or is your eye evil because I am good?' So the last will be first, and the first last. For many are called, but few chosen" (Matt. 20:1-16).

When Jesus said, "This cup is the new covenant in My blood, which is shed for you" (Luke 22:20), He introduced a new concept of life with God based on grace that, when compared to the old covenant requirements under the law, was so radical, transformative, and different it was very difficult for many to believe and accept. For centuries, Judaism had focused on a personal and national commitment to the religious laws and traditions of Israel as the only acceptable way to live in a covenant life with God. Every aspect of that relationship was earned through self-righteous works under the law, and no aspect of that covenant was viewed as a free, unmerited gift from God.

This belief is portrayed in the response of a man known in the gospel accounts as the "rich young ruler." Speaking to Jesus, he asked, "Good Teacher, what shall I do that I may inherit eternal life?" After Jesus had enumerated several basic commandments in response, the young ruler replied, "Teacher, all these things I have kept from my youth" (Mark 10:17-20). It was a very revealing answer.

A young Jewish male became a "son of the law" at the age of thirteen. He was then expected to fastidiously keep all of the laws and observe all of the religious rituals, and those demands became the dominating religious influence in his life. So, the young ruler revealed that he was a devout Jew clearly committed to personally adhering to and performing every requirement of religious worship. In effect, he was a perfect practitioner of the religious ritual of Judaism. Still, however, he knew no concept of eternal life, and he came to Jesus seeking clarification and guidance regarding what "I must do" to obtain that blessing.

It is sadly interesting that when told by Jesus to sell whatever he had and give it to the poor, this young ruler could not fathom doing that. Because of his wealth and status, he was presumed by others to be righteous, and because of his lifetime of compliance with the law, he thought so, too. Wealth was viewed as a sign of divine blessings, and the poor were considered to be out of favor with God. The rich man could not imagine giving up his wealthy status—which he had earned—and becoming poor himself, even though his wealth would have been a great blessing to many poor people, and he would have learned a great lesson about mercy. Those factors were not considered.

Thus, he struggled with a realization that the law brought him no inner peace about his life after death, and neither could he find peace in this life without the evidence of his self-righteous goodness and his presumed favor with God. His personal works and his wealth—over which he was the master—were his only means of finding favor with God, and they failed him. He could not imagine unearned divine favor, and neither could he imagine a relationship with God in which his own self-worth did not guarantee him acceptability.

The young man, with all his wealth and self-perceived goodness, sadly walked away. Jesus' admonition for him to rid himself of his wealth was not a blanket instruction requiring every Christian to live in poverty. Rather, His instruction was a test to see whether the young man could actually change from his life-long dependence on himself, his work, and his wealth and instead enter into a new covenant freely given to him without any personal reliance on religious ritual, work, and wealth. He could not.

Thus, Jesus uttered His powerful statement: "It is easier for a camel to go through the eye of a needle than for a rich man to enter the kingdom of God" (Mark 10:25). This is not a pronouncement that anyone with a large bank account cannot go to heaven, but rather a warning that those who viewed riches under the old covenant as a confirmation of their inheritance of the kingdom of God will be disappointed. To accent this point, Jesus said, "Children, how hard it is for those who trust in riches to enter the kingdom of God" (v. 24). Jesus well knew that the kingdom of heaven is a divine realm in which every blessing is given by God as an expression of His grace, and nothing is earned by religious works under the law. One may enter heaven freely; but one cannot work his way into heaven.

Startled by His statement, His disciples said to one another, "Who then can be saved?" (v. 26). They, too, were much like the wealthy young ruler: The reliance on wealth and earthly possessions as evidence of personal righteousness and favor with God was all they had been taught since youth, and it was all they knew.

Jesus radically altered this concept. When He spoke the Beatitudes in the Sermon on the Mount (Matt. 5:3-12), the first Beatitude focused on the issue of experiencing spiritual happiness and joy, not through personal wealth and self-righteous works, but rather through the exact opposite. Jesus described the spiritual joy within the kingdom of heaven of the "poor in spirit." The blessedness and joy they experience is greater than anything they had ever imagined, for "theirs is the kingdom of heaven." This promise of blessings is in direct contradiction to the belief that divine blessings and joy came from self-righteous works and the special ego-centered blessings that the wealthy were believed to receive from God. The first Beatitude was a radical departure from long-standing beliefs under Judaism.

Thus the new covenant in Jesus requires an inner spiritual transformation through repentance in which one abandons all concepts of self-worth, self-merit, and the belief that one's good works somehow obligate God to extend His favor and bestow His divine blessings. It is a covenant relationship in which the more one sees and acknowledges his spiritual poverty before God, the more he understands and appreciates the gift of grace and all the blessings that he freely receives because of his covenant life with Jesus, through which he is a "joint heir with Christ" (Rom. 8:17) to those heavenly blessings. Life with Jesus is a covenant life of grace in which all things are received as a free gift from God because of one's faith, and nothing is personally earned through self-righteous works of law.

Grace (*charis*) is defined as unlimited kindness and unmerited favor. There is no quid pro quo between the act of one and the response of the other. There is nothing bilateral about it: Grace is the unilateral act of one, without regard to the actions of the other, that accurately portrays the inherent kindness, goodness, and generosity of the one bestowing grace. It is simply a gift.

Under the new covenant, God grants to and bestows the righteous nature of Christ as a gracious gift upon all who believe in Jesus, and He then treats them as His adopted children. Through the blood of Christ and the covenant in His blood, God forgives every believer's sin, blots out the record of their transgressions, and then imputes to them the righteousness of Jesus. Just as He did with Abraham because of his faith, God "reckons" Christians to be righteous, not because any have earned it, but solely as an expression of His goodness and grace.

Therefore, ponder the challenge facing Jesus: The most fundamental tenant of His new covenant was so bold and audacious that, compared to the past, it was simply unbelievable to most people. How could that doubt, and disbelief be overcome? By strategically sharing a parable that was also so audacious that is was equally unbelievable.

The parable of the workers in the vineyard is astonishing in its portrayal of grace and unmerited favor. If it were presented as a truth from everyday life—compared to a parable to stimulate thought—it would be disbelieved because no vineyard owner would be so imprudent. It violates logic, contradicts common sense, is economically unfeasible, and is impractical as an employment and labor incentive. Viewed from the perspective of the rewards of labor and self-effort, the parable of the vineyard workers is foolish. So is grace when viewed from the perspective of those who attempt to relate to God only through self-righteous works.

The parable is a brilliant gem of divine truth cast amidst the familiar toil of everyday life. Any person who has worked for a living can relate to its truth and struggle with the point of its promise. Compensating workers in the manner described in the parable is unfathomable, as is the magnitude of God's grace in the new covenant. That is precisely what Jesus wanted His followers to consider and understand. The magnitude of grace divinely poured out into a Christian's life is simply hard to believe, but Jesus personally assures its truth.

The parable's setting would have been familiar to most people in Jesus' day. Many had either done physical work in a vineyard or had observed others, for it was a common occurrence. No doubt many vineyard owners had hired laborers in the same manner, with additional workers being added throughout the day to assist those hired first. It is possible that some aspects of the work would have been needed later in the day, rather than early morning, and thus the practice of hiring additional laborers at different intervals might not have been that unusual. However, the manner of compensation in the parable was certainly unusual and overtly shocking.

In the parable, the workday began about six a.m. when the first workers were hired. More workers were hired at nine a.m. (the third hour), at twelve noon (the sixth hour), at three in the afternoon (the ninth hour), and, surprisingly, still others were sent to the vineyard at five p.m. (the eleventh hour), so obviously the vineyard was large and productive. Significant meaning can be found in the hiring sequence. The landowner specifically agreed to pay the workers hired first a denarius, which was a coin normally given for one day's pay, and they had no other thought than personally earning the reward for their labor. That is a picture of the old covenant of law.

But, thereafter, each successive group that was hired was told by the landowner that he would give them "whatever is right." To the last workers sent to the vineyard at the eleventh hour, the landowner said, "whatever is right, you will receive." The workers hired first trusted only themselves to earn their pay; the workers hired at subsequent intervals trusted only the landowner to treat them right, based on goodness, grace, and fairness. Only those hired first were compensated as a matter of law because there was a specific agreement or covenant for pay. All others were compensated as a matter of grace.

The phrases "whatever is right I will give you" and "whatever is right you will receive" are significant. In the parable's language, "right" means that the vineyard owner's actions were just, righteous, and acceptable to God. But, unlike law, the owner did not define what he would give them because grace is beyond specific definition. The goodness, represented by what would be given, was to be put into the hands of the laborers and reckoned unto them without regard for merit. The laborers would receive it with joy as a welcomed gift and an expression of the righteousness and goodness of the vineyard owner.

At the end of the day, the landowner gave all of the workers the same pay, a denarius. Those who were hired first had earned it; those hired last, at the eleventh hour, were startled by the landowner's grace and generosity. Importantly, the hiring sequence does not teach some sliding scale of grace, but rather it portrays the great truth enunciated in the first Beatitude: The more one realizes that he has not earned the favor and grace of God, based on his self-righteous works, the more he understands grace.

The real focus of the hiring sequence is the attitude of the laborers hired first compared to the attitude of the laborers hired last. The first group worked all day; the latter group worked one hour. They each received the same, and the first group, assuming they would receive far more than any others because of their labor, bitterly complained over the generosity of the landowner, while the last group rejoiced over the landowner's grace and goodness, for they well knew their reward was a free gift.

This is not the only parable in which this resentful, legalistic attitude toward grace appears. In the parable of the prodigal son (Luke 15:11-32), the older brother was greatly offended at his father's grace and mercy shown to his younger son upon the young man's return to his father's house. Seeing the festive joy expressed and the mercy and grace displayed, the older brother bitterly commented to his father:

> *"... Lo, these many years I have been serving you; I never transgressed your commandment at any time; and yet you never gave me a young goat, that I might make merry with my friends. But as soon as this son of yours came, who has devoured your livelihood with harlots, you killed the fatted calf for him"* (v. 30).

The laborers hired first personified this expectation of reward because the landowner's determination of rightful reward was not considered. The first laborers could not conceive that their reward for labor was anything other than an obligation of the landowner to pay them for labor. The grace and goodness of the landowner was not a factor in their calculation. The same is true in a spiritual sense. If one believes that he has earned his reward, then he has no concept of that reward being a gracious, unmerited gift. In this view, the legalist is not indebted to God; God is indebted to him. Religious practitioners, both then and now, who truly believe they have earned God's blessings, have little understanding of and appreciation for the concept of unmerited grace.

Within the contrasting attitudes of the laborers who were hired first and the laborers who were hired last is the difference between life under the old covenant of law and life under the new covenant of grace. It is the difference between cold, calculating expectation of blessings for the unwavering performance of a duty—with no concern for anyone else—compared to the joyous thanksgiving of praise for unmerited favor and blessings.

The attitude of those hired first is pure law: I have earned all that I receive, and I have no appreciation for those who expect to receive equal blessings for doing little or nothing. It is the condescending, judgmental attitude of the scribes and Pharisees who condemned anyone they viewed as imperfectly keeping of the law.

But life under the new covenant of grace is entirely different. The landowner's words reveal an enormous truth: God will give to us what He considerers as a worthy expression of His righteousness and goodness. The kingdom of heaven is entirely His to do with as He wishes, to freely bestow its blessing on whomever He desires, and to whatever degree He determines. All Christians stand before Him without merit; none have earned His blessings. As the first Beatitude describes, we indeed stand before God poor in spirit, yet we are blessed with the riches of the kingdom of heaven. Our only response is praise and thanksgiving, not cold calculation of expected meritorious reward.

There are many verses in the New Testament which describe the blessings of grace. The following provide a revealing insight into the redeemed spiritual life in Christ, which is freely bestowed on every Christian through faith in Jesus. These passages provide a brief description of the covenant life of grace:

- "But God, who is rich in mercy, because of His great love with which He loved us, even when we were dead in trespasses, made us alive together with Christ (by grace you ave been saved), and raised us up together, and made us sit together in the heavenly places in Christ Jesus, that in the ages to come He might show the exceeding riches of His grace in His kindness toward us in Christ Jesus. For by grace you have been saved through faith, and that not of yourselves; it is the gift of God" (Eph. 2:4-8).
- "…being justified freely by His grace through the redemption that is in Christ Jesus" (Rom. 3:24).
- "For sin shall not have dominion over you, for you are not under law but under grace" (Rom. 6:14).
- "…For if by the one man's offense many died, much more the grace of God and the gift by the grace of the one Man, Jesus Christ, abounded to many" (Rom. 5:15).
- "For the grace of God that brings salvation has appeared to all men" (Titus 2:11).
- "But to each of us grace was given according to the measure of Christ's gift" (Eph. 4:7).
- "And He said to me, 'My grace is sufficient for you, for My strength is made perfect in weakness'" (II Cor.12:9).
- "Let us therefore come boldly to the throne of grace, that we may obtain mercy and find grace to help in time of need" (Hebrews 4:16).
- "But He gives more grace. Therefore He says: 'God resists the proud but gives grace to the humble'" (James 4:6).
- "But may the God of all grace, who called us to His eternal glory by Christ Jesus, after you have suffered a while, perfect, establish, strengthen, and settle you" (I Peter 5:10).

The deeper meaning and message of the New Testament is best learned through study and contemplation. However, that often does not capture the raw human emotion felt by one transformed by the grace of God. Oftentimes it is beneficial to simply imagine the emotions of a person identified in scripture who has forever been changed by the love, mercy, and grace of God.

And so it is with the laborers hired at the eleventh hour. Were they impoverished, hungry, or had a family to feed? Were they in debt to creditors and desperately trying to find a way to ease the worry and anxiety over obligations they could not meet? They were not lazy because they were in the marketplace looking for work. But the law of self-effort had failed them. Now, all they had was one hour of work, and that was inadequate to give them much relief, leaving them frustrated, anxious, and uncertain. Those are all too often the fruits of our endeavors, both spiritual and physical.

It was then, in their hour of greatest need, they experienced something unimaginable that filled them with joy, thanksgiving, praise, and hope for the future—grace. The vineyard owner had promised to give them "whatever is right" and told them that is what they would receive, but none of them understood the full meaning of his promise. At the end of the day, to their utter amazement, the landowner's focus was on them, not those who had labored all day. It was a complete reversal from the ordinary. What an incredible, uplifting experience to suddenly realize that all of the vineyard owner's thoughts were on those who had labored the least, who had no hope, no reason to expect or demand his favor, yet who had been promised to be treated right.

But what did the promise to treat them "right" really mean? If he treated them right under the law, the workers would expect only one-twelfth of a day's pay, leaving them hungry, unsatisfied, and yearning for more. However, he had not promised to pay them according to law, but rather to treat them right, as he alone viewed rightness. They had never experienced that and had no idea what to expect.

Amazingly, these workers hired last were called forward first. Expecting to receive only a small pittance, they were shocked and surprised at the amazing, indescribable grace of the vineyard owner who gave them a denarius—a full day's pay—for only one hour, and he did so without hesitation or reservation. They were filled with unbridled joy and thanksgiving. That is what being treated right truly meant—not the self-centered wages of labor according to law, but the generosity, grace, and goodness of the vineyard owner whose heart was on those who deserved it the least. Motivated by mercy and compassion for those who had no merit, the vineyard owner's righteousness was an expression of his grace and goodness and brought him great pleasure in giving his blessings as he desired, not as his workers demanded. Indeed, as Jesus said, "the last shall be first and the first last."

Seeing the vineyard owner's generosity toward the laborers hired last, the laborers who were hired first were outraged when they too received a denarius, just as they had been promised, for they now expected to receive far more for working the full day. Their attitude was an upsetting and confusing effort to combine law and grace, which is not possible. Surely, they reasoned, if the vineyard owner's generosity and grace so abundantly rewarded the laborers hired last, then surely he is obligated to bless us even more for our day-long tireless efforts. But grace cannot be modified to become an obligation. It is forever a gift and can never be viewed as a reward for labor. Regardless of how long and tirelessly one works in Christian service, God will never be our debtor.

The vineyard owner's grace produced joy, thanksgiving, and celebration for those hired last because their entire focus was on his compassion and generosity. However, the laborers hired first focused only on themselves, their labor and merit, and the vineyard owner's obligation to them. These laborers did not share in the joy of the others, did not understand the vineyard owner's generosity, and were filled with jealousy and resentment. The contrasting emotions of the two groups were totally opposite and are a vivid picture of life under the covenant of law and life under the covenant of grace.

Every Christian must realize that the redeemed church of Jesus Christ is the laborers sent to the vineyard last. We are the recipients of God's abundant, amazing grace. In 1911, Julia H. Johnston penned these words, which became the great hymn, "Grace Greater than Our Sin":

> "Marvelous grace of our loving Lord,
> grace that exceeds our sin and our guilt,
> yonder on Calvary's mount outpoured,
> there where the blood of the lamb was spilt.
>
> Dark is the stain that we cannot hide,
> what can avail to wash it away?
> Look! There is flowing a crimson tide;
> whiter than snow you may be today.

Marvelous, infinite, matchless grace,
freely bestowed on all who believe;
all who are longing to see His face,
will you this moment His grace receive?

Grace, grace, God's grace,
grace that will pardon and cleanse within;
grace, grace, God's grace,
grace that is greater than all our sin."

The sullen, self-centered laborers who were hired first left the vineyard mad and filled with hostility. The laborers who went to the vineyard last left joyous and filled with the goodness and holiness of the righteous vineyard owner. The first struggled with life under the old covenant of law; the latter celebrated life under the new covenant of grace.

Every Christian should thank God we went to His vineyard at the eleventh hour!

A New Standard for Forgiveness

For centuries, Israel had known about *Lex Talionis*, or the limitation of retribution, which in many ways is an act of mercy. Prior to this divine law being ordained by God, there was no limit on revenge or retribution that one might inflict on another. Thus, if one accidentally broke another's arm, nothing prevented the infliction of wholesale bodily harm and permanent injury in return.

However, Old Testament law restricted the degree of revenge in a manner that is often misunderstood: "But, if any harm follows, then you shall give life for life, eye for eye, tooth for tooth, hand for hand, foot for foot, burn for burn, wound for wound, stripe for stripe" (Exod. 21:23-25). This was not a justification for the infliction of harm, but rather the opposite. For the first time, punishment was made to fit the crime and excess revenge was restrained.

However, Jesus took the concept further. In the Sermon on the Mount, He stated:

> *"You have heard that it was said, 'An eye for an eye and a tooth for a tooth.' But I tell you not to resist an evil person. But whoever slaps you on your right cheek, turn the other to him also. If anyone wants to sue you and take away your tunic, let him have your cloak also. And whoever compels you to go one mile, go with him two"* (Matt. 5:38-41).

Are turning the other cheek and going the extra mile reactionary attitudes or rather strategic determinations made in advance about how one will respond to insult and abuse? That is a key question regarding forgiveness. Mercy and forgiveness are freely given; they are not compelled. One grants mercy to another; he does not become resigned to it. Thus, if turning the other cheek and going the extra mile are predetermined attitudes, then one willingly turns the other cheek and forgets the insult of the first slap on the cheek. If one willingly walks the second mile, he does not bear a grudge for having walked the first mile. The attitude is intentional and not reactionary.

Jesus also spoke about forgiveness in the Lord's Prayer when He stated, "Forgive us our debts, as we forgive our debtors" (Matt. 6:12). This is not a statement of economics, but rather an expression of mercy rooted in the ancient history of Israel. It is interesting to note the conditional nature of Jesus' statement about mercy and forgiveness. "Blessed are the merciful, for they shall receive mercy" indicates that one's experience of mercy from God directly relates to how mercy is shown to others. "Forgive us of our debts, as we forgive our debtors" again conveys the reality that understanding personal forgiveness is premised on mercifully granting forgiveness to others. Forgiving another's debt was one mercifully and willingly granting another the opportunity of a second chance, a new beginning debt-free. But very few are that merciful.

The forgiveness of debt owed by another was a central component of the Jubilee Year ordained by God. Every fifty years there was to be a nationwide observation of redemption, restoration, and freedom in Israel in which lost property was returned to its rightful owner, slaves in bondage were released, and debts were forgiven (Lev. 25:8-17). It was to have been a national expression of mercy glorifying God for the mercy he had shown to Israel.

However, Israel never declared a Jubilee Year because for many the forgiveness of debt was so difficult. Greed trumped mercy, and it still does. When Jesus read from the scrolls at Nazareth about "the acceptable year of the Lord" and declared that it had come true in their presence, He was referring to the true meaning of the Jubilee Year. The people jeered, ran Him out of town, and tried to throw Him over a cliff (Luke 4:16-30).

Forgiveness is not emotional pretense, as if one could pretend that hurt never happened. Forgiveness is not psychological denial, as if one could eliminate pain by denying its existence. Forgiveness is not a funeral, as if one could bury past pain so that it never hurt again. Instead, forgiveness is the dynamic spiritual power of mercy, rooted in covenant, redeeming love, to take hurt—even the most grievous, life-changing kind—and place it outside the bond of love that binds two people together. The pain is not forgotten, nor is it buried, and no one pretends it did not occur. Rather, the power of redeeming love renders the hurt inconsequential to the relationship, and no lasting harm is done.

Forgiveness is the power of preservation poured out in limitless quantities when needed on a daily basis. Forgiveness is not an emotional defeat that one is forced into; conversely, it is a dynamic, powerful, aggressive assertion of one's determination to protect a bond, preserve a promise, and secure guaranteed blessings. It is a powerful, proactive force fortifying a covenant union that is taxed by indiscretion, unfaithfulness, and untruth.

Forgiveness is the opposite of revenge and retaliation. In simple positive and negative terms, forgiveness is the power of love that enables one to set aside the negatives in order to protect the positives. Forgiveness is the power and ability of divine covenant love to recognize and deal with sin, infidelity, and untruthfulness in a loving manner, unmotivated by anger, resentment, or revenge. It is the process ordained by God to deal with sin and permanently secure the sanctity of His divine covenant with man. It is also the means divinely given to man to preserve the bonds of matrimony and the sacredness of friendship when those bonds are stretched to the breaking point.

The divine emotional power enabling forgiveness is mercy—mercy that is neither pretentious nor feigned, but rather is personal, powerful, and flows from the deepest chamber of divine goodness within our heart. Mercy takes that which would tear a relationship apart and makes the bond of love stronger through loving acceptance of another's faults and foibles. Mercy casts aside the impending failure of a relationship and instead gives birth to new fidelity, loyalty, and love that strengthens and sustains the bond of love into perpetuity. The two pillars supporting the arc of forgiveness, under which we all pass in our relationships with God and one another, are mercy and redeeming love.

Judaism has a rich history regarding forgiveness dating back to the beginning of God's covenant with Israel. The language of the Old Testament describes God's ability to take away sin and pardon inequity, and Exodus 34:7 enumerates forgiveness as one of God's basic spiritual characteristics. When God entered into a covenant with Israel, He knew there would be failure of fidelity caused by the appeal of pleasure, sensuality, and wealth. He understood that the glitter of a golden calf can hold more sway than the righteous goodness of an unseen God; that the goddess of pleasure can seductively sidetrack the most fervent promise of faithfulness; and that the allure of personal wealth and power can undermine pledges of humility and servanthood. The problem of sin is not new to God, and neither is His means of defeating it and negating its impact. That is the power of forgiveness borne out of mercy.

The Old Testament describes forgiveness in an interesting manner. In his capacity as High Priest, Aaron was commanded to take two goats and cast lots upon them. One would be chosen as a sacrifice and sin offering, but the High Priest would put his hands on the head of the other goat, symbolically placing the sins of the people on the animal and release it into the wilderness in order for it to escape and take away the sins of the people (Lev. 16:7-10). It is from this ancient ritual that the term "scapegoat" is derived—one who takes the blame and punishment for the actions of another and allows the guilty to go free.

From a Christian perspective, that was a very rudimentary method of symbolically putting aside the guilt of sin. Jesus, however, took the blame of all believers upon Himself and bore their punishment so that their covenant bond with God would be preserved (Heb. 9:11-15). The Old Testament prophet Isaiah spoke of God's "Suffering Servant" who would bear our sorrows, for "by His stripes we are healed" (Isaiah 53:5). The New Testament speaks of Jesus as the substitution for believers by saying that "He is the propitiation for the sins of the people" (Heb. 2:17), thus taking the wrath of sin upon Himself.

Mercy motivates forgiveness. It is not misty-eyed, mercurial mercy subject to sudden reversion back to anger, but rather dynamic, focused mercy, compassion, and lovingkindness that prepares in advance for the failures, short-comings, and disappointments inherent in a relationship between two people. The Bible presents the essential characteristics of God as love, mercy, and grace. Think of them in this manner: Love redeems what is lost; mercy mends what is broken; and grace makes the old new. The end result puts sin to the side, as if it never happened.

But law is a jealous suitor for the soul of man. Law defines conduct and consequences and is uncompromising and unyielding. Guilt guarantees punishment without compromise. The only way punishment may be lessened is through mercy, or the intentional withholding of legally prescribed punishment. No person facing sentencing for a crime asks the judge to show redeeming love or grace; he simply asks for mercy.

Therein is the contrast: Law and mercy are based on two different value systems. Law does not provide for mercy. Law defines the crime, describes the punishment, and directs its imposition. Law does not contemplate mercy, and neither does it prescribe compassion, forbearance, longsuffering, and forgiveness. Law is mental and physical and comes from one's head; mercy is spiritual and comes from one's heart. Law is action; mercy is attitude. Law does not generate joy; mercy does.

A society focused on law, especially religious law, without mercy is a cold, dogmatic, cruel, and unkind place. A person, or people, focused on the demands of religious law see themselves as God's agent for carrying out and executing the demands of the law, believing that God will be pleased with and bless their actions. That idea is very alive today in certain churches and denominations. In their religious fervor and zeal, they are totally blind toward, indifferent to, and unmindful of Jesus' specific admonition, "But go and learn what this means, 'I desire mercy and not sacrifice...'" (Matt. 9:13).

The ancient religious code of Israel was very strict and uncompromising, as revealed in the following provisions:

- Disobedient son – "If a man has a stubborn and rebellious son who will not obey the voice of his father or the voice of his mother, and who, when they have chastised him, will not heed them...then all the men of the city shall stone him to death with stones..." (Deut. 21:18-21).
- Blasphemy – "And whoever blasphemes the name of the Lord shall surely be put to death" (Lev. 24:16).
- Murder – "Whoever kills any man shall surely be put to death" (Lev. 24:17).
- False prophesy – "But that prophet or that dreamer of dreams shall be put to death..." (Deut. 12:5).
- Negligent homicide – "But if the ox tended to thrust with its horn in times past, and it has been made known to his owner, and he has not kept it confined, so that it has killed a man or a woman, the ox shall be stoned to death and its owner also shall be put to death" (Exod. 21:29).
- Loss of virginity – "But if the thing is true, and evidence of virginity are not found for the young woman...then the men of the city shall stone her to death with stones..." (Deut. 22:20-21).
- Adultery – "If a man if found lying with a woman married to a husband, then both of them shall die..." (Deut. 22:22).

- Breaking the Sabbath – "You shall keep the Sabbath, therefore, for it is holy to you. Everyone who profanes it shall surely be put to death…" (Exod. 31:14).

As Jesus taught in the temple one day, the scribes and Pharisees brought before Him a woman caught "in the very act" of adultery, and they judgmentally placed her in their midst. Testing Him, they said, "Now Moses, in the law, commanded us that such should be stoned. But what do You say?" Jesus tended to ignore them at first, but finally said, "He who is without sin among you, let him throw a stone at her first" (John 8:3-11). Jesus used the moment to inject a radical new dimension into the concept of mercy and forgiveness. None of her accusers could cast a stone because of their sin, but Jesus could have because He alone was sinless. Thus, those who judgmentally wanted to stone her could not; He who could have mercifully did not. Cold religious law finally met the warmth of compassionate mercy, and, for Christians, the law lost its grip on our life, just as it did for the adulterous woman.

The standard of forgiveness demanded by Jesus is hundreds of times greater (if it could be quantified) than anything previously known in Israel. The parable of the unforgiving servant is premised on the master mercifully forgiving a debt beyond calculation (10,000 talents), and yet the forgiven servant would not forgive a fellow servant of a minor debt of one hundred denarii, or about twenty dollars.

Instead of revealing his master's mercy to others, he acted entirely opposite. He had no compassion for his fellow servant and showed him no mercy. Even though he had abundantly received the spiritual blessings of mercy, he nevertheless continued to treat others with the cold, unyielding demands of law. In his legalistic attitude, he would not allow himself to reflect to another even an infinitesimal fraction of the mercy that his master had shown to him. Because of his obsession with law, the master's mercy did not faze him. Unfortunately, that is a sad but true picture of the attitude of many Christians today.

If one assumes that in our salvation there are no sins that God has not mercifully forgiven—regardless of their magnitude or number—then how can a Christian justify not forgiving another of wrongs that have been committed against them? If the mercy of God is poured out on us without limit, then every Christian must do no less in their relationship with others.

Peter once asked Jesus, "Lord, how often shall my brother sin against me, and I forgive him? Up to seven times?" Jesus shocked Peter by responding, "I do not say to you, up to seven times, but up to seventy times seven" (Matt.18:21-22). One should avoid literal calculation and not assume that Jesus was speaking of forgiving 490 times. Even if that were the case, it would have been far greater than anyone could imagine. But, seven in biblical numerology is equated with fullness and completion. Thus, seventy times seven is a demand for total, absolute, and unwavering forgiveness. It is a standard that is difficult to fathom, but that is how God forgives us, and He expects no less from covenant Christians in our relationship with others.

In addition to Jesus' own compassionate acts, His strategic method of making people rethink the issue of forgiveness and mercy was powerful, piercing parables that drove new truths into the cold, rock-hard hearts of religious zealots. It was against this harsh, unforgiving, and unmerciful religious and social background that Jesus spoke three parables that transformed the purpose and power of mercy and forgiveness.

The Parable of the Unforgiving Servant

"Therefore the kingdom of heaven is like a certain king who wanted to settle accounts with his servants. And when he had begun to settle accounts, one was brought to him who owed him ten thousand talents. But as he was not able to pay, his master commanded that he be sold, with his wife and children and all that he had, and that payment be made. The servant therefore fell down before him, saying, 'Master, have patience with me, and I will pay you all.' Then the master of that servant was moved with compassion, released him, and forgave him the debt.

But that servant went out and found one of his fellow servants who owed him a hundred denarii; and he laid hands on him and took him by the throat, saying, 'Pay me what you owe!' So his fellow servant fell down at his feet and begged him, saying, 'Have patience with me, and I will pay you all.' And he would not but went and threw him into prison till he should pay the debt. So when his fellow servants saw what had been done, they were very grieved, and came and told their master all that had been done. Then his master, after he had called him, said to him, 'You wicked servant! I forgave you all that debt because you begged me. Should you not also have had compassion on your fellow servant, just as I had pity on you?' And his master was angry and delivered him to the torturers until he should pay all that was due to him. So My heavenly Farther also will do to you if each of you, from his heart, does not forgive his brother his trespasses" (Matt. 18:23-35).

"Lord, have mercy" is often used as an expression of hope, fear, or even humor, but, in many ways, it has lost its original meaning. Jesus also faced a similar loss of the original meaning of this basic religious concept. Israel was founded on the mercy of God, and His mercy and compassion ensured Israel's survival during many nationwide cycles of sin and repentance. The Book of Judges, for example, describes repeated instances of Israel's wavering commitment to God.

Mercy stems from the Hebrew word *chesed*, one of the most fundamental Old Testament concepts. *Chesed* is compassion in action and describes lovingkindness and mercy expressed toward others in meaningful ways and not simply through thought or attitude.

For example, Abraham was old, childless, and his elderly wife, Sarah, was unable to bear children, yet God promised Abraham that he would be the father of a multitude of descendants. God demonstrated mercy toward Abraham and blessed him with a miracle son with Sarah, who they named Isaac, and Isaac later became the father of Jacob. Jacob's sons became the founding fathers of the twelve tribes of Israel. God's gracious covenant promise to bless Abraham with descendants more numerable than the stars of heaven—out of which emerged the Jewish nation—was based on mercy and compassion.

When the Israelites were toiling in Egyptian bondage, God said to Moses:

"I have surely seen the oppression of My people who are in Egypt, and have heard their cry because of their taskmasters, for I know their sorrows. So, I have come down to deliver them..." (Exod. 2:7-8).

As a result, God used Moses to miraculously lead the Israelites out of Egypt in a great exodus to the Promised Land. From the foundation of the Jewish faith, freedom from enslavement was founded on God's mercy.

God's compassion enabled many who were taken captive by the Babylonians in 587 B.C. to later return and re-establish their religious practices in Jerusalem, and the Old Testament books of Ezra and Nehemiah chronicle this historic return. Once again, God's mercy was displayed in a marvelous outpouring that provided the means for the exiles' return to their native land.

Jeremiah, the prophet, wrote about God's mercy on Israel in the Book of Lamentations. Looking at the destruction and suffering in Jerusalem caused by the Babylonian invasion, Jeremiah stated, "Through the Lord's mercies we are not consumed, because His compassions fail not. They are new every morning; great is your faithfulness" (Lam. 3:22-23). The great prophet realized that divine mercy is not just a theological concept, but rather a daily experience with God and a constant and continuous reality.

However, religious law has a peculiar feature: The receipt of mercy does not always motivate one to be merciful to others. Often those who boast of having been forgiven by God are the most unforgiving toward others, and those who have personally experienced God's compassion are the most condemning and cold-hearted toward those whom they judgmentally shun.

That is why Jesus established a direct connection in the Beatitudes between showing mercy and receiving mercy, but He did so in reverse order from the ordinary. It was a shocking contrast. Most would think when God shows mercy to an individual, they would logically and gratefully show mercy to others. But Jesus changed that by saying, "Blessed are the merciful, for they shall obtain mercy" (Matt 5:7). In effect, He said, "If you are not going to show mercy to others, then do not expect to receive mercy from God."

By the time of Jesus' life and ministry, Israel had become shockingly unmerciful in her cold, legalistic attitudes toward others, despite her receipt of boundless mercy from God. For example, it was unlawful to have relations with Gentiles, the poor were neglected, the sick were often abandoned and left to fend for themselves through begging, lepers were left in colonies filled with hopeless despair, and sinners were unmercifully condemned, as exemplified by the woman caught in adultery (John 8:4).

Although people asked many things of Jesus, the most consistent request expressed openly to Him was a plea for mercy. The following are moving examples:

- Two blind men crying out to Jesus, "Have mercy on us, O Lord, Son of David" (Matt. 20:30-31).
- A father's plea for his epileptic son, "Lord, have mercy on my son…" (Matt. 17:15).
- Ten lepers pleading, "Jesus, Master, have mercy on us!" (Luke 17:13).
- A blind man near Jericho begging, "Jesus, Son of David, have mercy on me!" (Luke 18:38).
- The mother of a demon-possessed daughter pleading, "Have mercy on me, O Lord, Son of David…" (Matt. 15:22).

Jesus was deeply burdened by realizing that those who had been more blessed by God's mercy than any other people had become coldly uncaring and unmerciful and seldom reflected God's mercy to others. He was determined to change that attitude, and He began the process of change with a shocking parable about an unforgiving servant.

Although the main thrust of this parable relates to forgiveness and is in response to Peter's question about how often he should forgive, the motivating emotion for forgiveness is mercy. In that respect, the parable contrasts God's mercy shown to Israel and the people's refusal to reveal God's mercy to others in return.

The parable contrasts two opposite and extreme views of compassion and mercy. A servant owed his master ten thousand talents that he was unable to pay, and for good reason. Its enormity was beyond calculation. The talent was the largest measurement of weight (about seventy-five pounds) and also the greatest monetary measurement. Thus, if the parable's talent represented a valuable, such as gold or silver, the value of ten thousand talents would have been astronomical. Visualize, for example, that one talent was seventy-five pounds of gold. Ten thousand talents of gold would be 750,000 pounds, or 375 tons of gold.

The talent has also been defined as the value of labor, with one talent equal to the compensation for many years of labor. Conservatively calculated, if one talent in the parable represented only one year of labor (and that would be less than some theorize), the servant would have had to work 10,000 years to repay the debt.

If the servant made a denarius each day worth about twenty cents, he would have earned $73.00 per year. If the talent was one year's pay at that rate, then the debt would have been $730,000. However, in order to make the magnitude of the indebtedness more meaningful for modern readers, if the parable were applicable to contemporary standards, and the current minimum wage of $7.25 per hour were used as a basis, one year's pay would be $15,080 and the total debt would be $150,800,000.

However the obligation is calculated, the servant faced a huge, insurmountable debt that he had no hope of repaying through his own efforts. Unable to pay, the master directed that he and his entire family, and all that he had, be sold. The servant begged for the master's patience, assuring him that, "I will pay you all." Even though he promised, he fully knew that was impossible—and so did his master.

It is important to grasp the impasse here. The debt could never be paid, even if he and all he possessed were sold. Self-effort was not the solution. The servant's promises to do better were fruitless, for he could never repay the debt, even if he gave his master all he had and all he earned for the rest of his life. He was in total bondage with no answer and no hope. This is a picture of the grip of sin on each of us and the futility of our self-righteous effort.

The answer to the servant's desperate situation was shocking. The solution came not from the servant's hollow promises and ineffective labor, but rather from the heart of the master. Seeing the servant's hopeless plight, the master was "moved with compassion." The master's compassion and mercy were visceral and touched the very core of his emotions, literally "his inward parts." He was deeply moved and emotionally compelled to release the servant and forgive the unpayable debt. The concept is very important, for it denotes a level of mercy so deep the master found it impossible not to act in a compassionate and merciful way. That is a poignant picture of God's merciful attitude toward those trapped in bondage to sin.

One would assume the servant was filled with gratitude, thanksgiving, and praise, but he was not. The parable contains no language describing the servant's joy or his expression of gratitude for his master's mercy shown to him. It is as if he felt he had earned it, with no reason for praise and thanksgiving. Sadly, obedience to religious law can also leave one with that feeling of entitlement.

Neither did the receipt of mercy make him more merciful toward others—another negative side effect of religious law. In his self-absorbed focus on himself, he directed his attention not to the merciful master, but rather on a fellow servant indebted to him. The man owed him a hundred denarii, which was a modest debt. A denarius was worth about twenty cents and was the normal daily wage for laborers and Roman soldiers. Thus, one hundred denarii would be approximately $20.00. Even if the second servant had given the first servant all he made, the debt could have been repaid in one hundred days, or slightly more than three months. But, instead of showing mercy as had been shown to him, mercy was denied to the other in a mean-spirited manner because of an inability to pay.

The forgiven servant's attitude is both shocking and unfathomable. He had been mercifully forgiven an enormous debt that would have taken multiple lifetimes to repay (if such were possible), yet he was unwilling to show equal mercy to another indebted to him for $20.00, which could have been repaid quickly and easily.

The merciful master was outraged and gave him to "the torturers until he should pay all that was due him." That would have been the rest of his life, more like eternity. It is a sobering thought, but mercy is the one spiritual aspect that is described in the New Testament as conditional. After describing the action of the master due to the servant's refusal to be merciful and forgiving, Jesus warned, "So My heavenly Father also will do to you if each of you, from his heart, does not forgive his brother his trespasses" (v. 35). Jesus' statement in the Beatitudes, "Blessed are the merciful, for they shall obtain mercy" (Matt. 5:7), causes one to wonder what the unmerciful will receive when they do not show mercy.

The parable accurately pictures Israel during Jesus' earthly life. There are no verses in the four gospels describing a merciful act by a religious leader of Israel toward another—or love and grace for that matter.

Jesus faced a major spiritual obstacle in making the people who were called to be God's intermediaries in the world and who had received abundant outpourings of God's mercy realize how cold, intolerant, judgmental, and unmerciful they had become through their obsessive commitment to the law. How could He do that? Directly telling an unmerciful person to be more merciful is counter-productive, for they will not listen. What strategy would vividly shock people into thinking about their own unmerciful attitudes? Parables—parables that would forcefully convey the need for mercy and would forever remain compelling word-pictures stimulating introspective thought.

The Parable of the Pharisee and the Tax Collector

> *"Two men went up to the temple to pray, one a Pharisee and the other a tax collector. The Pharisee stood and prayed thus with himself, 'God, I thank You that I am not like other men – extortioners, unjust, adulterers, or even as this tax collector. I fast twice a week; I give tithes of all that I possess.' And the tax collector, standing afar off, would not so much as raise his eyes to heaven, but beat his breast, saying, 'God, be merciful to me a sinner!' I tell you; this man went down to his house justified rather than the other; for everyone who exalts himself will be humbled, and he who humbles himself will be exalted"* (Luke 18:10-14).

This one parable alone would have generated unusual anger and resentment among the Pharisees toward Jesus because it is a pointed denunciation of their arrogance and unmerciful attitude. The parable is also shocking in its contrast between the two people involved and the complete reversal of their public status and persona. It likewise would have bordered on unbelievable for many because it shattered every religious concept that most people had about Pharisees and tax collectors. The parable may not have changed everyone's long-standing opinions, but it certainly made people think differently about mercy, just as Jesus intended.

Pharisees were one of two major religious parties in Israel, Sadducees being the other. Pharisee means "the separated ones," and all devout Pharisees prided themselves in their steadfast, fundamentalist commitment to both the religious laws of Israel and also the customs and traditions of Judaism. It was their unyielding, uncompromising devotion to righteousness under the law that separated them from both the world and from all other people. As the parable states, they trusted only their legalistic, religious ritual to provide themselves with divine righteousness.

Pharisees were also among the most admired men in Israel and were viewed as morally upright, religiously perfect, and the ultimate example of righteousness—and they constantly crafted and enhanced that image. However, their spiritual pride and arrogance made them hard-headed, cold-hearted, uncompromising, judgmental, and unmerciful in their attitudes toward others who they viewed as sinners and imperfect keepers of the law. They took great pride in their righteous public persona and fostered their status and standing by regularly engaging in public prayer, acts of charity, and other religious rituals on street corners and in markets, or other public places, in order to be seen by others (Matt. 6:1-5). Spiritually, however, they were dead, and Jesus told them so—and they hated Him for speaking the truth.

Jesus warned His disciples not to follow the Pharisees' example. He denounced their attitudes and actions as hypocrisy, compared them to tombs filled with dead bones (Matt. 23:27) and called them "the blind leading the blind" (Matt. 15:14). In return, they labeled Him an illegitimate, demon-possessed radical who was worthy of death. Throughout His ministry, the Pharisees unmercifully hounded Jesus in every negative way possible, ultimately joining in the conspiracy to kill Him.

In comparison, a tax collector was one of the most despised and hated men in Israel. In terms of public trust and respect, Pharisees and tax collectors were on the opposite ends of the social spectrum—the first being admired and respected and the latter being detested, rejected, friendless, and deeply ridiculed. For clarity, this attitude resulted from the governing structure imposed by Rome and does not apply to modern-day officials in charge of public revenue.

Israel was a vassal state of the dominant Roman Empire. Rome regularly assessed many different taxes, and occasionally a general census of the empire's population was ordered to maximize tax revenue. It was during such a taxation census that Joseph and Mary journeyed to Bethlehem, Joseph's ancestral family hometown, where Jesus was born (Luke 2:1-7). The people of Israel chaffed at the Roman rule and longed for the day when the messiah would appear, rid the country of its enemies, and restore national pride and power.

Roman taxation policies were most often implemented by local tax agents who contracted with Rome and served as tax collectors.

Their authority was widespread, unchecked, and backed by Roman legions garrisoned in the area. Everything possible was taxed in some way, and whatever amount collected over the base assessment was kept by the collector as a fee for services. This system produced harsh and coercive collection methods and allowed many tax collectors to become very wealthy, such as Zacchaeus (Luke 19:2). As long as Rome received its assessed taxes, there was little concern about collection methods.

Tax collectors were viewed as traitors, cowards, and infidels and were considered as greedy, unprincipled, uncaring, and unmerciful. To the utter amazement of everyone, Jesus befriended them and even insisted on going to Zacchaeus' house to fellowship with him, calling him a "son of Abraham" because of his faith, which was a title reserved only for the most devout Jew (Luke 19:1-10). Notably, Jesus called Matthew, a tax collector, to be a disciple, and he later wrote the Gospel of Matthew, one of the foundation documents of the New Testament.

Thus, the very premise of portraying truth about mercy with these two figures was totally surprising and shocking. In terms of common expectations, God would have showered the Pharisee with mercy, and the tax collector would have received none. But Jesus portrayed the exact opposite in the parable: The Pharisee, viewed publicly as the most righteous, was described as the most unmerciful, while the tax collector, viewed publically as the most unmerciful, was portrayed as the recipient of God's mercy and love, making him justified and righteous. Why would Jesus cast them in such a puzzling and contrasting manner? The actions and statements of both in the parable reveal the answer.

The pious Pharisee lifted his hands to heaven in an apparent gesture of praise and submission. Numerous Old Testament passages describe lifting one's hands to God in this manner. However, the same gesture of uplifted hands was described as an abomination to God if done while filled with sin and inequity. In describing God's disgust with meaningless religious ritual, the prophet Isaiah said:

"When you spread out your hands, I will hide My eyes from you; even though you make many prayers, I will not hear. Your hands are full of blood" (Isa. 1:15).

The series of "woes" declared by Jesus against the scribes and Pharisees enumerated in Matthew chapter 23 reveal the nature of the unclean hands raised by the hypocritical Pharisee. Filled with all kinds of ungodly thoughts and attitudes, he nevertheless lifted his hands to God and thanked Him that he was "not like other men," and specifically pointed to the tax collector as an example.

This is one of the most graphic examples in the gospels of the unrepentant audacity of religious perfectionists to arrogantly and piously elevate and posture themselves as godly, while coldly and unmercifully condemning one viewed as morally and religiously inferior. According to Isaiah's statement, God hid His eyes from the Pharisee and would not hear him. But the Pharisee would not have known that. Because of his bloated spiritual pride, he would have assumed that he had God's undivided attention while he prayed—even though Jesus said, "he prayed to himself."

On the other hand, the tax collector did three significant things indicating his humility, submission, and true worship of God. First, he stood "afar off." This is an important statement. In the Sermon on the Mount, Jesus specifically condemned the hypocritical habit of scribes and Pharisees praying in public places, such as street corners and markets, "in order to be seen by men" (Matt. 6:5). Their prayers were not petitions to God, but rather public performances of false piety for their own benefit and ego. One would assume that the Pharisee sought an equally noticeable position with his Temple prayer.

In direct contrast, the tax collector prayed in a totally opposite manner. Jesus once told His disciples to go into a closet to pray—not a literal instruction, but an admonition to pray privately to God without concern for others' perception. That is how the tax collector prayed. Rather than seeking a prominent, noticeable position, he found a quiet, secluded place as far away from the crowd as possible where he could be alone with God.

Secondly, unlike the Pharisee, the tax collector not only refused to lift his hands toward heaven, but he also chose not to lift his eyes heavenward. His physical response of guilt and repentance is significant. Just as a guilty child finds it difficult to look their parent in the face, the tax collector was so aware of his guilt before God that he could not lift his eyes. A downcast, remorseful look signifies the crushing reality of guilt, and the tax collector fully experienced that spiritual condition.

Thirdly, he beat himself on the chest. Often this physical gesture is employed in a ritualistic act of grief or mourning. But there is a deeper physiological significance implicit in his act. The human circulatory system has an amazing capacity to constrict arteries in the body during times of extreme fear, grief, anger, or other intense emotional causes, often resulting in headaches, coldness, fainting, or the onset of shock. These physical reactions are occasionally accompanied by intense chest pain as the oxygen supply to the heart is reduced.

What if that is what the tax collector experienced? Then beating his chest was not some shallow gesture of sorrow and repentance, but rather the reality of his sin caused him such grief and sorrow that he nearly had a heart attack, and he pounded on his chest to get relief from the physical pain. Anyone who has endured an angina attack knows how he was suffering. Perhaps that intense level of personal grief, sorrow, contrition, and mourning is what Jesus meant when He said, "Blessed are those who mourn, for they shall be comforted" (Matt. 5:4).

David, the great King of Israel, was a gifted psalmist, and in a moment of utter contrition over sins that he had committed, he penned these words:

"The sacrifices of God are a broken spirit, a broken and a contrite heart—these, O God, You will not despise" (Psalm 51:17).

The spiritual contrast between the Pharisee and the tax collector is both startling and thought-provoking, and that was Jesus' strategic intent. The tax collector understood the meaning of David's psalm; the Pharisee did not. The tax collector saw himself as a sinner; the Pharisee reserved that category for others, but never for himself, and instead pointed out the sins of other people, whom he condemned, as he boasted of his self-righteousness. The tax collector saw the magnitude of his sin debt and knew he could never be righteous through his own effort; the Pharisee boasted of his religious accomplishments as he enumerated for God all the good things he had done. The tax collector pleaded for mercy; the Pharisee saw no need for mercy for, in his estimation of himself, he had done no wrong. The tax collector left justified; the Pharisee left entrapped in the web of his egotistical self-righteous sins.

The Old Testament concepts of sorrow, contrition, and mercy are closely related to the idea of spiritual comfort. The mission of God is to bring comfort to His repentant people through His mercy and compassion (Isaiah 40:1-2). King David powerfully declared in a psalm that because the Lord was his shepherd, "surely goodness and mercy shall follow me all the days of my life..." (Psalm 23:6). In fulfillment of that, the Holy Spirit takes the mercy of God made available to all Christians through faith in Jesus and brings eternal spiritual comfort to them. Thus, the Holy Spirit is the "Great Comforter." The tax collector knew the reality of God's mercy and comfort; the Pharisee had no concept of its meaning.

The Parable of the Prodigal Son

"A certain man had two sons. And the younger of them said to his father, 'Father, give me the portion of goods that falls to me.' So he divided to them his livelihood. And not many days later, the younger son gathered all together, journeyed to a far country, and there wasted his possessions with prodigal living. But when he had spent all, there arose a severe famine in that land, and he began to be in want. Then he went and joined himself to a citizen of that country, and he sent him into the fields to feed swine. And he would gladly have filled his stomach with the pods that the swine ate, and no one gave him anything. But when he came to himself, he said, 'How many of my father's hired servants have bread enough and to spare, and I perish with hunger! I will arise and go to my father, and I will say to him, Father, I have sinned against heaven and before you, and I am no longer worthy to be called your son. Make me like one of your hired servants.' And he arose and come to his father. But when he was still a great way off, his father saw him and had compassion, and ran and fell on his neck and kissed him. And the son said to him, 'Father, I have sinned against heaven and in your sight, and am no longer worthy to be called your son.' But the father said to his servants, 'Bring out the best robe and put it on him and put a ring on his hand and sandals on his feet. And bring the fatted calf here and kill it and let us eat and be merry; for this my son was dead and is alive again; he was lost and is found.' And they began to be merry" (Luke 15:11-23).

Anyone listening to the unfolding events in the parable would have been shocked at the conclusion. One can imagine the ire building, especially among fathers devoted to the law, as they pictured the attitude of this rebellious and ungrateful young man. He was certainly worthy of death, or at least severe punishment, from his father, and that punitive action would have been heartily supported. Regardless of what his legal punishment entailed, he would not have been entitled to the leniency and mercy that he received.

The young man's initial demand to his father for his inheritance portion was shockingly impudent. Under Jewish law, the first-born son was entitled to a double portion of his father's estate (Deut. 21:17)), and in the case of two sons, the older son would have received two-thirds of the total. Control over the inheritance and the estate was primarily between the oldest son and the father. Younger siblings simply shared the remainder. For whatever reason, however, the father granted the younger son's unusual request for early distribution. Perhaps in his wisdom, he sensed the younger son's rebellious nature and, knowing that experience is often the best teacher in life, simply gave him the freedom to learn from his mistakes. We do not know the rationale for his decision.

Clearly, we do know from the parable that the younger son squandered the entirety of his inheritance in loose living within a short time, and legally he was entitled to nothing more from his father. However, to his amazement, he was to learn that his father was motivated by mercy and forgiveness and not by law, and he could have never imagined what he would receive from his father—neither could those listening to Jesus' parable.

The abuse of his rights of inheritance was not the young man's only problem. He openly and defiantly violated the religious law and customs of Israel in several ways. Because of his rebellious and demanding attitude, he would have easily fit the category of a rebellious son worthy of death according to the Jewish law. At any time after he boldly and disrespectfully demanded his inheritance in advance of his father's death, and certainly after his return, he could have been stoned to death (Deut. 21:21).

After receiving his inheritance, he then journeyed to a distant country and joined himself to a foreigner. In doing so, he betrayed his Jewish heritage and brought shame upon himself, his family, his nation, and his religion by violating the prohibition against contact with Gentiles. The relationship with the foreigner greatly exceeded basic employment. It was deeply personal, and the original language implies that this young Jewish man glued himself to his Gentile employer in a close-knit bond of friendship prohibited by Jewish law (Acts 10:28).

Compounding matters further, the younger son worked feeding swine, and would have eaten their feed because of his hunger, thus becoming religiously unclean. Swine were specifically declared to be an unclean animal under Jewish law, and anyone working with them or eating pork was considered unclean and accursed (Lev.11:7-8).

The young man's actions had sealed his fate. He was in an emotional and physical dilemma because he faced the reality of either death by starvation in a foreign land or death by stoning if he returned home. His only hope of leniency from his father was limited to confessing his unworthiness to be considered his son again and pleading that he be viewed only as a servant. In effect, he was willing to become his father's indentured slave under the law—with no rights whatsoever—in order to live, and that was the best hope. Because of the magnitude of his sin, he had sadly abandoned all concepts of himself as the son of his father.

Mired in the pigpen of his sins, the prodigal son was a victim of religious law in two ways: Not only was he guilty of his own sinful actions, but he was also victimized by the limitations of religious law. The unyielding law had never taught him about mercy and forgiveness because it did not envision those alternatives. The law of stoning said that a father shall stone his disobedient son to death, with no lesser penalty being permitted. The prodigal son could not conceive that a father's love is not controlled by the legal obligations to punish, but instead can transcend merciless law through boundless, merciful love—a level of mercy that compels redeeming love to become both attitude and action regardless of the magnitude of sin.

Under ordinary circumstances, neither the young man's father, his family, nor his friends would have greeted him upon his return. He was a sinner worthy of death, and that is what anyone hearing the parable would have anticipated. But then Jesus injected a radically transforming new dimension—the father's mercy and forgiveness—and the parable moved in a direction no one would have anticipated.

Customarily, in a patriarchal society where a father's word is unquestioned and he is entitled to reverence and respect, one would have anticipated the father being stern, unforgiving, reserved, and judgmental toward the younger son upon his return. His harshness would have vindicated both his authority and the loyalty of the older son. That is the image of God in a legalistic religious environment; that is how Israel viewed God's attitude toward sinners and law breakers; and that is how they would have expected the father in the parable to act. That is also how religious zealots today expect God to act toward those whom they condemn and shun.

However, Jesus portrayed the father—and indirectly portrayed God—to be the exact opposite. It is challenging to think how the role of the father, in relation to his sinful child, could have been portrayed more dramatically. The attitude of the father in this parable is godly, and it was Jesus' intent through the parable to present God in a merciful, loving way seldom considered.

It must also be noted that the oft-discussed issue of spiritual life and death adds a dimension to this parable that is not readily apparent, but it is alluded to by the father. Because of his defiant attitude and actions, the young man was presumed physically, socially, and religiously dead. By closely and intimately attaching himself to a Gentile, the younger son turned his back on his Jewish heritage and faith and renounced his Jewish identity. As a Jew, he died.

Further, it is unknown how long he resided in the foreign country, but it was obviously long enough for him to both waste away his inheritance and for a severe famine to develop. With no contact from his son, the father could have easily presumed that he was dead.

But redeeming love, mercy, and grace would not allow the merciful father to accept that as his son's final fate, and he continued to hope and look for his return. The father's mercy and forgiveness provided for the triumph of life over death, and that is the amazing truth of Christianity.

The Apostle Paul, in writing to the Ephesian church, described God's mercy:

> *"And you He made alive, who were dead in trespasses and sins, in which you once walked according to the course of this world, according to the prince of the power of the air, the spirit who now works in the sons of disobedience, among whom also we all once conducted ourselves in the lusts of our flesh, fulfilling the desires of the flesh and of the mind, and were by nature children of wrath, just as the others. But God, who is rich in mercy, because of His great love with which He loved us, even when we were dead in trespasses, made us alive together with Christ (by grace you have been saved)"* (Eph. 2:1-5).

That is the experience of every Christian with God's mercy. Even while we were spiritually dead in our trespasses and sins, Christ died for us that He might give eternal life to all who believe (Rom. 5:8). In the parable, the father did not see his son as dead. He saw him as alive and forgiven through his mercy, and that is how God sees us.

It is important to note the father's forgiving attitude as he waited. He determined in advance how he would react. For the father, mercy and forgiveness were not emotional afterthoughts once the son returned. Instead, mercy and forgiveness were intentional spiritual attitudes to which the father committed himself well in advance of his rebellious son's return.

As a comparative note of history, Abraham Lincoln was determined to preserve the bond existing between the states prior to the Civil War. He was asked how he intended to treat the rebellious Southern states once they returned to the Union, and he replied, "I will treat them as if they never left." That is the father's attitude in this parable.

Although the parable is most often referred to as the parable of the prodigal son, other names have been suggested, such as the parable of the forgiving father and the parable of the two sons. In a broader sense, however, it is a parable about the triumph of mercy over religious law, and that was the point Jesus was strategically emphasizing. There are vital lessons about mercy and forgiveness that are evident in the parable:

- The father's compassion and mercy for his sinful son were much greater than the harsh constraints of law.
- The father's compassion and mercy never allowed him to consider his son dead, but rather he believed in the power of life over death.
- The father's compassion and mercy caused him to continue to look for and seek his son's return, even when the young man was far away.
- The father's compassion and mercy poured out through redeeming love as he embraced and kissed his repentant son.

- The father's compassion, mercy, and redeeming love became grace as he clothed his son in the best robe and put a ring on his finger and sandals on his feet.
- The father's compassion and mercy turned his repentant son's return into a joyous celebration for all—except his merciless, legalistic brother.
- The father's compassion and mercy transformed the son's status from a slave into a redeemed son.

There are also powerful truths about mercy versus law that are apparent in the parable:

- The law gave the older son a double portion of the father's inheritance, and he took control of the father's estate. The father's mercy and grace, however, compelled him to instead place his signet ring on the younger son's finger, which granted him authority to act for his father rather than the older son. The signet ring normally was engraved with a small personal seal, initials, or other identifying marks. In historical transactions, melted wax was often placed on a document and the emblem of the individual's signet ring was pressed into the wax, thus sealing it with authority.
- Through the father's mercy and forgiveness, the characteristic of the redeemed son's life and the father's estate became boundless joy, celebration, and thanksgiving that had never been known before.
- Through the father's mercy and forgiveness, he cast aside the religious unclean nature of his son—imposed upon him by law because of the pig-pen lifestyle he had lived—and embraced his uncleanness with no concern for becoming unclean himself because of his loving welcome.
- Through the father's mercy, his regal robe covered over the son's sinful stains of past sins, and he re-entered his father's house with full acceptance. He was neither punished nor put on probation; he was fully forgiven.

The father's signet ring is profoundly important to the parable's meaning. Through mercy and grace, the father's entire estate was given to the younger son by virtue of the ring, and mercy, grace, and redeeming love forever took priority over cold, unyielding religious law. The rules of inheritance were forever changed. When the father put his ring on the younger son, he not only gave him control over his estate, but he also granted him power of attorney to act as his father's ambassador and speak on his father's behalf.

This single gesture presaged the unfolding concept of Christians inheriting the kingdom of heaven. The entirety of God's heavenly kingdom does not belong to the self-righteous, religious perfectionists with an inflated sense of entitlement, but rather it is given as an unmerited gift to the most undeserving who will truly understand the nature of grace. Jesus succinctly captured this amazing truth when He said, "Blessed are the poor in spirit, for theirs is the kingdom of heaven" (Matt. 5:3).

In truth, this parable is not so much about the prodigal son as it is about his loving father. Through this parable, Jesus transformed the concept of a father's authority from the legalistic obligation to punish to the loving and merciful opportunity to forgive, redeem, and restore. Nothing in the law of Judaism would have bestowed such love upon a sinner, and no one would have imagined that God's mercy was portrayed in the action of the father. However, that is the amazing truth of the parable.

Yet, in the midst of such mercy and love, the parable also portrays a sad and sobering dimension in the older brother's opposite attitude. He is the embodiment of religious legalism:

- The older son had written off his brother as a worthless sinner. He expressed no love or concern for him, and he showed no interest in his return and repentance.
- The older son expressed no joy over his younger brother's return; instead, he continued to reveal only a cold, judgmental condemnation of him.
- The older son was resentful of the mercy and love shown by his father.
- The older son was jealous over the joyous reception given to his younger brother but realized that nothing he had

done in lawfully serving his father had produced such joy and happiness.
- The older son refused to acknowledge the younger son as his brother, speaking of him to his father only as "this son of yours."
- The older son was angry over the younger son being given the robe and ring of his father due to love, mercy, and grace. He presumed he had earned those as a matter of law.
- The older son was bitter, cold, harsh, and unmerciful and could neither fathom nor engage in the joy of one who had been presumed dead because of his sins, but was now alive, and of being lost, but now found. He was cold-blooded and condemning, and none of the father's loving, merciful action touched him emotionally or spiritually.
- The older son is a classic example of the scribes, Pharisees, and other religious leaders in Israel who had no concept of mercy and forgiveness and who placed all their religious expectations on their own self-righteous works under the law and their presumed entitlement to the blessings of God.

The parable of the prodigal son is far more than a classic description of a defiant, rebellious young man returning home. It is a strategic gem that portrays the consequences of sin, the mercy of God, and the coldness of judgmental legalism. In its powerful portrayal of the contrast between law and mercy, its greatest impact lies in its ability to make us see ourselves as either the older brother or the younger son.

For example, when I consider my own sins, it is easy to see myself as the younger son. But, when I look at the sins of others, am I like the merciful, forgiving father, or the unforgiving, unmerciful brother? Do I love and forgive others as the father did? Am I filled with joy over their repentance and return, or does doubt and skepticism dominate my thoughts?

Every Christian in his relationship with God is the younger son. But the real test of this parable is whether, in our relationship with others, we are like the father or the older son. Which one am I, really? This parable shocked Jesus' listeners into thinking more deeply about mercy and forgiveness, and it should do the same for us.

A New Definition of Neighbor

The Parable of the Good Samaritan

> *"A certain man went down from Jerusalem to Jericho, and fell among thieves, who stripped him of his clothing, wounded him, and departed, leaving him half dead. Now by chance a certain priest came down that road. And when he saw him, he passed by on the other side. Likewise a Levite, when he arrived at the place, came, and looked, and passed by on the other side. But a certain Samaritan, as he journeyed, came where he was. And when he saw him, he had compassion. So he went to him and bandaged his wounds, pouring on oil and wine, and he set him on his own animal, brought him to an inn, and took care of him. On the next day, when he departed, he took out two denarii, gave them to the innkeeper, and said to him, 'Take care of him; and whatever more you spend, when I come again, I will repay you.' So which of these three do you think was neighbor to him who fell among the thieves?"* (Luke 10:30-36).

No parable is better known than the parable of the Good Samaritan. Its iconic name has been used to describe compassionate and generous individuals; it has inspired countless acts of ministry; and numerous hospitals and other charitable institutions and organizations bear the name. The Good Samaritan is synonymous with compassion, personal sacrifice, and selfless caring for others.

Yet, Jesus did not tell the parable for that purpose. It was told as a calculated confrontation with a religious legalist who sought to define the dividing line between the obligation to love and the opportunity to hate, and that emotional line hinged on the definition of "neighbor." The ancient religious law of Israel required that one should "love your neighbor as yourself" (Lev. 19:18). The law did not specifically authorize animosity toward one who was not a neighbor, but over time legal interpretations stipulated that just as one loved his neighbor, he was conversely free to hate his "enemy" and to feel completely justified before God in doing so. Jesus radically challenged this divisive attitude by telling His disciples to "love their enemies" rather than hating them (Matt. 5:43-44). Thus, precisely who fell into the category of neighbor had significant meaning.

Definitions are important in law. A "neighbor" was not necessarily one who lived next door or in close proximity, but rather one with whom one had a bond of mutual interest, tribal identity, or the sharing of common customs and beliefs. An "enemy" was essentially everyone else. "Love" was not emotional, erotic feelings, but rather the bond of kinship, friendship, and mutual commitment and support. "Hate" was simply the absence of any such positive feelings and usually the presence of animosity, indifference, rejection, and coldness. All of these are important in understanding the parable of the Good Samaritan.

For the religious legalists, however, the line between the two was significant, and therefore the lawyer posed the question to Jesus, "Who is my neighbor?" (v. 29). He was seeking clarification and designation of those he had to love, and those he was free to shun, condemn, reject, and hate without violating the religious law and compromising his righteousness with God.

Jesus, in His characteristic fashion, did not issue a clarifying edict which would validate the lawyer's prejudices. Instead, He told a parable that totally shocked and challenged the lawyer and eternally redefined the word "neighbor," and He used one of the most despised people of His day as the central figure in the parable—a Samaritan.

Contrary to modern descriptions of the Samaritan's goodness, he was actually viewed as very bad. There are different theories regarding the Samaritans' origin, but historically they have been viewed as the descendants of foreigners brought into central Israel after the Assyrian conquest of the area in 722 B.C., where they were assimilated into the population, married, and established families. Their descendants, however, were regarded as "half-breeds" by the Jews and were bitterly hated. Following the Assyrian conquest of northern and central Israel, Samaritans were so despised and rejected that Jewish citizens would not journey through central Israel where Samaritans primarily resided. A Jewish traveler would usually cross over the Jordan River and journey along its eastern shore when traveling from one end of Israel to the other.

Jesus pointedly challenged this deep-seated prejudice by insisting on personally journeying through Samaria on His way from Judea to Galilee (John 4:3-4), and by sharing some of the deepest truths about His divine nature with a Samaritan woman at a water well in Sychar (John 4:5-26). But it was Jesus' radical use of a Samaritan in this parable that is considered one of His most challenging and ingenuous statements.

The basis of the parable begins with a demand for a legal, limited definition of neighbor and ends with a spiritually powerful new understanding of mercy. The contrast between the lawyer's question and Jesus' answer, as defined by the actions of the Samaritan, is riveting, and the lawyer would have been shocked and mystified by Jesus' statements because they contradicted every idea, prejudice, and presumption he had known all his life.

The parable portrays a traveler who had been robbed by thieves, beaten, and left half dead. He is first found by a priest who, as a member of the priestly tribe of Levi, should have revealed God's compassion and mercy to the wounded man, but he did not. Instead, he "passed by on the other side," implying that he got as far away from the wounded man lying in the pathway as possible.

Why would he do that? The religious laws stipulated that if one touched a dead body or bodily discharge they were rendered unclean and must ceremonially purify themselves from the contamination. Since the wounded man was left half dead, the priest, not knowing whether he was dead or alive, would not have wanted to touch the traveler's body in order to avoid the inconvenience of purifying himself in the midst of his journey.

Next, a Levite came along. All priests were Levites, but not all members of tribe of Levi were priests. Others had duties associated with the priesthood and with maintenance of the temple worship ritual, and this man was apparently in that category. So, even though he was not a priest, the Levite was viewed as one directly involved in and responsible for leading others in the worship of God.

But, rather than revealing the caring nature of God to the wounded traveler, he, too, passed by as far away from him as possible. Both the priest and the Levite, men who were ordained to reveal the nature of God to others and who were greatly admired and respected as devout, righteous, religious leaders, were in fact trapped in the restraints of religious law and were uncaring, pitiless, cold, and indifferent—the exact opposite of God.

Then, along came the despised Samaritan, viewed by Jews as the scum of the earth and scornfully referred to as a dog. However, one major thing distinguished him from the priest and the Levite: He was not bound by the merciless dictates of religious law that made a mockery of mercy. He was free to love his enemy, not hate him, and he did. Here is the sheer irony of this parable: The ones who should have reached out to the wounded man as a neighbor in fact treated him like an enemy, and the one who could have treated him as an enemy instead treated him as a neighbor and loved and cared for him like he would his own self. The motivation was mercy and compassion unfettered by religious law.

It is noteworthy that the first legalistic instinct of both the priest and the Levite was to get away from the wounded man as far as possible in order not to defile themselves. They experienced no sense of mercy for him. On the other hand, the first instinct of the Samaritan was compassion that compelled him to mercifully care for the wounded man's needs as he would want to be cared for if he were the victim.

Religious law has a pernicious effect upon the determination of friend or foe, neighbor, or enemy. That was true during Jesus' earthly life, and it still is. Our contemporary religious and social attitudes are greatly influenced by it. Those who are like us, those who share similar beliefs, and those who have comparable values are considered as friends and neighbors. Those who do not possess those values are not. Most of us are not like the Samaritan, and that is one reason the parable remains so challenging.

The Samaritan invested himself in the traveler's life and needs without concern for legalistic religious restrictions. He was not concerned with being religiously unclean, but instead focused on cleaning the traveler's wounds and bandaging them. It was costly compassion in action. He took the man to an inn and personally cared for him. Upon leaving, he gave the innkeeper two denarii and instructed him to care for the wounded man, assuring the innkeeper he would repay him if additional time and money were spent on the wounded man's care.

A denarius was a coin commonly used for one day's pay for a laborer. Thus, the Samaritan gave the innkeeper two days' wages and promised more if needed. Quite frankly, that was unheard of in Israel and was so shocking it would have been hard to believe, but that is how Jesus created new understanding and insight about God and shattered centuries-old religious attitudes and traditions.

Jesus redefined the definition of "neighbor" through a description of unprecedented mercy—mercy free from religious law, social custom, and cultural traditions. The parable is a word picture of mercy without racial or ethnic prejudice and without concern for the gossip, cynicism, and skepticism of others. It was a description of divine mercy that transcended the cold-hearted religious rules of man and made mercy a life transforming experience for both the Samaritan and the wounded traveler, for neither ever thought of the other again as they had previously.

Through the experience of mercy, enemies became neighbors, not because they lived nearby or because of a technical, legal definition, but through the common bond of compassion, caring, and "doing unto others as you would have them do unto you" (Matt. 7:12). When Jesus asked who of the three men was a neighbor to the wounded traveler, the inquiring lawyer was compelled by the power of the parable to respond, "He who showed mercy on him" (v. 37).

If every Christian prayerfully considered the truth of the parable of the Good Samaritan, their rigid, robotic, religious life would be transformed. When the mercy of God becomes unrestricted by the opinions of man and our Christian faith becomes divine compassion in action, then the world changes. When our definition of neighbor becomes every fellow human being, regardless of race, creed, or color, who struggles with cultural, social, economic, and religious beatings and wounds inflicted on them by others; when we ignore the judgmental, unmerciful religious perfectionists who denounce us for investing ourselves in their lives; and when we are willing to compassionately commit ourselves to their struggle and to alleviating their pain, our life, and our understanding of mercy changes.

When the divine mercy of God flows unimpeded from our heart because of a deep sense of compassion for the hurt and suffering of others, then enemies become neighbors and our attitude toward all others radically changes. It is through our mercy and redeeming love for one another—even our enemies—that we demonstrate to the world that we are disciples of Jesus (John 13:35). It is only when we are merciful to others that we best understand how merciful God is to us (Matt. 5:7). Amazingly, when the truth of the parable of the Good Samaritan becomes a living reality in our life, then we become a neighbor to all others, and we have no enemies.

Words can define action, and action can define attitudes. In re-examining who he viewed as a neighbor, the inquisitive lawyer was no doubt speechless when Jesus told him to act like the hated Samaritan rather than the admired priest or Levite. No one in Israel would have dared use a Samaritan as a role model for godly conduct, but Jesus did. Jesus' statement, "Go and do likewise" (v. 37), essentially means to act in a similar fashion with the same attitude shown by the Samaritan.

It is fascinating that through the power and genius of this parable, Jesus compelled the lawyer to evaluate his own attitude and actions and to admit that he—a man well-versed in the religious law—actually had less understanding of the true meaning of neighbor than the most despised, ungodly man he could imagine—a man who would forever be known as the Good Samaritan.

None of us can eliminate hurting and suffering in the world. But we can try with at least one other person, and then others. "Blessed are the merciful, for they shall obtain mercy" is Jesus' eternal promise that when we purge our heart of the cold, judgmental attitudes of religious law and stop "passing by on the other side" when we see someone in need and instead put compassion into merciful action, we experience more mercy ourselves. Mercy becomes multiplied, and in the words of Jeremiah, there is new mercy to be experienced every morning and new mercy to be shared.

Mercy is not a one-time event. It is a never-ending divine attitude flowing from us to others that turns compassion into action. There is no greater kinship with Christ than being a Good Samaritan to our neighbors—whoever they may be.

The Value of One

The Parable of the Lost Sheep

> *"What man of you, having a hundred sheep, if he loses one of them, does not leave the ninety-nine in the wilderness, and go after the one which is lost until he finds it? And when he has found it, he lays it on his shoulders, rejoicing. And when he comes home, he calls together his friends and neighbors, saying to them, 'Rejoice with me, for I have found my sheep which was lost.' I say to you that likewise there will be more joy in heaven over one sinner who repents than over ninety-nine just persons who need no repentance" (Luke 15:4-7).*

The parables of Jesus strategically challenged entrenched social and religious attitudes in Israel. They vividly revealed new truth against the backdrop of old habits and attitudes and portrayed the nature of God with clarity and freshness that surprised Jesus' listeners. The parable of the lost sheep revealed God's interest in individuals and His joy over their return to Him in ways not envisioned by the religious principles of Judaism. The parable's description of God's concern for individual sinners was radical and shocking.

Judaism is premised on a covenant between God and Israel based upon legalistic concepts found in the Ten Commandments, other Old Testament legal codes, and the interpretations of those laws over several centuries. In a general sense, the covenant of the Old Testament was between God and the nation of Israel, and no individual was the recipient of God's covenant promise.

That concept is reversed in the New Testament. Jesus declared that the new covenant in His blood is with each individual Christian, and no specific nation is the recipient of His covenant blessings. Anyone in the world may believe in faith and enter into the new covenant with Christ. It is a total reversal of covenant focus and requires re-evaluation of the role and importance of individual believers under the new covenant compared to their minimized role and importance under the old covenant of law.

The parable of the lost sheep is not just a nice little story about a caring shepherd's search for a lamb. Admittedly, that is the common perception of the parable, and that is what one generally thinks at first reading. But the parable has a less conspicuous message that is a radical and revolutionary story about the value of every person to God, regardless of how sinful they may be, and about the spiritual joy that results when anyone returns to Him in faith. It was this hidden message, skillfully woven into the fabric of the shepherd's search for one sheep, which is the real strategic gem of the parable. That truth is not what one thinks about when first reading the parable; it is what one ponders for a long time afterward.

It is important to grasp Jesus' challenge in transforming and refocusing the understanding of his listeners away from the value of the laws of Israel to the value of the life of one lost individual. To comprehend its original impact, the parable should be read as a daring and dramatic presentation of new truth about God that would have shocked and angered Jewish listeners and forced them to rethink their own attitudes about individuals they condemned as sinners. We should do the same as we read and study this amazing parable.

The transition of thought from the whole to the one is similar to the rights and powers contained in the Constitution of the United States. Indeed, the Constitution provides the governmental basis for the nation and all its citizens, and that is how most view it, but the amazing feature of this great document is its focus on protecting the rights and privileges of each citizen. It may be argued that the greatest document of civil government in the world, governing the greatest and most powerful nation in the world, is actually intended to protect the rights of one person—and all people of the nation collectively. That was an amazing concept of government when it was adopted, and it remains so today. The same may be said of Jesus' teaching about the value of one sinner in the eyes of God.

Perhaps the best way to conceptualize this parable is by imagining a scenario under American law. Visualize a fundamentalist, nationalistic group that defines American citizenship as unwavering and fastidious compliance with every requirement of law contained in the Constitution, all federal laws and regulations, and every applicable state law and municipal ordinance, and they vehemently condemn anyone who does not comply as being unpatriotic. Imagine their cold contempt toward violators and their harsh desire to penalize them to the maximum extent of the law. One can virtually hear their boastful assertions regarding their own loyalty and citizenship, and also hear their scathing, vitriolic condemnation of those who did not follow the law as closely as they did. In their judgment, the nation would be stronger, more powerful, and socially at peace if only the lawbreakers could be permanently removed from society.

What would be their attitude toward a young reformer who declared the Constitution was actually intended to protect the interests and rights of each individual scoundrel and lawbreaker they detested and bitterly judged? One can mentally see the hard, piercing glare of disbelief and rejection on their stony faces. Now, visualize Jesus projecting the same truth to the religious legalists of Israel through a simple parable about a shepherd and a lost sheep. The parable did not produce sighs of approval and understanding; it most likely produced outrage among the scribes and Pharisees because it projected an image of sinners and God's love for them that was the exact opposite of their cold, entrenched attitudes.

The fundamentalist Pharisees, who prided themselves in their adherence to the law, categorized those less devoted as "People of the Land," and the phrase, or variations of it, is still used today to define different categories of adherents to Judaism. Dr. William Barclay, the noted Scottish New Testament theologian, provides a revealing discussion about this judgmental attitude:

> "The Pharisees gave to people who did not keep the law a general classification. They called them *the People of the Land*; and there was a complete barrier between the Pharisees and the People of the Land. To marry a daughter to one of them was like exposing her bound and helpless to a lion. The Pharisaic regulations laid it down, 'When a man is one of the People of the Land, entrust no money to him, take no testimony from him, trust him with no secret, do not appoint him guardian of an orphan, do not make him the custodian of charitable funds, do not accompany him on a journey.' A Pharisee was forbidden to be the guest of any such man or to have him as his guest. He was even forbidden, so far as it was possible, to have any business dealings with him. It was the deliberate Pharisaic aim to avoid every contact with the people who did not observe the petty details of the law….the strict Jews said, 'There will be joy in heaven over one sinner

who is obliterated before God.' They looked sadistically forward not to the saving but to the destruction of the sinner."[1]

This level of judgmental bitterness by supposedly religious people is hard to comprehend. Unfortunately, it was not limited to the scribes and Pharisees during Jesus' ministry but continues today.

A member of my immediate family died a few years ago at age ninety-one. He was a very religious man, and he took pride in memorizing all the books of the Bible and numerous scripture passages. His Bible was filled with underlined verses, margin notes, and personal comments. He quoted from it often, and he used his biblical wisdom in most of his decisions.

He also used his Bible to judge others in the community, including his family, neighbors, and friends. He would quickly condemn them for what he considered unrighteous and ungodly actions, and he even made a list of men in the community, dividing them according to whether he thought they were going to heaven or hell. When any of them died, he mentally checked their name off his list. He was exceedingly religious in his demeanor, yet coldly unmerciful in his denunciation of others.

He was usually the first to arrive at church and the last to leave, and he never missed a Sunday unless he was ill. He enjoyed his perception among church members as a godly man and a pillar of the church. But he was an intensely unhappy man. In all the years that I knew him, he never told a simple joke or enjoyed any kind of merriment. Anything of that nature was sinful to him. Not once did I hear him laugh heartily.

He did not watch television or listen to music. He never took his wife or family out to dinner, and he did not enjoy sports or have any recreational activities, for those were of the devil. To my knowledge, he never read a book and had no idea about current interests or affairs. He knew nothing about sports, colleges, trends, or fashion. Other than service travel when he was drafted, he never journeyed more than one hundred miles from home in his life. He knew nothing about the world and had no interest in it, for it belonged to the devil.

---

[1] William Barclay, *The Gospel of Luke, The Daily Study Bible Series,* Rev. ed. (Philadelphia, PA: Westminster, 1975) 199-200.

He was truly a joyless man. He was stern, dour, demanding, uncompromising, unyielding, and judgmental, yet very religious. He seemingly viewed himself as God's agent in pointing out the sins of others, while not acknowledging his own. He consistently found fault in others and piously told them they were being judged by God and going to hell, even his own children.

He was married twice, and neither of his wives had any love or respect for him because of his harsh, abusive attitude. He often said to each of them, "I am the man of the house, and you will do as I say." He never sat down with his family for a meal without a verbal confrontation resulting. He began each day fussing and complaining at his wife and children about some trivial matter, often while reading the Bible aloud to them. He beat his children unmercifully with limbs and switches in the belief that sparing the rod would spoil the child. None of his three sons had any emotional bond with him, and each of them avoided him whenever possible.

He showed no interest in his children's accomplishments and refused to attend any school activities in which they participated. All of that was of the devil, he said. His youngest son enrolled in a state university, but he never called him while he was away at school, never inquired about his interests or his plans, and offered no meaningful financial assistance. The young man eventually received a bachelor's degree and two post-graduate degrees over seven years of study. Throughout all those difficult years of financial struggle to obtain an education, this man contributed a total of forty dollars in financial support to his son. Rather than encouraging him, he wrote his son letters condemning his desire for an education and knowledge and urged him to drop out of school and avoid the temptation of the devil. He condemned his son's interests, appearance, and desires and pointedly told him he was going to hell because of them.

The youngest son eventually entered the ministry and served as a pastor for twenty years. This man attended only a very few services in which his son preached, but instead wrote him lengthy letters condemning his religious beliefs and telling him that only the strict, fundamentalist denomination to which he belonged was the true faith and all others were wrong.

Despite his harshness toward his sons, he constantly reminded them of the Bible verse requiring them to respect and honor him as their father, so that their days would be long on the earth. That was his way of saying, if you do not honor me, you can die an early death, and I will not grieve. Because of his actions and attitudes, none of his children have any happy memories of their childhood.

He lived a long, miserable, unhappy life of rigid, religious fundamentalism. Although he read his Bible every day and went to church without fail, he was the most humorless, joyless man I have ever known, and I knew him well. He was my father, and I am his youngest son—the one he considered a wayward prodigal.

As I consider this parable, I can think of no better example of the joyless, stern, critical attitude of the Pharisees than my own father. I have often wondered if he even had the physical and emotional capacity to experience joy. If he did, I never saw it. Jesus did not see it in the Pharisees, either. David, the psalmist, asked God to restore to him the joy of his salvation (Psalm 51:12), but the scribes and Pharisees never did.

Jesus often had a unique way of boxing people in with logic, as he stated a religious point to them, and He began this parable in such a manner: "What man of you, having a hundred sheep, if he loses one of them, does not leave the ninety-nine in the wilderness, and go after the one which is lost until he finds it?" It was a direct appeal to their sense of responsibility as adult men and to their stewardship over their property. None of them would have answered, "Not me. I would not go after the one sheep." In doing so, Jesus had them focused on the worth of the individual sheep, and not on the worth of the ninety-nine left behind, before they even realized His intent.

There is an aspect of this parable that I find challenging and difficult to understand, and it enhances the focus on the value of the individual sheep to the shepherd. The shepherd left ninety-nine other sheep in the wilderness, unguarded and unprotected against thieves or prowling animals, in order to search for one. What happened to the other ninety-nine? During the time that it took for him to find the lost sheep, bring it home, and call all his friends together to rejoice with him, the other ninety-nine sheep could have scattered, been attacked, or wandered far from where he left them. In some ways, that does not seem very practical or prudent. Why would the shepherd do that?

Jesus provided an answer. In the Gospel of John, Jesus described Himself as the true shepherd, and He equated His interest in each individual person to the knowledge that a shepherd had about his individual sheep:

> *"But he who enters by the door is the shepherd of the sheep. To him the doorkeeper opens, and the sheep hear his voice; and he calls his own sheep by name and leads them out"* (John 10:2-3).

That is an amazing truth. The focus of the shepherd was not primarily on the entire flock as a whole, but rather on each individual sheep, and he intimately knew the personality and traits of each one, including its name. Under the new covenant of grace, the focus is on the individual and not the nation of Israel, or any nation, but every individual in the entire world. The deep meaning of John 3:16 comes to mind: "For God so loved the world that He gave His only begotten Son, that whoever believes in Him should not perish but have everlasting life." Is God's love for every person in the world so great that He would give His Son if only one of them believed? The scripture sets no minimum number requirement for believers in order for God to act.

With the flock of one hundred sheep grazing and moving, how did the shepherd know that one was missing? If his focus was on the entirety of the herd, then one sheep could have easily disappeared. But, because of his love for each sheep, the shepherd counted them constantly and called each of them by name. He left the ninety-nine because his love for the one lost sheep compelled him to search for it until he found it, and as he went, he no doubt called its name. What a beautiful, vivid, and moving picture of God's love for every individual. Thus, the Bible says, "The Lord is not…willing that any should perish but that all should come to repentance" (2 Peter 3:9).

When the shepherd found the lost sheep, he did not drag it back to the flock in anger due to the arduous task of finding it. Instead, he rejoiced with exceeding happiness and lovingly carried it on his shoulders, even if it occasionally bleated and kicked. His joy was contagious, boundless, and unreserved. He brought it home—not to a people who wanted to stone it to death for leaving—but to a village-wide eruption of unrestrained happiness, joy, and thanksgiving because it had been found. This joy was not over the entire flock coming safely back to the sheepfold at the end of the day, but, amazingly, over the return of one erring lamb. That kind of heavenly joy over an individual sinner repenting was simply incomprehensible to the Pharisees.

Jesus could not have painted a more striking contrast between the attitude of the Pharisees and the attitude of God concerning the value of one individual. The Pharisees would have rejoiced to see a sinner condemned to death and forgotten. But Jesus shocked them by stating, "I tell you that likewise there will be more joy in heaven over one sinner who repents than over ninety-nine just persons who need no repentance."

It was to these sullen, sour-faced judgmental zealots—the ones who intensely criticized Him for eating with and befriending sinners—that Jesus directed this parable focusing on the value of one life and the joy that should be experienced over the salvation of every person. One can readily surmise that not a single scribe or Pharisee had ever placed any value on a sinner's life nor experienced any spiritual joy over their repentance. In fact, there is no record in the four gospels of any scribe, Pharisee, or priest expressing any emotion of joy or praise, even over Jesus' miraculous healings or the power and clarity of His teaching. When Jesus raised Lazarus from the dead, there was no joyful response from the Pharisees for this divine power of life over death. Instead, they only intensified their plans to kill Him (John 11:46-53).

How can the nature of spiritual joy be conveyed to a joyless person and how can praise, thanksgiving, and spiritual happiness be injected into cold, lifeless, religious ritual? Jesus used these parables to paint a picture of joy never before experienced in Israel.

The Parable of the Lost Coin

> *"Or what woman, having ten silver coins, if she loses one coin, does not light a lamp, sweep the house, and search carefully until she finds it? And when she has found it, she calls her friends and neighbors together, saying, 'Rejoice with me, for I have found the piece which I lost!' Likewise, I say to you, there is joy in the presence of the angels of God over one sinner who repents"* (Luke 15:8-10).

Which brings greater joy—determined effort or desperate effort? Although both the parable of the lost sheep and the parable of the lost coin focus on joy, they are different, and the resulting joy was different. The shepherd was determined to find his lost sheep, but the woman was desperate to find her lost coin. His search defined the love of a shepherd; her search defined the life of a woman.

The lost coin was a drachma, which was a Greek coin still used in parts of the Roman Empire and was roughly equivalent to a denarius, or a day's wage. But this parable is not about the economic loss of one coin out of ten, or else it could have been easily addressed to men, as was the parable of the lost sheep. Jesus specifically directed the parable to the women who were listening, and they would have uniquely understood the joy He described.

Israel was a patriarchal society, and men dominated every social, economic, and religious aspect. A woman had very few rights and very few possessions. A man could divorce his wife for the most trivial reason and send her away from home helpless and destitute. There were few things that were unquestionably a woman's possession, and her wedding garland was one of them. It was unique to her, and it was treasured above all else. Often it was a family heirloom passed from mother to daughter on their wedding day—a personal family treasure with a special meaning and value known only to women.

The wedding garland was uniquely constructed. Regardless of its design, the garland's distinguishing feature was ten drachma coins arranged in order and woven into the garland material creating a special meaning and value that every married woman treasured. The garland denoted the wearer as a married woman, indicating to others her status of acceptance and love, and she wore it openly and proudly.

However, misfortune had befallen the woman in the parable. One of the drachma coins was missing and lost. It was not the value of a single coin she had lost, but rather the symbol of her life as a married woman—a special honor in a male-dominated society. Until the missing coin was found, she would not wear a disfigured wedding garland, and without it, she was horrified at the thought of public reaction.

The wedding garland was the one thing that gave her a sense of self-worth, dignity, and acceptance. Losing the coin and losing use of the ten-coin garland was much like losing her life. She was desperate to find the lost coin, and her desperation reached levels not readily understood nor appreciated today.

Given the importance of the missing coin, her intense search efforts become more understandable. Lighting a lamp for better illumination, she searched every corner, crack, and crevice in the house while no doubt softly saying to herself, "Where is it? Where is it?" She then took a broom made from brush and swept the floor, searching carefully through the debris. Understanding her desperate search helps one better understand her joy over finding the lost coin. It restored her life.

It is unknown how long she searched nor where she found the coin. However, one thing is certain: When she found it, pure joy erupted in that little house! Her joy was unrestrained and contagious. She repeatedly called out to her friends and neighbors, inviting them to come and rejoice with her because she had found the lost coin. Her joyous reaction, Jesus said, is how God's angels react when one sinner repents.

Comparing the quietness of her house while she searched to the joyful shouts when she found the coin is exhilarating. But, thinking of the hushed quiet in heaven compared to the reverberation of angelic joy when one sinner repents is spiritually spine tingling. Such heavenly joy over one sinner was beyond the comprehension of those listening. But, through these parables, Jesus led them to begin thinking differently about the value of every individual and the widespread joy that should be experienced over their salvation.

It is easy for any human activity to become routine through repetition, and that includes religious worship. Worshipping God should neither be lifeless ritual, dogmatic condemnation of others, nor superficial, exaggerated, exuberance. Worship should be a joyous experience flowing from the gratitude of every sinner over the assurance of their salvation and the inestimable gift of everlasting life. The magnitude of that joy should inspire every Christina to share the good news of the gospel of Jesus.

In the hectic rush of religious activities, it is easy to forget that the first angelic message to the frightened shepherds was "good tidings of great joy" for all people of the world (Luke 2:10) because a savior had been born bringing salvation to any who would believe in Him. There is no greater spiritual joy than finding one lost sinner and leading them home to God. Every Christian should share that joy, just as it is shared in the presence of God by the rejoicing angels in heaven.

The Value of All

The Parable of the Great Supper

> *"A certain man gave a great supper and invited many and sent his servant at supper time to say to those who were invited, 'Come, for all things are now ready.' But they all with one accord began to make excuses. The first said to him, 'I have bought a piece of ground, and I must go and see it. I ask you to have me excused.' And another said, 'I have bought five yoke of oxen, and I am going to test them. I ask you to have me excused.' Still another said, 'I have married a wife, and therefore I cannot come.' So that servant came and reported these things to his master. Then the master of the house, being angry, said to his servant, 'Go out quickly into the streets and lanes of the city, and bring in here the poor and the maimed and the lame and the blind.' And the servant said, 'Master, it is done as you commanded, and still there is room.' Then the master said to the servant, 'Go out into the highways and hedges, and compel them to come in, that my house may be filled. For I say to you that none of those men who were invited shall taste my supper'" (Luke 14:16-24).*

Unlike the Old Testament focus on the nation of Israel, the New Testament focuses on both the value of one and the value of all individuals. It vividly presents both God's love for only one sinner and also His redeeming love for all mankind. The religious ideology of Israel and the attitude of her leadership—especially the conservative scribes and Pharisees—opposed both views. There was widespread condemnation of all individual sinners who did not keep the law and deep-seated antagonism toward all non-Jews. There was no concern for the spiritual salvation of either.

Frank Pollard, the noted Baptist pastor, once wryly remarked that the prayer of a devoted Pharisee could easily have been, "Oh God, bless me and my wife, our son and his wife, us four and no more." Therefore, Jesus sought to instill a greater understanding of God's love for those outside one's immediate circle of family, friends, and neighbors in the constricted minds of these religious zealots. In the parables about the lost sheep and the lost coin, Jesus stressed both God's love for each individual sinner and the heavenly joy over their repentance and salvation. Through this parable of the great supper,

Jesus portrayed God's love for all people, especially the poor, sick, and maimed—the very ones the Pharisees wrote off as being under God's judgment because of their life status. As with many of the parables, Jesus boldly confronted the core of Jewish religious beliefs, and this parable, as did others, would only have increased the religious leaders' animosity toward Him.

The parable of the great supper should be studied within the context in which it was stated. Joyous gatherings among intimate family and friends were significant in Jewish social life. Such meals also play an important role in the New Testament. For example, Jesus wanted to visit the home of Zacchaeus the tax collector (Luke 19:5), and He often dined with sinners, for which He was harshly condemned (Matt. 9:10-11). Jesus' first great miracle of turning water into wine occurred at a wedding feast in Cana (John 2:1-10).

In addition, meals associated with Jewish festivals were greatly anticipated, especially Passover, and Jesus' last Passover meal with His disciples (the Last Supper) is particularly meaningful. The great union celebration of Christ and the redeemed church is referred to as the Marriage Supper of the Lamb (Rev.19:7-9) and is eschatologically important.

Through preferential treatment, obsequious comments, choice seating, and expensive gifts, feasts and large dinner gatherings were a way to solidify and strengthen friendships, form new bonds and relationships, and curry favor with influential friends and guests. The setting of this parable was a dinner hosted by a Pharisee, who most likely invited Jesus so that guests might question Him and hear His intriguing answers. Perhaps the Pharisee simply invited Jesus as the entertainment for the evening since He met none of the social and economic criteria for a personal invitation.

But Jesus did not entertain. Instead, He did three things that would have antagonized both the Pharisee host and his guests, who intended to spend the evening pandering to one another with fake, fawning flattery.

First, it was a Sabbath gathering, and the law provided that no labor should be performed on the Sabbath, including healing (Luke 13:14). However, Jesus noticed a guest suffering from dropsy, and His compassion compelled Him to heal the man. Dropsy is a form of edema in which excess fluid collects in the body, or specific organs, and is painfully debilitating. Jesus violated the Sabbath law by healing the man, but there was no joy, praise, or amazement from the guests for the miracle—only silence.

Secondly, Jesus noticed how the guests were moving around and choosing the best seats, likely as close as possible to the most influential individuals and the host. He spoke an initial short parable about ego, exalting oneself, and inviting only "your friends, your brothers, your relatives… (and) rich neighbors," so they will return the invitation and continue the quest for personal power, prestige, and social status. It was all so pretentious and superficial to Jesus. To the astonished guests, Jesus said, "When you give a feast, invite the poor, the maimed, the lame, the blind" (vv. 12-13). That comment did not win Him any friends, only more people who were uncomfortably challenged by His comments.

Finally, Jesus told a longer parable about a certain man who hosted a great supper and invited many people. There are two things readily apparent: the significance and preparation of the great supper and the shallow, illogical responses of those declining the invitation. It portrays the contrast between God's long preparation of Israel for the messianic kingdom of Jesus and their obstinate, unjustifiable refusal to believe. The parable would have stunned and angered the Pharisee host and his assembled guests.

Preparation for the great supper would have taken considerable time, and it cannot be envisioned through the lens of modern shopping. Instead, animals that were served for food would need fattening, plus their slaughter and preparation would have to be done on the day of the feast to ensure freshness. All other incidentals would need arranging—invitations, seating arrangements, location, wine preparation, and other factors necessary for a joyous occasion. The host would also have thoughtfully selected his guests based on friendship, interests, and mutual respect and would have anticipated total response and enthusiastic acceptance. He was wrong—embarrassingly, hurtfully wrong.

Those that he loved and treasured the most coldly turned him down, and their excuses are a pretentious absurdity. The invitations had gone out earlier, so there was ample time for the guests to arrange their other affairs, or to properly and respectfully decline in a timely fashion, but they did neither. When time for the meal arrived, the host's servant went to each guest informing them that the meal and other arrangements were ready. It was a gracious reminder of their invitation to a great, joyous meal prepared especially for them.

Then, the excuses began. Anyone studying this parable should put themselves in the place of the host and sense his disappointment, frustration, and hurt as his servant reported the excuses given for not attending the great supper he had lovingly and laboriously prepared. Visualize him realizing that these guests placed a greater priority on senseless personal reasons for not attending than on the meaning of his invitation.

The first stated that he had bought a piece of land and must go view it. That meant he had bought a piece of property before seeing it, and now, suddenly, he must go at night and inspect it. That could easily have waited until the next day when he could actually see the property in the daylight.

The second was similar. The guest had bought five yoke of oxen and was going to test them. To accept his excuse, the host would have to believe this man had bought ten oxen—a significant investment—without knowing whether he could even plow with them. Were they trained? Were they fit for the job? Suddenly, he needed to drive five yoke of oxen out to a field at night and see if he could plow with them.

A yoke of oxen is two oxen bound together side-by-side by a wooden yoke around their necks. If five yoke of oxen were connected as a ten-oxen team, driving them single-handedly at night to test them would have been a tremendous challenge. If, on the other hand, the oxen were five separate two-oxen teams, then he would have had to make five separate trips at night in order to test them. If you had been the host, would you have accepted this implausible excuse?

The third guest falls into a different category. "I have married a wife, and therefore I cannot come," he replied. Really? Could he not bring his wife or tell her that he had to attend the supper and would immediately return? Or did this third guest actually have the audacity to tell the host, "I have just gotten married, and I would rather stay at home with my bride and enjoy the pleasures of matrimony than attend your great supper"?

It is obvious that shallow, superficial reasons focusing on personal wealth and pleasure were more important to the guests than fellowship with a caring host at a great supper prepared especially for them. The rejected host became understandably angry.

It is not clear how many were invited, but the parable states that "they all with one accord began to make excuses." Does "one accord" simply mean they all excused themselves? Or is there a more sinister meaning that they were in one accord in deciding not to attend the supper? Was there a calculated, cold-hearted conspiracy among them to steadfastly refuse to attend and thwart the host's plans for the supper, regardless of what trivial excuses they had to give?

Applying the parable to the message of the New Testament, what excuses could Israel give for refusing to accept Jesus as the messiah? Despite the wisdom of His words, the miraculous, wonder-working power of His works, and His willingness to die for their sins, what valid reason could be given for rejecting and crucifying Him? Would either "He has a demon;" "He eats with sinners"; "He eats with unwashed hands"; "He heals on the Sabbath"; or "He claims that God is His father" be an acceptable excuse to God? The lengthy build-up under the old covenant of law for the divine revelation of Christ compared to the superficial reasons for Israel rejecting Him is projected in this parable.

In response to the invited guests spurning his invitation, what options did the host have? Those declining presumed they were invited because of their social and economic status, their self-worth, their recognized status in the community, and their righteousness with God. Despite their rejection, they were always invited to the biggest and most elegant suppers, and they assumed that would continue because no one else was worthy of such invitations.

However, in a surprising reversal of roles, the host turned instead to those who were never invited to a supper and were deemed socially unworthy of an invitation. They would have expected it the least but appreciated it the most. They had no wealth, social status, or economic clout. They were invited to the great supper solely because of the mercy and grace of the host. Who were they? They were a cross-section of humanity unloved by man but cherished by God. They existed then, and they exist now:

(1). The poor – Pharisees, scribes, and other religious leaders were inordinately obsessed with wealth as an indicator of God's blessings, and there was intense desire to be rich so that others would consider them righteous and blessed of God. Often arraying themselves in the finest purple linen, these religious practitioners publically wore lavish robes as an ostentatious display of wealth (Luke

16:19). When Jesus stated that it would be easier for a camel to go through the eye of a needle than for a rich man to enter heaven, His disciples asked in surprised disbelief, "Who then can be saved?" (Luke 18:26).

Conversely, the poor were presumed to be unrighteous and cursed by God, and that is why they were poor. Shunned, ignored, left to beg for survival, the religious and social elite would never consider the poor to be their friends and invite the poor to dinner as guests. The rich man, dressed in his expensive purple linen, would not even give the beggar Lazarus the food crumbs from his table (Luke 16:19-21). These were not poor individuals who had modest subsistence, but rather beggars who had no means whatever to survive, except for the generosity of those who occasionally gave them food. It is this category of poor that Jesus identified when He said, "Blessed are the poor in spirit, for theirs is the kingdom of heaven" (Matt. 5:3).

The spiritual blessings of the poor in spirit are not based on economic poverty, but on spiritual poverty that made them realize their complete lack of merit to receive God's blessings, and thus they best understood the gift of God's redeeming love, mercy, grace, and the nature of the kingdom of heaven. They do not see themselves as earning God's blessings; rather, they accept His gift of grace joyously and with thanksgiving and praise. They would not pridefully gloat over an invitation to a great supper; they would rejoice with humility and heart-felt gratitude. However, the Pharisee host would have been horrified at the thought of inviting the poor to his banquet.

(2). The crippled and maimed – Israel had a historic animus toward individuals who were crippled, and it surfaces in some of Jesus' most specific statements. The attitude is rooted in the ancient law that declared a maimed animal unfit for use as a sacrifice to God (Lev. 22:12). This prohibition became gradually extended to physically crippled and maimed individuals who were considered inferior.

The rejection and ridicule they experienced must have been palpable and emotionally devastating and paralyzing. For example, Jesus said, "If your right hand causes you to sin, cut it off and cast it from you; for it is more profitable for you that one of your members perish, than for your whole body to be cast into hell" (Matt. 5:30). He made the same comment about plucking out your right eye (v. 29). Consider this: Was Jesus saying, "If you think the physical and emotional pain of being blind and maimed caused from losing your right eye or your right hand is bad, it is nothing compared to the agony of your whole body being cast into hell caused by sin?"

The Old Testament contains a beautiful and poignant account about a physically maimed man. When David, the great leader of ancient Israel, sought a way to reveal his covenant love for King Saul's son, Jonathan, he asked, "Is there still anyone who is left of the house of Saul, that I may show him kindness for Jonathan's sake?" A servant informed David that Jonathan had a son, Mephibosheth, who was still living, but he was lame in his feet. His nurse had dropped him when he was an infant, injuring and severely deforming his feet and leaving him crippled for life.

Mephibosheth well knew the stigma in Jewish society of being maimed and crippled. When he came before David, Mephibosheth asked, "What is your servant, that you should look upon such a dead dog as I?" What a heart-wrenching statement by a man burdened by years of scornful rejection and ridicule. David, however, was moved by great compassion for Mephibosheth and restored to him the land of Saul, his grandfather, that had been lost. But that was not all. David bestowed a greater blessing on Mephibosheth by inviting him to eat at the king's table for the rest of his life (2 Sam. 9:1-10).

David's merciful and gracious kindness was an early picture of Jesus' attitude toward the crippled and maimed. They are included among those who Jesus miraculously healed to the astonishment of observers (Matt.15:30-31). One may find a slight variation in meaning between those who were intentionally maimed and those crippled by disease or injury, but the attitude toward them was the same. In this parable, Jesus specifically invited them to the great supper, much to the consternation of those hearing Him.

(3). The blind – The same cruel predisposition to condemn another for physical deformity or debilitating condition also applied to blindness, again stemming from the law against blind animals being a worthy sacrifice to God. The harshness of the Pharisees' attitude toward the blind is shockingly revealed in the account of Jesus healing a blind man, who was apparently facially deformed (John 9:1-34).

Sickness and disability were believed to be God's punishment for sin. Thus, when Jesus and His disciples encountered this disfigured blind man, the disciples asked, "Rabbi, who sinned, this man or his parents, that he was born blind?" In response, Jesus spat on the ground and made a small amount of clay, which He applied to the man's eyes, and then told him to go wash in the pool of Siloam. He did, and he returned, seeing for the first time in his life.

The blind man was not only healed, but his facial appearance was so transformed that he was unrecognizable to those who knew him, even his parents. It is speculative, but Jesus may have made him new eyes out of the clay, not only giving him sight but also changing his appearance and giving him a new life free from scorn and ridicule. It is one of Jesus' most powerful and emotionally touching miracles, and the man was filled with praise and gratitude.

The Pharisees saw it differently. Because the miraculous healing occurred on a Sabbath, they were indignant, saying, "This man is not from God, because He does not keep the Sabbath." But others countered, "How can a man who is a sinner do such signs?" There was considerable division and discussion among them about the miracle, and they persistently asked the man to identify who had healed him. He was equally insistent that it was Jesus. The Pharisees demanded that the blind man give God the glory for his healing and questioned his parents about whether he had indeed been born blind, and, if so, who had healed him. The exchange grew more intense, and the healed man bluntly said to the Pharisees:

> "…we know that God does not hear sinners, but if anyone is a worshipper of God and does His will, He hears him. Since the world began it has been unheard of that anyone opened the eyes of one who was born blind. If this Man were not from God, He could do nothing."

The Pharisees angrily retorted, "You were completely born in sins, and you are teaching us?" They angrily excommunicated the healed man from his Jewish faith because of his testimony about Jesus.

This hypocritical attitude toward blindness is also documented in the Old Testament. The prophet Malachi accused Israel of despising the name of the Lord and defiling His altar by offering animals that were blind and lame in direct violation of the law. Malachi denounced their actions and dared them to offer the same animals to their governor and see if he would be pleased and favorably accept them. If the governor would be offended, then surely God was also offended by offering Him the blind and lame as a sacrificial gift (Mal.1:7-8). With no spiritual concern for their hypocrisy, they unmercifully condemned their fellow man for being blind and lame while simultaneously offering blind and lame animals to God as an acceptable sacrifice.

Imagine the host Pharisee's surprise and disgust when Jesus specifically said that the invitation to the great supper included the blind. Just as with beggars and the maimed, the blind would have never been on anyone's guest list.

Without let up, Jesus continued His confrontation with His startled host and those in attendance. As the parable unfolded, even after inviting the poor, crippled, and blind, there was still room for more guests, so the host of the great supper sent his servant into "the highways and hedges" to compel others to come in "so that my house may be filled." Again, this comment would have infuriated the Pharisee host.

The ideological legalists methodically and illogically applied the religious clean-versus-unclean doctrine to every aspect of daily life. Only those who devotedly followed the law and were free and clean from any contact with the common everyday life of others were acceptable to God, and all others were unclean and unacceptable. Consequently, if a Pharisee went into the streets and markets, it was necessary to ritualistically wash in a precise manner upon returning home in order to cleanse themselves from the common defilement around them. Pharisee means "the separated one," and complete separation from human life, except for others like them, was their goal. Even a speck of dust or a grain of sand from the common areas was sufficient to defile them. The wealthy often had a servant who would wash their master's feet upon his returning home to cleanse him of the residue of worldly contact. It was this practice that inspired Jesus to gird himself as a servant and wash the feet of His disciples as a gesture of His ability to cleanse them of sin (John 13:3-9).

Ceremonial washing in a precise procedure was also required before and during each meal, often between courses of food. At any dinner, the host would have an ample supply of water for ritualistic washing. For example, the host at the wedding feast at Cana had six large pots, each holding twenty to thirty gallons of water, for the guests to use for washing when they arrived and before and during the meal. Jesus turned these pots of water into new wine, symbolizing the transformation from law to the new covenant of life in Him (John 2:1-10).

The Pharisee host would also have had water for his guests to ceremonially wash away contact with those from the highways and hedges, as well as the streets and lanes of the city. But it was these very people—unclean and condemned under the law—who Jesus said would be invited to the great supper, a great supper where there would be no ceremonial water to wash away the defilement before God. The Pharisee host and guests would have been outraged at such an assault on their cherished beliefs and traditions.

The parable scenario was started by a legalist's exuberant expression, "Blessed is he who shall eat bread in the kingdom of God!" (v.15). However, by the end of the parable, this religious exuberance had turned into stunned silence. Regarding those who proffered spurious excuses for declining to attend the great supper, Jesus' final words were sobering, "For I say to you that none of those men who were invited shall taste my supper." In effect, Jesus said to the judgmental gentleman who started it all, "Those eating bread and drinking wine at My great supper will be the poor, blind, lame, lost, and lonely who rejoice with unbridled praise and thanksgiving for their unmerited, gracious invitation. But, sir, it won't be you." The silence was deafening.

The parable of the great supper stressed God's love and acceptance of the very ones in Jewish society that had long been disparaged and discarded as unholy and unfit. The parable would have forced the Pharisee and his guests to decide whether this man, Jesus, was a true prophet speaking new truths from God or a crazed, demon-possessed man speaking religious nonsense and blasphemy. It may not have changed many hearts and minds at the dinner, but the parable made them begin to think about the magnitude of God's love for all people—a divine love far exceeding the law of Israel—and that was Jesus' intent. It should also make each of us rethink our own understanding of God's love for mankind.

This parable projects two great truths about the kingdom of heaven: the merciful love and concern of the host for those who had no hope or expectation of receiving an invitation and the indescribable joy the guests would have experienced in being invited. That would have never occurred under the law of Israel.

When John the Baptist was imprisoned and facing execution, he sent messengers to Jesus asking, "Are You the Coming One, or do we look for another?" Jesus responded:

> *"Go and tell John the things you have seen and heard: that the blind see, the lame walk, the lepers are cleansed, the deaf hear, the dead are raised, the poor have the gospel preached to them"* (Luke 7:22).

All these manifestations of God's love for the lonely, lost, and left-behind are the exact opposite of the merciless constraints of Israel's religious laws and traditions. The prejudice, hatred, scorn, and mean-spirit of the law have been overcome by the redeeming love of God and the power of the gospel. In contrast to the loving shepherd looking for one erring sheep and the woman searching for one lost coin, the host of the great supper invited all who would respond to his joyous feast and sent his servant out searching for them.

As a verbal image of the kingdom of heaven, to whom is this parable ultimately addressed? The answer lies in the description of the host. The parable describes him as "a certain man," but the phrase may also mean "someone or anyone." God's redeeming love for mankind is so great and the kingdom of heaven is so open to all believers that anyone, anywhere may serve as a host and invite others into the kingdom by faith in Christ. The gospel encourages all believers to serve as Jesus' messengers and go into the lanes, highways, and hedgerows of ordinary life with Christ's invitation to repent and believe. Anyone and everyone is encouraged to invite anyone and everyone to the "Great Supper" of our Lord, for that is God's view of the value of all.

A New Level of Humility

The Parable of the Lowest Seat at a Feast

> *"When you are invited by anyone to a wedding feast, do not sit down in the best place, lest one more honorable than you be invited by him; and he who invited you and he come and say to you, 'Give place to this man,' and then you begin with shame to take the lowest place. But when you are invited, go and sit down in the lowest place, so that when he who invited you comes he may say to you, 'Friend, go up higher.' Then you will have glory in the presence of those who sit at the table with you. For whoever exalts himself will be humbled, and he who humbles himself will be exalted"* (Luke 14:8-11).

It was a large, festive Christmas banquet attended by employees of a religious organization where I was employed. There were several circular dining tables across the brightly decorated room, each arranged for eight people to comfortably sit. Most guests were accompanied by their spouse, and thus four couples sat at each table. It was intended to be an enjoyable time of Christian fellowship as friends and coworkers celebrated the birth of Jesus. However, the evening left me embarrassed and embittered.

I arrived early. Only the executive director and his wife were there, seated at the head table, and I joined them. Soon, other administrative level guests arrived, and a couple of them sat at our table. Since I was alone, it quickly became obvious I was disrupting the seating arrangement because of the empty seat beside me. I noticed the director kept looking at me, as he commented about who was arriving and who he wanted at his table and the adjoining tables. Finally, I commented I could move to another less occupied table, thereby freeing up two places for a couple to sit. With noticeable irritation, he replied, "Yes, that is a good idea." Embarrassed by other table guests looking at me, I got up and moved—and I did not stop until I arrived at my home. Although I understood the situation, nevertheless, the director's insulting tone of voice, especially in the presence of other employees, left an emotional hurt that did not quickly heal.

In retrospect, however, the experience would have been entirely different if I had sat alone at an empty table when I arrived. If the director had then invited me to sit with him and other administrative employees at the head table, it would have been an honor rather than the embarrassment that developed. The pain was not as much the director's fault as it was mine. It was a lesson in humility for me, and this parable helped change the thoughts of my heart about the experience.

It is noteworthy that Jesus told this short parable about a wedding feast seating arrangement at a dinner hosted by a Pharisee. The Sabbath dinner was unrelated to a festive wedding gathering, and it begs the question why Jesus used a wedding feast scenario for His parable. At least two significant truths emerge, and each relates to the attitude of pride versus humility: One is physical and emotional and relates to the relationship between individuals, while the other is spiritual and relates to one's relationship with God.

Several religious festivals were held in Israel throughout the year, and they were boisterously celebrated. Gatherings of families, along with friends and guests, were common social events, complete with expansive meals and festivities. However, wedding celebrations took priority in social engagements. They were joyous, elaborate, carefully planned, and were attended by all of one's family, friends, and invited guests. The guest list included the most important and influential people within the community. A joyous wedding procession would be joined by many people, as an expression of support and celebration, and virtually all activities temporarily stopped for the procession.

An elaborate dinner was the central focus of the wedding festivity. The best food and wine were abundantly available, and the host carefully determined the seating arrangement in order to provide proper recognition and respect for important guests. Being placed at the best location near the host and the bride and groom was a prime honor and was greatly coveted.

However, dining customs to which Jesus referred greatly differed from present-day banquet seating arrangements. The honored guests reclined on a small couch, somewhat like a padded bench, rather than sitting at a table. In the Greek and Roman world, this padded couch was known as a *lectus triclinaris*, and both the custom of reclining while dining and the placement of the *lectus triclinaris* add significant meaning to this parable. Other less notable guests often reclined on blankets or mats placed on the floor. An interesting example of this custom is "the disciple whom Jesus loved" reclining against Jesus' breast while they dined (John 13:23-25).

The term "best place," as used in the parable, means the chief place or the first dining couch and describes the place and position of greatest honor at a banquet. One must visualize honored guests being escorted by the host to the designated *lectus triclinaris* where they would recline comfortably and be attended by servants. The first couch, however, was the most coveted, and the guest placed there received special recognition and honor.

The arrogant and egotistical scribes and Pharisees relished invitations to wedding banquets, which provided an opportunity for them to be courted and feted as if they were royalty. Jesus castigated them for expecting the best place at a banquet where they could recline in the presence of other guests and be personally catered. Note the tone of the following verses:

- *"But all their works they do to be seen by men. They make their phylacteries broad and enlarge the borders of their garments. They love the best places at feasts…"* (Matt. 23:5-6).
- *"…Beware of the scribes, who desire to go around in long robes, love greetings in the marketplaces, the best seats in the synagogues, and the best places at feasts"* (Mark 12:39).

With that in mind, Jesus' parable becomes more vivid. One must visualize a proud, self-centered Pharisee dressed in his finest robe of purple linen arriving at a wedding feast. But, rather than waiting to be seated according to the host's desires, he arrogantly proceeds to the choice *lectus triclinaris* closest to the host and reclines with an ostentatious display of wealth and status. With unfettered pomposity, he comforts himself on the couch and waits for the host to welcome him and for servants to begin serving him food and wine. One must grasp the mindset of such a self-absorbed individual glorying in his own sense of self-importance. Jesus directed the first beatitude, which focuses on the blessings of those who see themselves as spiritually impoverished, toward this haughty attitude.

For some individuals, however, life deals out painful moments in which the shaky pedestal on which one's human ego rests comes crashing down. The pivotal moment when pride and humility clash for control of one's soul can be both emotionally and spiritually sobering. That is the thrust of this short parable.

In order to understand the parable's impact, imagine the emotions of a proud, selfish individual who arrogantly strides unescorted to the choice *lectus triclinaris* at a wedding feast and positions himself on the couch in all of his finery, waiting to be recognized and served, while he notes those of lesser importance who are enviously gazing at him. But, in a moment of utter shock, the host instead instructs him to get up and give the best place to someone more important. Shamefacedly, he moves from the highest place of recognition and honor to the lowest. Literally, he is told to move from first place to last place. More specifically and graphically, in front of all other guests, he must move from the place everyone wants to the place no one wants—the last place available.

Grasping the extent of his humiliation and embarrassment is challenging. However, that is the image presented in this parable. It is that shocking, singular moment when the arrogant, reclined, presumptuous individual is told that he is not the most important guest, but rather the least important, that defines this parable. In that moment, his pride is pummeled, his arrogance becomes embarrassment, and his haughtiness becomes humiliation.

Jesus consistently emphasized an attitude of personal humility, both in one's relationship with others and with God. He demonstrated this attitude in His own life and stressed its importance to His disciples. In contrast to the obsessive focus on temporary worldly wealth and status, Jesus focused on the eternal spiritual riches of the kingdom of heaven and how they could be obtained. He had no interest in personal wealth, nor did He have any desire for personal social standing. His only desire was to glorify His heavenly Father and do His will.

Within the social structure of Israel, what example could Jesus have used to most vividly project the difference between glaring personal pride and quiet personal humility? What would have been the most meaningful way for a proud, arrogant, self-glorifying person to experience and reveal the opposite emotion? Jesus provided an answer in the second part of this parable.

Rather than presumption and arrogance that make one desire the best seat—the first *lectus triclinari*—Jesus stated that one should instead choose the last place without assuming a greater level of importance. If the host says, "Friend, go up higher," it would be an honor that is unearned and undeserved, and the recognition would be an experience of joy, thanksgiving, and gratitude. The journey from a couch to a pallet is one of humiliation; the journey from a pallet to a couch is one of jubilation.

The meaning of this parable is underscored by Jesus' statement "The last will be first, and the first last," which He often used (Matt. 20:16). The kingdom of heaven is a gift bestowed by God through His grace on all who believe. Jesus said it was the Father's "good pleasure" to give the kingdom as a reward of faith and not payment for work (Luke 12:32). The kingdom of heaven is not for sale: It cannot be bought nor bartered for. It is not given in exchange for good work or good conduct. It is a divine gift of love and grace.

The transition from arrogant pride and presumption to spiritual humility and poverty wherein one receives God's blessings as a gift of grace is a major focus of repentance. That transformation truly involves a complete change in the direction of one's spiritual life and imparting that understanding of repentance was a great challenge for Jesus.

Jesus' first beatitude is a lesson in humility. Overall, the Beatitudes focus on the blessedness—the spiritual joy—of Christian life. The first step is an attitude of humility, not presumptuous pride, and arrogance. The kingdom of heaven is given to those who see themselves as possessing no spiritual basis in which to expect or demand blessings from God. They only see themselves as spiritual paupers completely devoid of spiritual merit. Only then can one appreciate the kingdom as a divine gift. To them, the kingdom is both given and received as a gracious gift providing spiritual joy and gratitude—the experience of blessedness.

Coming before God filled with pride and spiritual boasting produces nothing but shame, humiliation, and being moved from first place—which was expected—to last place. But, if one comes before God filled with a sense of spiritual poverty and looking only to Christ for His blessings, then his reward is the fullness of the heavenly kingdom. He is the last to expect the kingdom based on merit, but he is the first to understand the kingdom of heaven as a gift. God moves him from last place to first place, and he is served by the angels of heaven. That journey is the fruit of repentance, and it is the joy and blessedness of Christianity.

The Priceless Value of the Kingdom

The Parable of Treasure Hidden in a Field

> *"Again, the kingdom of heaven is like treasure hidden in a field, which a man found and hid; and for joy over it he goes and sells all that he has and buys that field" (Matt.13:44).*

On October 1, 1939, Sir Winston Churchill famously described the uncertainty of Russia's future action in World War II as "…a riddle, wrapped in a mystery, inside an enigma." The parable of treasure hidden in a field falls into a comparable category. The parable has three noteworthy aspects, all related to the actions and attitudes of the man who found the hidden treasure: He initially discovered the treasure; he bought the field; but then he kept the treasure hidden and never attempted to describe or reveal its nature in physical terms. Thus the parable is a tri-level mysterious masterpiece of wisdom that uniquely reveals great truths about the kingdom of heaven.

The man's actions provide an unambiguous description of Jewish law regarding the rights of a treasure finder. Israel did not have banks or other safe depositories for funds, and people routinely buried their valuables for protection against loss. If one purchased property, Jewish law recognized the purchaser's right to whatever might be buried there. The good-faith purchaser had no obligation to return to the previous owner anything of value that he found.

Unless the purchaser was a servant of the owner and had a fiduciary duty of loyalty to his master, or unless he was under a contractual obligation to divulge his knowledge of the treasure to the owner when he purchased the property, the seller would have had no breach of duty claim against the buyer for failing to divulge knowledge about the buried treasure. An old, elementary expression regarding lost property states, "Finders keepers, losers weepers," and that was the essence of Jewish law in the parable's scenario.

Interestingly, in his wilderness sermon, John the Baptist provided insight into the practice of burying valuables. When he concluded the sermon, various individuals, including Roman soldiers, asked what they should do in response to the proclamation of John's message and his demand for repentance. John told the soldiers to be content with their wages and stop intimidating and coercing people (Luke 3:14). Apparently, it was common practice to extort money and other valuables from citizens, and one measure of protection was burying the valuables. Occasionally, owners would move away or die before removing the property or revealing its location to others. In those situations, it became a buried treasure and belonged to whoever found it, provided the finder had valid title to the property on which the treasure was buried.

Understanding the nature of the parable's undescribed mysterious treasure is challenging. The concept of treasure denotes both a valuable and the storehouse in which it is kept. Therefore, one should not think treasure only means gold nuggets or a container filled with money. In a broad sense, treasure means both the things that are of greatest value to an individual and the trusted place where he lays those up for safekeeping. As Jesus used the word, it applies to both physical and spiritual values.

Accounts of finding a buried treasure are fascinating, and imagining our own reaction is interesting introspection. However, the parable is not about going on a hunt for physical treasure. It is not a search for the glitter of a pot of gold; rather, the parable, in its true meaning, describes the search for the glory of the kingdom of heaven. The focal interest is obviously on the search for a buried physical treasure and the resulting action of the finder, but one should not lose sight that Jesus said searching for and discovering the treasure of the kingdom of heaven is like finding a valuable physical treasure.

Through the contrast of the parable, Jesus said the emotional and spiritual reaction to discovering the glory of the kingdom of heaven is not unlike the physical reaction of discovering a pot of gold. One must, therefore, read the parable with a dual focus: the physical discovery of the treasure and extrapolating that to the meaning of the spiritual discovery of the treasure of heaven.

Initially, the purchaser became aware of the buried treasure before buying the property. Again, the depth of the parable emerges in the finder's actions. Indeed, he may have simply stumbled upon the treasure. But the parable concept of "finding" is the conclusion of an ongoing process. The treasure was something the man had been searching for a long while and discovering its location and value had become a consuming passion that only added to his joy of discovery.

In the Sermon on the Mount, Jesus spoke to His disciples about the ongoing search for a greater understanding of the kingdom of heaven: "Ask, and it will be given to you; seek, and you will find; knock, and it will be opened to you…" (Matt.7:7). Discovering the spiritual treasure of the kingdom of heaven is a continuing experience of discipleship akin to a prolonged search for a buried treasure in a field. If one is to find the treasure, he must not give up until it is found and placed in a storehouse guaranteed to protect it. Just as one would do with the glitter of gold, he must also do with the glory of God.

Jesus had a clear and specific view about the meaning and value of one's treasure. Again, in the Sermon on the Mount, He stated, "…where your treasure is, there your heart will be also" (Matt. 6:21). Significantly, Jesus stressed the unique relationship between one's heart and one's treasure. But there is a very important truth underlying this treasure concept: The treasure and the storehouse both must be of the same nature, for their meaning is essentially the same. They cannot be interchanged. One cannot put physical treasure in a spiritual storehouse, and neither can spiritual treasure be placed in a physical storehouse, even though the Pharisees tried.

That distinction is at the heart of Jesus' teaching about treasures. One can lay up physical treasure on earth, or he can lay up spiritual treasure in heaven. He cannot do both, because he cannot serve two masters with equal devotion, for he will inevitably prefer one over the other (Matt. 6:24). Whichever of the two treasures—either physical or spiritual—is most important to him is where his heart and his motivation for life will be found.

Unlike the ostentatious display of wealth favored by the Pharisees and scribes, Jesus stated the true treasure of life—one's relationship with God—is a treasure hidden within one's heart whose true value is known only by the beholder, and it motivates all of one's actions in life. The heavenly treasure, which is revealed by words and works for God and not gaudy displays of material wealth, is a special blessing given by God that enriches and transforms life.

Within the parable's spiritual context, the value and relationship between the field and the hidden treasure must be considered. The field is not just a fertile, tillable piece of ground where crops may be grown. It represents more than that. It is something of physical value, and its purchase would denote financial success and accumulation of earthly treasures. It represents the never-ending desire of many people for more possessions to prove their self-worth to themselves and others. If that is all the field and the treasure meant, then the parable would end there, and we would applaud the finder's acquisition—just another shiny tinsel added to the glitter of an apparently successful life.

But that is not why the man bought the field. In fact, its physical value had nothing to do with his decision. His sole motivation was acquiring the visible field so that he might possess the invisible treasure within it and experience the joy it would bring him. His motivating desire was not to acquire treasures to be seen by others; his motivation was to acquire a treasure known only to him and God. That, Jesus said, is the nature of the kingdom of heaven.

It is unknown how long the man had been searching for the treasure or how it was discovered. All we are told is that it was hidden. That means more than just a buried treasure. The concept can mean something that is simply hidden from view, but it may also mean something that is "laid up" and stored out of sight from others. In truth, the treasure had been laid up for the man to find for an unknown period time while he searched, and it only awaited his discovery. The Apostle Peter wrote:

> *"Blessed be the God and Father of our Lord Jesus Christ, who according to His abundant mercy has begotten us again to a living hope through the resurrection of Jesus Christ from the dead, to an inheritance, incorruptible and undefiled and that does not fade away, reserved in heaven for you, who are kept by the power of God through faith for salvation ready to be revealed in the last time"* (1 Pet. 1:3-5).

God promises every Christian an invisible spiritual treasure that is incorruptible and undefiled, which is reserved for us and laid up out of the physical sight of others, and we, through faith in Jesus, shall discover its full value. How long has that treasure been laid up? Consider the following:

> *"Blessed be the God and Father of our Lord Jesus Christ, who has blessed us with every spiritual blessing in the heavenly places in Christ, just as He chose us in Him before the foundation of the world, that we should be holy and without blame before Him in love..."* (Eph. 1:3-4).

The unseen treasure of the heavenly kingdom has been divinely stored up for us in Christ since before the foundation of the world. Every spiritual blessing in heaven is buried in the field of Christian life and awaiting our discovery. That is an absolutely amazing promise!

Also, consider Jesus' guaranteed reward: "Blessed are those who hunger and thirst for righteousness, for they shall be filled" (Matt. 5:6). The promise of Christianity is the divine assurance of being filled with every spiritual blessing that God can envision, and those blessings have been safely stored, undefiled and incorruptible, in a divine spiritual storehouse since the beginning of time. Words cannot describe the magnitude of that treasure. One should remember this promise when the focus of the parable turns to the experience of joy.

In the parable, the treasure finder did something unusual. Upon finding the treasure in the field, he immediately hid the treasure. That may seem devious, but it is logical. If he had informed the owner, the treasure would have been the landowner's. Under the law, his most secure and defensible access to the treasure was remaining silent and first securing his personal ownership of the field, which he did.

But, after buying the field and the buried treasure, he did something even more unusual: He never told anyone it was there. He did not dig it up and display it, nor did he disclose its nature or its location. Perhaps he did that for safety, knowing that thieves would try to steal it. However, there may be another explanation that provides a deeper understanding to both the nature of the parable and nature of the kingdom of heaven.

The finder realized the treasure had been laid up for him by another. He did not earn it, nor did he create any of its value through his own works. He had no boasting or bragging rights, nor could he feel more deserving than others. The treasure was a divine gift of grace that had been graciously revealed to him, and his only justifiable response was overwhelming humility, gratitude, and thanksgiving flowing from within his heart.

That spiritual blessing would have been ruined if he had tried to convert it to a physical blessing. He would have taken a spiritual treasure and tried to lay it up in a physical storehouse on earth. That does not work, even though countless Christians try, openly disregarding Jesus' admonition that "…one's life does not consist in the abundance of the things he possesses" (Luke 12:15). Most professing Christians do not believe Jesus on this subject, and their daily search for more physical treasure proves it.

If the finder had converted the hidden treasure into a visible physical treasure once he obtained title, the treasure would have produced "works of the flesh," such as pride, arrogance, material idolatry, envy from others, and greed. The Apostle Paul, writing to Christians in Galatia, stated, "…those who practice such things will not inherit the kingdom of God" (Gal. 5:19-21).

Since this parable reveals how one may inherit the kingdom of heaven, the focus therefore shifts to the "fruits of the Spirit" and the spiritual joy and peace the hidden treasure provides. Thus, the finder took the unusual step of again burying the treasure so it would remain unseen. He carefully considered his two choices of storehouses for his treasure and chose to personally layup treasure for himself in the unseen storehouse of God. He wanted what could not be seen more than he wanted what could be seen by others.

The finder knew it was a spiritual treasure that could not be converted into the riches of personal property. No aspect of the treasure could be revealed through an opulent lifestyle, possessions, abundant food, or physical necessities. It was all spiritual and hidden within. The finder fully realized he might outwardly appear poor and humble by worldly standards because he had sold all that he had to obtain the field and the treasure, but inwardly, he was spiritually rich.

The Apostle Paul described this truth to the Corinthian church by saying:

> *"For it is the God who commanded light to shine out of darkness who has shone in our hearts to give the light of the knowledge of the glory of God in the face of Jesus Christ. But we have this treasure in earthen vessels, that the excellence of the power may be of God and not of us"* (2 Cor. 4:6-7).

Paul realized our earthy bodies are "hard pressed on every side, yet not crushed; …persecuted, but not in despair;…struck down, but to destroyed" (vv. 8-9). Within the fragile, easily broken, clay-pot field of our Christian humanity is buried a heavenly treasure of inestimable value. The blessedness—the inner joy—of a fruitful spiritual pauper is knowing that he truly possesses nothing in this world, yet he is a joint-heir with Christ to the fullness of the riches of the kingdom of heaven (Rom. 8:17).

However, seeking the unseen treasure of heaven is not the motivation of most people, either then or now. One of the challenges Jesus faced was conveying the difference to His disciples between the value of temporary physical treasures and the value of eternal spiritual treasures. Repentance involves a life-transforming shift in personal priorities from the former to the latter.

In the Sermon on the Mount, Jesus addressed obsessive worry about wealth, possessions, food, and clothing, the abundance of which was considered a blessing from God. Many Pharisees desired material possessions for both physical comfort and as a sense of spiritual security. It was physical proof of divine favor and blessings, or so they thought.

Jesus taught His disciples an opposite view, and His words are challenging: "…do not worry about your life" (Matt. 6:25). From a human perspective, how can one not worry about life? This is one of Jesus' most demanding statements, because He obviously realized the universal anxiety and concern over life's basic necessities. Jesus told His disciples that, if they were consumed with worry, rather than standing out differently through their faith—like a city on a hill—they would be no different than the Gentiles, in effect comparing them to the rest of the world (v. 32).

Jesus then established a new treasure standard for His disciples that would transform their spiritual life, "…seek first the kingdom of God and His righteousness and all these things shall be added to you" (Matt. 6:33). Unlike the kingdom of David, which was political and military in nature, the kingdom of heaven was a new concept that Jesus' disciples struggled to understand. But Jesus told them, even as He stated to Pilate, "My kingdom is not of this world" (John 18:36), and He assured them it was His Father's "good pleasure" to give them the kingdom (Luke 12:32). But it was Jesus' statement that "the kingdom of God is within you" (Luke 17:21) that left them perplexed and spiritually challenged. That statement is important in understanding this parable.

It was difficult for Jesus' disciples to comprehend the kingdom as an inner, transforming spiritual power that gives life new meaning and purpose. The kingdom of heaven was a divine realm within each of them manifested by redeeming love and not ritualistic religious law.

No longer would they seek to impose their religious beliefs on others by force, but instead they would reveal God's redeeming love for all people by their love for them, not religious laws used against them. That inner transformation from law to love is one of the major characteristics of spiritual repentance. Jesus assured His followers this divine transforming power was neither a past experience to be nostalgically remembered nor a future experience to be excitedly anticipated, but it was a dynamically present reality, for "the kingdom of heaven is at hand" (Matt. 4:17).

The treasure of this heavenly realm would not be physical and placed in an earthly storehouse where it could be stolen by thieves, but rather spiritual and placed in a heavenly storehouse where it would be guarded by the angels of heaven (Matt. 6:19-20). Through repentance and faith in Jesus as Lord and Savior, the treasure would be the assurance of the forgiveness of sin; justification before God; the fullness of divine righteousness; sanctification in the life of Christ; adoption as a child of God; a spiritual renewal akin to being born again; and the full inheritance of the kingdom of heaven as a joint heir with Jesus. All of that treasure would be buried within them spiritually but revealed through redeeming love for others in their words and works that glorified God and proved them to be disciples of Jesus. It would not be revealed through the glitter of gold in their life, but rather through the glory of God in their life.

The strategic challenge facing Jesus was that nothing in Judaism compared to this. It was a new and startling truth, and He had to find a means of not only imparting this concept but also inspiring His disciples to ponder its meaning until they had some grasp of this transforming, divine truth. To accomplish His goal, Jesus shared a short parable about the reactions of a man who found a treasure buried in a field.

The great challenge of discipleship—both then and now—is how badly one wants this hidden treasure compared to the visible treasures and wealth of the world. Most people then—as they are now—were obsessed with obtaining abundant guarantees of food, clothing, and other physical blessings. But Jesus bluntly said, "Don't worry about all that," adding that if they truly sought first the kingdom of heaven, all these things would be added to their life.

What does "added" mean? It does not mean what many Christians think: It is not step one in a long-term investment strategy.

The concept describes a process in which things are gathered together and set forward for a purpose or goal. Therefore, if one seeks first the kingdom, then the necessities of life become additions to the overall purpose and goal of one's spiritual life. They are not the goal of life, and obsessively putting together physical treasures is not the substance of life. They are of secondary importance and should be viewed as "additions" to the overall purpose of Christian discipleship. If one's goal is the glory of heaven, the treasures of this earth are merely "add-ons" in life's journey.

So, if a disciple of Jesus seeks first the kingdom of heaven, and he wants to lay up his true treasure where thieves cannot steal it and rust and moths cannot destroy it, and if his heart is where his treasure is, what does he do when he finds the treasure of the kingdom and realizes it is possible for him to possess it? In that moment of life-transforming discovery, what decisions does he make? How one reacts to discovering heavenly glory "is like" how one reacts to discovering earthly gold. The treasures and the storehouses may be different, but the reaction is essentially the same:

(1). It is a life-changing discovery – The moment when the treasure is discovered is emotionally meaningful. The gripping moment when the finder realizes its true value leaves him shocked, numbed, and emotionally frozen, and he immediately knows that his discovery is life changing. His perspective on life, his value system, and that which he deems most important will never be the same. The value of the treasure will thereafter dominate his life and dictate his actions and attitudes.

There is an interesting phrase in the Lord's Prayer that is important and relevant to the parable's meaning and impact. In the prayer, Jesus taught His disciples to pray, "…Your kingdom come…," stressing the importance of immediate action and not a delayed and debated response (Matt. 6:10). It was that kind of reaction to the value of the kingdom that compelled Matthew to leave his lucrative tax collector's booth (Mark 2:14) and Peter, along with his brother Andrew, to abandon their fishing nets and become "fishers of men" in response to Jesus' invitation to "Follow Me" (Matt. 4:19).

The phrase does not condone irrational, ill-conceived, and rash conduct. It demonstrates, however, that once one perceives the value of the kingdom of heaven, compared to all other earthly treasures, there is no good excuse for unwarranted delay in becoming a committed Christian. The kingdom of heaven's treasure compels immediate commitment and total dedication to Christ.

The parable does not specify what financial resources the finder had, but the value of the treasure suddenly outweighed all else he possessed. He was willing to immediately sell all that he had in order to buy the field containing the treasure. He was willing to become poor in order to become rich in a manner known only to him and God.

The treasure finder's actions contrast with the response of the "rich young ruler." Having asked Jesus what he must do in order to inherit eternal life, Jesus instructed him to sell what he had and give it to the poor, "and you will have treasure in heaven" (Matt. 19:16-22). The young ruler had a chance to become poor in order to become spiritually rich, but he refused to do so, choosing instead earthly treasure over heavenly treasure. He walked away physically rich, but spiritually poor, when he could have been spiritually rich through giving up reliance on earthly treasures.

(2). It is a value-altering discovery – The finder of the treasure in the field was immediately confronted with a choice between what he presently possessed compared to what he could possess if he bought the field and the buried treasure. He sold everything he had that was visible to others in order to acquire something that was invisible and known to only him! That is mind-boggling.

Discovering heavenly treasure raises similar issues and questions of a deeply personal nature: Is the spiritual treasure I have discovered of greater value than the physical treasure I presently possess? Which treasure captures my heart and my imagination—what I can presently acquire on earth, or what I am divinely promised in heaven? Does the promise of a heavenly tomorrow hold greater attraction than the earthly reality of today? The answers are significant because whichever treasure controls one's heart also controls his life and his eternal destiny. The spiritual treasure within you must be of greater value than the physical treasure around you, for where your treasure is, there your heart will be, and it will govern both your motivation for life and the resulting fruit you bear. This comparison compelled Jesus to ask, "For what will it profit a man if he gains the whole world, and loses his own soul?" (Mark 8:36).

Discovering the treasure reduces all other things in life to secondary importance. If one first seeks the kingdom of heaven, then knowing and experiencing the spiritual nature of the heavenly realm becomes one's greatest passion. Priorities change from physical to spiritual, the concept of work changes from advancing one's own interests to advancing the work of Christ, and earthly rewards pale in comparison to the spiritual rewards of the kingdom of heaven.

(3). It is a mysterious discovery – Unlike the value of the field that could be easily calculated, the value of the buried treasure was unknown. The finder did not weigh it, measure it, have it analyzed, or subject it to any physical measurement, but he intuitively knew it was of greater value than all he possessed. He could not determine its future impact on his life, nor could he gauge its potential to shape his destiny. All of that remained a great mystery, yet he was willing to give up all in order to possess it.

The finder's actions in selling his possessions to acquire this one field were no doubt mysterious to others. Why it held his total interest and commitment when it produced no measurable physical reward confused and confounded many. The sudden change of priorities in his life looked foolish, for others could neither see nor comprehend the value of the treasure hidden in the field. Unlike the Pharisees and scribes who loved to publicly display their wealth, the treasure was never revealed "in order to be seen by men." Rather, its nature and value remained known only to the finder.

When the angel Gabriel revealed to Mary that she would conceive and bear a Son who would be the Christ, she did not rush out telling this glorious news to everyone. Instead, "she kept all these things and pondered them within her heart" (Luke 2:19). One cannot imagine her emotions or her joy over this miracle in her life, yet she hid the treasure within her. In many ways, the finder of the treasure in the field did the same.

The parable is based on an astounding premise: The treasure finder's action was motivated by a deep desire to experience something he had never known. The parable uses a phrase with a unique meaning: "…and for joy over it he goes and sells…." The emphasis is on "he," and it implies the joy he experienced was his alone, and he alone decided to sell all that he had and buy the field. He consulted no one, and he allowed no one to neither alter nor influence his decision. Regardless of what others thought, he committed himself to experiencing the inner joy of possessing the treasure, and he allowed nothing and no one to deny him that blessing.

That speaks volumes about his life. It was joyless, despite possessing "all that he had." No material possession, no ritual of his faith, and no effort of self-righteousness under the religious laws that dictated his life brought him a sense of inner joy, for it was all methodical and meaningless. The finder was willing to sacrifice all that he knew in order to experience an unknown inner joy. He transformed his life, his priorities, and sold all that he had in order to obtain a treasure known to only himself and to experience boundless joy only he realized. That is an amazing truth about the kingdom of heaven.

Most Christians do not consider this underlying characteristic of Christian life. Obviously, salvation is the primary blessing, but our salvation is bathed in the experience of joy. Consider the angel's opening declaration to the frightened shepherds: "Don't be afraid, for behold, I bring you good tidings of great joy which will be to all people" (Luke 2:10). That could be paraphrased, "Do not be afraid of what you see and hear. I have the most amazing, good news for you that will bring more joy into your life than you have ever imagined, and into the life of everyone who believes."

Jesus said to His disciples, "These things I have spoken to you, that My joy may remain in you, and that your joy may be full" (John 15:11). That statement demands our deepest thought. Despite all His earthly struggles, Jesus possessed an inner joy known to only Him that transcended every other earthly experience. The word "remain" describes both Jesus' desire for His disciples to experience the fullness of His spiritual joy and for His joy to be their permanent experience.

The second aspect of Jesus' statement is even more challenging. "Full" describes a maximum capacity that leaves room for nothing else. Jesus' desire for His disciples is a life so joyful that fear, worry, and anxiety associated with everyday life are totally blotted out, thus producing an inner peace that passes all understanding (Phil. 4:7). This level of spiritual joy is not obtainable through earthly treasures or worldly pursuits but is found only in one's relationship with God through faith in Jesus. Unconditional, boundless, spiritual joy is the fundamental characteristic of citizenship within the kingdom of heaven.

What kind of joy did the treasure finder experience? The answer is surprising. It was not his joy. He did nothing to earn it; he simply discovered it. Only two people fully understood the joy of the treasure: the one who created and hid it and the one who found it, and a common bond of indescribable joy uniquely linked them. The finder's joy was the continuation and fulfillment of the joy known by the one who laid up the treasure.

The good news of Jesus' birth and of the gospel is the joyous experience of believers. But the startling truth is that it is Jesus' joy that is given by God to Christians as a divine gift, and not their own. Our Christian joy in discovering the treasure of the kingdom of heaven is the same joy of Christ in storing it up for us, and it is given to us through our covenant life with Him.

The finder made his work secondary to the work of the one who created the treasure, and thus he reaped the full benefit of the purpose, passion, work, and joy of another. The treasure was a gift of grace laid up for the finder's discovery at an earlier, unknown time. Its full value had been there waiting to be discovered by one who realized its priceless nature. The one who hid the treasure invested his life in creating joy for another.

The finder of the treasure transformed his life, his priorities, his value system, and his life's work, so that he could experience the fullness of the joy that had been created for him by the one who buried the treasure. The indescribable treasure brought enormous joy to both. "The kingdom of heaven is like that," Jesus said. "Allow My joy to remain in you, so that your joy may be full."

The Parable of the Pearl of Great Price

> *"Again, the kingdom of heaven is like a merchant seeking beautiful pearls, who, when he found a pearl of great price, went and sold all that he had and bought it"* (Matt. 13:45-46).

What is wisdom? Many would define it as knowledge, insight, intuitive understanding, and sage advice. The Jews, however, historically viewed wisdom much deeper than merely intellectual acumen. Wisdom was a level of life incorporating a broad understanding of the relationship of physical life and spiritual life. Wisdom was the rational understanding of the control over everyday forces in physical life by the mind, will, and purpose of God. Ultimate wisdom would be personified through a life of divine righteousness.

The importance of wisdom in Judaism may be seen in the structure and language of the Old Testament. The Books of Wisdom, which include Job, Proverbs, Psalms, Ecclesiastes, and Song of

Solomon, are central to Old Testament theology. King Solomon, who was known for his unusual wisdom, is credited with writing three of these, Proverbs, Ecclesiastes, and Son of Solomon. Solomon described the importance of spiritual wisdom in the introductory verses to his Book of Proverbs:

"To know wisdom and instruction, to perceive the words of understanding, to receive the instruction of wisdom, justice, judgment, and equity; to give prudence to the simple, to the young man knowledge and discretion—a wise man will hear and increase learning, and a man of understanding will attain wise counsel, to understand a proverb and an enigma, the words of the wise and their riddles. The fear of the Lord is the beginning of knowledge, but fools despise wisdom and instruction" (Prov. 1:2-7).

Wisdom thus took on a mythic personification in Solomon's writings, and he described "her" power and influence in the very creation of life and the universe:

"I, wisdom, dwell with prudence, and find out knowledge and discretion. The fear of the Lord is to hate evil; pride and arrogance and the evil way and the perverse mouth I hate. Counsel is mine, and sound wisdom; I am understanding, I have strength ...The Lord possessed me at the beginning of His way, before His works of old. I have been established from everlasting, from the beginning, before there was ever an earth. When there were no depths I was brought forth, when there were no fountains abounding with water. Before the mountains were settled, before the hills, I was brought forth; while as yet He had not made the earth or the fields, or the primeval dust of the world. When He prepared the heavens, I was there, when he drew a circle on the face of the deep, when He established the clouds above, when He strengthened the fountains of the deep, when He assigned to the sea its limit, so that the waters would not transgress His command, when He marked out the foundations of the earth, then I was beside Him as a master craftsman; and I was daily His delight, rejoicing always before Him, rejoicing in His inhabited world, and my delight was with the sons of men" (Prov. 8:12-31).

There is an amazing parallel between these verses and John's description of Jesus written centuries later:

> *"In the beginning was the Word, and the Word was with God, and the Word was God. He was in the beginning with God. All things were made through Him, and without Him nothing was made that was made. In Him was life, and the life was the light of men"* (John 1:1-4).

Thus, in both the Old Testament and New Testament, wisdom is revealed as a spiritual "life" that has been present with God from the beginning of time and is never-ending. Solomon's description of wisdom is an early revelation of the life Jesus later described as "eternal life" or "everlasting life." This eternal life of ultimate wisdom, goodness, and righteousness completely unifies God and man and has been with God since the world began.

Amazingly, Christianity is premised on this one life. Christianity is not about many good lives, or the lives of saints, or servants of God. Christian belief is founded on this one perfect life of wisdom, goodness, and righteousness that is ordained by God. It is His one means of redeeming mankind to the level of spiritual perfection from which he fell through sin. There are no other philosophies, doctrines, or beliefs that have been with God since the beginning of time that have such an inherent ability, but this life does. The entire promise of salvation rests in the power of this one life of wisdom, truth, and divine goodness that alone was possessed by Jesus. In contrast to the sinful darkness of the world, John thus stated, "In Him was life, and the life was the light of men."

Eternal life should not be considered in physical terms, as if one lived in his present consciousness forever. Rather, eternal life is a concept in which one's spiritual life is so complete that he is in perfect union with God, and therefore through the divine covenant bond with God, he spiritually exists as long as God exists—forever.

Because of His unique spiritual "oneness" with God, Jesus possessed eternal life and promised His everlasting life to all Christians as a gift of grace. Consider the following promises of Jesus to believers:

> *"For God so loved the world that He gave His only begotten Son, that whoever believes in Him should not perish but have everlasting life"* (John 3:16).
>
> *"And this is the will of Him who sent Me, that everyone who sees the Son and believes in Him may have everlasting life; and I will raise him up at the last day"* (John 6:40).

> *"Most assuredly, I say to you, he who hears My word and believes in Him who sent Me has everlasting life, and shall not come into judgment, but has passed from death into life"* (John 5:24).

> *"And whoever lives and believes in Me shall never die. Do you believe this?"* (John 11:26).

> *"As the living Father sent Me, and I live because of the Father, so he who feeds on Me will live because of Me. This is the bread which came down from heaven—not as your fathers ate the manna, and are dead. He who eats this bread will live forever"* (John 6:57-58).

> *"…I have come that they may have life, and that they may have it more abundantly"* (John 10:10).

Amazingly, the everlasting life of Christ is given to all Christians by faith, and everlasting, abundant life is mutually shared by all believers within the kingdom of heaven. We may not presently know and live its fullness on earth, because now "we see in a mirror, dimly," as the Apostle Paul stated to the Corinthian church (1 Cor. 13:12). But, in the ages to come, we will discover this life of wisdom, goodness, and righteousness has been safely stored and laid up as a divine treasure since before the foundation of the world, and it will be given to us, according to King Solomon, as a "crown of glory."

Thus, Solomon in his Book of Proverbs states:

> *"Wisdom is the principal thing; therefore get wisdom. And in all your getting, get understanding. Exalt her, and she will promote you; she will bring you honor, when you embrace her. She will place on your head an ornament of grace; a crown of glory she will deliver to you"* (Prov. 4:7-9).

Since the eternal life of divine wisdom is a spiritual treasure, how can its value be understandably described physically? Solomon stated:

> *"For wisdom is better than rubies, and all the things one may desire cannot be compared with her"* (Prov. 8:11).

"Rubies" may also mean "jewels" or "pearls." It denotes something smooth, round, and significantly valuable. It is from these ancient Hebrew writings that the phrase "pearl of wisdom" is derived, and wisdom of the greatest life-transforming value was referred to as a "pearl of great price." Solomon stated that nothing physical in the world can be compared to its value. It is from these ancient Jewish concepts of wisdom that Jesus drew His parable.

After He shared the parable about the treasure buried in a field, Jesus immediately spoke this parable. His transition from one parable to the other is interesting and enlightening. He stated, "Again, the kingdom of heaven is like…." Jesus had just described the value of the kingdom as comparable to a treasure that transformed the finder's life. He then added a further descriptive dimension.

However, "again" does not repeat the previous concept. Rather, it describes an added dimension of thought of a different nature. As Jesus finished the first parable and connected it to the second parable, it is as if He were saying, "Not only that, but think about this also." It denotes a further concept of even deeper and more challenging meaning.

Jesus struggled to change the basic mindset of Israel regarding righteousness with God. Historically, Judaism placed importance on earning righteousness through obedience to the law and the traditions of the elders of Israel. But Jesus stressed an opposite view. The true meaning of life was found not in the abundance of things possessed or one's adherence to the law, but rather in the spiritual attitudes of his heart. Jesus specifically stated, "For out of the heart proceed evil thoughts, murders, adulteries, fornications, thefts, false witness, blasphemies. These are the things which defile a man…" (Matt. 15:19-20).

Repentance, as Jesus saw it, was a fundamental change in one's understanding that a right relationship with God was not based on physical acts, but rather spiritual attitudes. Repentance involves such a complete inner transformation that it is like being spiritually recreated into a different person in Christ's image, and thus one is born again. The life that a believer receives as a result of his spiritual regeneration is the eternal life of Jesus—His everlasting life—the life that Solomon described centuries earlier as "wisdom." It is the one life that has been with God since the beginning of time. The challenge of repentance, both then and now, is changing the thoughts deeply buried within one's heart in order for this divine life of wisdom to live and thrive within his earthly humanity.

Unlike living under the religious laws of Israel, which were stagnant, Jesus viewed the life of Christian discipleship as a dynamic life of spiritual discovery that, like a mustard plant, begins small but grows to an unimagined size. He therefore encouraged His disciples to always "ask, and it will be given to you; seek, and you will find, knock, and it will be opened to you. For everyone who asks receives, and he who seeks finds, and to him who knocks it will be opened" (Matt.7:7-8). Similarly, Solomon stated that among all the things one might desire in life, "wisdom is the principal thing." Christian discipleship is the never-ending spiritual journey searching for the deepest understanding of the eternal life of "wisdom" revealed in Jesus.

Through His genius as a teacher, Jesus shared this parable comparing the kingdom of heaven to a merchant, searching for pearls, who found a "pearl of great price." That discovery changed his life, for he then sold all that he had in order to acquire this one pearl, whose value to him was greater than all things he possessed in life. Discovering the kingdom of heaven "is like that," said Jesus.

A parable derives its name from the comparison of two truths in which the facts of the first are used to teach the truth of the second. That is important in understanding this parable. On the surface, the parable describes a merchant on a mission to find pearls that he might buy and re-sell. However, he discovered one pearl that was so valuable he was immediately compelled to act completely opposite to his intention. Instead of adding this pearl to his existing inventory of earthly valuables, he sold all that he possessed in order to acquire it. One pearl suddenly became more important to him than all other pearls that he had seen and owned, and no earthly treasure mattered to him anymore or controlled his life any longer.

Interestingly, the parable does not say that he ever resold the pearl. He gave up all he now treasured in order to acquire something he would never give up in the future. That is amazing. Its value was not measured by what others might offer him; its value was known only to him and was treasured within his heart.

However, the merchant was not an ordinary shop owner dealing in pearls. In the parable, "merchant" denotes someone on a journey, such as a passenger on a defined journey or a trader with a specific mission. The merchant was searching for pearls, and his journey took him wherever he thought he might find pearls of exquisite beauty and value. It is unknown how far or how long he traveled and searched. Likewise, it is unknown how many pearls he handled and examined, only to lay them down as unworthy of his investment.

The merchant is a sobering picture of many in the journey of life. He was searching for something of greater value than what he possessed. Regardless of his accumulated wealth, or the number of pearls that he possessed or could acquire, they did not produce happiness and inner peace, and so he continued to search.

But, at a time arranged by destiny and fate, his journey ended. How he found the priceless pearl is not stated, but his reaction is described in the parable. We can only surmise that his action was similar to the man who found the treasure buried in the field. Overcome and numbed by the reality of what he had found, he immediately made life-transforming decisions to give up all that he had in order to personally acquire and possess the "pearl of great price." His life was never the same afterward.

The parable's meaning is not about a merchant on a mission to find pearls. It is about anyone on a journey searching for ultimate spiritual truth and wisdom that brings true peace and rest to his soul and fills him with such understanding that he looks no further. Along the way on his journey of life, he finds numerous wise, truthful sayings and pearls of wisdom that inspire, encourage, and even comfort him. But they do not bring lasting spiritual peace, and the journey and the search continue.

Only God knows the date and time of one's fateful encounter with spiritual destiny. But, in his search for wisdom and truth, the spiritual sojourner hears these words:

"For God so loved the world that He gave His only begotten Son, that whoever believes in Him should not perish but have everlasting life" (John 3:16).

"In the beginning was the Word, and the Word was with God, and the Word was God, He was in the beginning with God...And the Word became flesh and dwelt among us, and we beheld His glory, the glory as of the only begotten of the Father, full of grace and truth" (John 1:1-2, 14).

"...God was in Christ reconciling the world to Himself, not imputing their trespasses to them, and has committed to us the word of reconciliation. Therefore, we are ambassadors for Christ, as though God were pleading through us: we implore you on Christ's behalf, be reconciled to God" (2 Cor. 5:19-20).

"Then the King will say to those on His right hand, 'Come, you blessed of My Father, inherit the kingdom prepared for you from the foundation of the world'" (Matt. 25:34).

Each of these verses is a significantly valuable pearl of wisdom. But, when their truth is combined and applied to an individual's life, an overwhelming sense of divine wonder and mystery unfolds. It is a spiritual truth so overwhelming that one is compelled to assess its value in relation to all other concepts and dimensions of life. If one is searching for a higher purpose and meaning in life, consider their combined wisdom:

- God, in His mercy, was so motivated by redeeming love for the world and for every person that He willingly gave Jesus, His only begotten Son, to die on the cross in full atonement for man's sins, so that anyone anywhere in the world who believes in Him would not perish but instead have "everlasting life."
- Salvation is no longer based on human self-effort and works of the law. It is not based on religious creeds or denominational beliefs. Through faith in Christ alone, salvation is freed from man's restraints and his prejudices and mean spirit. Salvation is a free gift of grace given by a loving God to anyone, anywhere on earth who believes in Jesus as Lord and Savior.
- Jesus was not just some interesting and commanding historical figure who was a brilliant teacher, social activist, and religious reformer. He was God in human flesh. He was the total physical manifestation of every aspect of God's spiritual nature, and He dwelt among mankind, and humanity was allowed the opportunity to visibly see the full

grace and truth of God. Thus, Jesus said, "…He who has seen Me has seen the Father…" (John 14:9).
- God was in Christ. Through Jesus' work and life on earth, and through His death on the cross, God provides a way for man to be fully reconciled to Him, forgiven of sin, and justified before God as if no sin had ever been committed.

Amazingly, God calls and commissions every Christian to be an ambassador for Christ to the world around them. Every disciple is empowered by the Holy Spirit to speak for God, as if He were speaking through them, pleading with others to be reconciled to God. That is our calling in life as a Christian and that is the ministry of reconciliation that he has given to each Christian. Continuing the earthly redemptive work of Christ becomes our work, our purpose, and our passion in life.

Every Christian's citizenship is moved from the physical realm of this world to the spiritual realm of the kingdom of heaven where he realizes the sovereignty of God over His creation. The value of gold on earth does not compare to the treasure of the glory of this heavenly realm. Each Christian is an adopted child of God and is a joint heir with Jesus to all the riches of the kingdom of heaven. That is our guaranteed inheritance in Christ, and it has been laid up for us before the foundation of the world was formed.

That overall truth is not just a pearl of wisdom; it is a pearl of wisdom whose value exceeds all other treasure to be found on earth. It is a pearl of wisdom of the greatest price. Its truth grips our soul in a loving embrace and bids us to take up our cross and follow Christ. Its wisdom strips away the foolish pride and vanity of all other human endeavors. Its holy purpose reveals a divine calling in life as Christ's ambassador that far exceeds any dream of human ambition.

Its potential impact on the life of others around us far exceeds any act of benevolence that we might undertake. It provides an unbroken covenant relationship of human life with the divine life of God in which the very person and power of God lives in us and through us by faith in Christ. We are transformed and spiritually reborn in the image of Christ. His life becomes our life, His work becomes our work, and His resurrected power becomes the empowering spiritual force in life. When God looks at each of us, He does not see our frail, sinful humanity. Instead, He only sees Christ in us.

This life is not a fleeting human experience; it is our life for all eternity, and it is the very nature of God's everlasting life. This everlasting divine life is given to every Christian as a gift of grace because of faith in Jesus, and it produces a spiritual sense of joy, peace, thanksgiving, and praise that exceeds all other human emotions.

This pearl of wisdom can only be called a "Pearl of Great Price." When we find it, we look no further.

Spiritual Growth

The Parable of the Leaven

> *"The kingdom of heaven is like leaven, which a woman took and hid in three measures of meal till it was all leavened"* (Matt. 13:33).

Jesus possessed an unmatched ability to teach a deep truth using a simple object, and this parable is a prime example. Because bread was such a common staple in everyday meals, anyone could visualize the difference between unleavened bread, which was prepared for religious observances, and leavened bread, which was prepared for daily meals. Jesus used the simple distinction between the two kinds of baked bread to illustrate a powerful truth about the kingdom of heaven.

The parable is best understood against the historic role of bread in Jewish religious rites because every Jew knew the sight and taste of unleavened bread. Also known was the observable difference the addition of leavening made. No one knew how it chemically and biologically worked to produce change in the dough, but no one questioned that leavening dramatically altered the internal nature of flat, unleavened bread. That was why Jesus used leavening for His strategically important parable.

The use of unleavened bread dates back to the Hebrew exodus from Egypt under Moses' leadership. The Jews were divinely instructed to bake unleavened bread and begin their journey to the Promised Land when the last plague—the death angel—was unleashed on the Egyptians.

A sacrificial lamb was slain by each household, and the lamb's blood was sprinkled on the doorpost of all Jewish homes. Because of the blood of the lamb, the death angel mercifully passed over each Jewish household, sparing them from the plague of death. Remembrance of God's mercy and deliverance is the historic basis of Passover and eating unleavened bread has continued to be a vital part of Passover memorial observances throughout the centuries.

Bread took additional meaning in Judeo-Christian theology through the manna that miraculously fell from heaven and divinely nurtured the Israelites during their forty-year wilderness journey.

Manna became the "bread of life" for the Jews in their exodus because of its life-sustaining power. Thus, Jesus identified with the ancient manna, and comparing His ability to give eternal life to the sustaining power of the wilderness manna, He said, "I am the bread of life. Your fathers ate the manna in the wilderness and are dead. This is the bread which comes down from heaven, that one may eat of it and not die. I am the living bread which came down from heaven. If anyone eats of this bread, he will live forever..." (John 6:48-51).

But this parable is not specifically about bread or leavening. Instead, it is a description of the kingdom of heaven using the visible effect of leavening in bread as the parallel physical truth to establish an unseen spiritual truth about the impact of heavenly spiritual values on an individual. The parable portrays the power of the kingdom of heaven to bring profound change in the thoughts of one's heart through repentance and how those changed attitudes impact his actions toward God and others.

However, a brief discussion about baking bread will better amplify the parable's meaning. Bread consists of flour made from grain, some kind of "shortening" such as oil or animal fat, a moistening agent like milk or water, and leavening. More simple bread consists only of flour and water that produces a very flat bread because it has no leavening. Bread traditionally used during the Jewish observance of Passover is made in this manner. Leavened bread significantly increases in size and has a different taste, while unleavened bread remains flat, slightly unpleasant tasting, and does not change form. The difference is created by the addition of leavening.

Leavening is any kind of ingredient added to bread dough that changes into carbon dioxide and emits small gas bubbles, causing the dough to expand or "rise," as the effect is commonly called. Leavening may include active yeast or baking powder, which is a combination of sodium bicarbonate (baking soda), cornstarch, and other ingredients. When combined with dry flour and a liquid, leavening releases carbon dioxide bubbles that are trapped by the cornstarch in the dough, and the combined effect causes the dough to expand considerably in size as it is heated.

Yeast also works as leavening. When added to dough, the fermentation of the yeast converts carbohydrates into carbon dioxide gas bubbles causing a similar rising effect. Although baking powder and yeast work similarly, yeast causes a greater reaction and produces a more appetizing taste.

However, the leavening described by Jesus was no doubt a small portion of dough kept over as a "starter" from a previous baking. In order to make the bread rise, the older, fermented dough was added to the flour mixture. The beneficial bacteria naturally occurring in the starter acted on the fresh flour dough, producing a rising effect throughout. When Jewish religious observances called for unleavened bread, the starter dough was not incorporated, and no rising effect occurred. The difference was unmistakable.

How leavening works cannot be seen visibly because it occurs internally within the bread dough. Although modern science provides a technical description of the process, centuries ago it was viewed as a mystery. Through some unseen and unexplainable means, leaven profoundly altered the shape and size—and even the taste—of bread.

Thus, as one thinks about the inner working of leavening on bread dough, he must also think about the mysterious, inner working of the spiritual kingdom of heaven on an individual's heart, for Jesus, in speaking of leavening, said that the kingdom of heaven "is like" leavening. It is an interesting and intriguing comparison.

Jesus told Nicodemus the Holy Spirit worked in a similar manner. In response to Nicodemus query about the spiritual impact of His teaching, Jesus replied:

> *"The wind blows where it wishes, and you can hear the sound of it, but cannot tell where it comes from and where it goes. So is everyone who is born of the Spirit"* (John 3:8).

Therefore, when Jesus told His disciples, "the kingdom of God is within you" (Luke 7:21), He established the premise that the Spirit works unseen within an individual to bring about profound inner change in a manner that is both mysterious and unexplainable. It is like leavening in bread dough.

These three parables—the parable of the hidden treasure, the parable of the pearl of great price, and the parable of the leaven—should all be examined together, for they focus on the nature and power of inner spiritual transformation that occurs in a person once his commitment to Christ becomes his paramount passion and purpose.

Why is that important to Christians? The life and ministry of Jesus is the most significant and transformative moment in history. It must not be forgotten that both John the Baptist and Jesus premised their preaching on the same words demanding spiritual change: "Repent, for the kingdom of heaven is at hand" (Matt. 4:17). Their messages clearly established that experiencing the kingdom of heaven—and Jesus' power to reveal the divine messianic age—is predicated on repentance, or the fundamental change in one's understanding of the spiritual nature of the kingdom of God.

Repentance involves much more than ceasing bad behavior. Instead, repentance involves a transforming redirection of the purpose, passion, and power in one's life from a physical orientation through compliance with religious law to a totally different spiritual orientation through commitment to Christ. Once that new direction is chosen through faith, the Holy Spirit works internally within a Christian's heart to transform religious law into redeeming love for others, obligation into opportunity, and legal compliance into spiritual consecration.

The Holy Spirit does not teach one how to impose religious law and beliefs on others. Instead, the Spirit teaches one how to reveal redeeming love to others. Only through repentance can one's life be redirected by the Holy Spirit toward the priceless spiritual treasure laid up in heaven for believers since the beginning of time. There is no limit on the internal change that takes place through repentance.

Understanding how difficult that change was for Jesus' disciples is challenging. The disciples—along with the rest of Israel—knew no other method of worship than devotedly following the religious laws of Israel. Israel was bound to the law and to the writings of the prophets, and the religious rules that tied them together could not be broken. No other concepts or interpretations of the law, other than the traditional views of the elders, were acceptable.

There is a significant difference between the internal impact of law and the impact of the Spirit. Law changes only when man changes it, and no religious law changes the thoughts of a person's heart, because law has no spiritual effect. It is stagnant, static, unyielding, and only makes one focus on strict obedience. Law has defined parameters and does not allow action and attitudes outside of set limits.

If one's focus is on law, he inescapably lives within a joyless emotional and spiritual box. No practitioner of the law ever rejoices and praises God because he has kept the law. There is only a smug sense of accomplishment feeding an attitude of spiritual superiority and condemnation of others. It fosters spiritual pride and arrogance through boasting about compliance, such as the rich young ruler who said of his obedience to the law, "All these things I have kept from my youth..." (Matt. 19:20).

No person spiritually matures as a disciple of Jesus through religious law. Saul of Tarsus (before he became the Apostle Paul) could boast of being blameless under the law because he perfectly complied with its demands (Phil. 3:6). But inwardly he was a mean, vicious man who coldly arrested and bound Christians in chains for their belief in Christ (Acts 9:1-2). Religious law does not make a person merciful; it just makes them mean-spirited toward others.

Jesus' disciples had no real basis for understanding the kingdom of heaven concept, especially the idea "the kingdom in within you." It was a totally alien concept. Thus, the strategic challenge underlying these parables was how to effectively convey ideas and ignite thoughts about spiritual concepts that were unseen, unheard of, and incomprehensible to the disciples yet divine truth.

I have often wondered how Anne Sullivan taught Hellen Keller, who was deaf and blind, to effectively communicate. How was it possible for Miss Sullivan to reveal truth to one who could not see instructions, hear words, or understand thoughts? She realized no traditional teaching technique would break through the dark silence of Hellen Keller's mind, and she resorted to methods that only a dedicated and loving teacher would create and employ.

With great patience, Anne Sullivan, who was also visually impaired, began using a braille method to tap the sounds and spelling of words with her finger into Hellen's palm. Through patience, dedication, and Anne Sullivan's innovative teaching techniques, Hellen Keller became an effective communicator. Ann Sullivan used a physical means to communicate emotional, intellectual, and spiritual truth, much like Jesus' use of a parable. Though she never physically saw or heard, Hellen Keller was inwardly transformed.

In like manner, how did Jesus teach truth to those who were spiritually blind, who did not have the ability to spiritually hear his words, and who believed it was a heretical violation of the law to even consider Jesus' words as divine truth? Jesus chose these parables as His fundamental teaching tool to begin changing the thoughts of their hearts and inwardly transforming the disciples.

If one is to understand the strategic importance of the parables to repentance and the birth of Christianity, the challenge Jesus faced as a teacher must be studied. These parables involve the concept of spiritual regeneration and the power of the Holy Spirit within a believer, which was unknown to the disciples. Those men no more understood Jesus' teaching initially than Hellen Keller understood Anne Sullivan's first touch. But they eventually became extra-ordinarily gifted communicators of the gospel. The parable of the leaven reveals how their understanding and ability gradually expanded.

Therefore, Jesus chose one of the most common and easily visible physical truths to teach a greater yet unseen spiritual truth. He chose the example of leavening in bread to inspire the disciples' thoughts about the power of the spiritual kingdom of heaven within them, not a physical military kingdom around them, and it was a brilliant choice.

This parable has subtle truths that powerfully emerge when closely examined. The woman took "three measures" of meal in which she "hid" the leaven. These phrases are significant. The volume of three measures, which greatly exceeds the amount normally measured for daily needs, immediately indicates this was no ordinary dinner she was preparing. A "measure" was the Jewish "seah," or one-third of an ephah, which was the equivalent of 5.75 gallons. Thus, one-third of an ephah was 1.91 gallons, and that would have been one measure. However, the woman used three measures of meal, or the equivalent of an ephah of flour (5.75 gallons). A gallon equals sixteen cups, so she measured out about ninety-two cups of flour. An ordinary loaf of bread contains approximately three cups of flour; therefore, she measured enough meal to bake thirty loaves of bread, which would have been sufficient for a feast.

The phrase "three measures of meal" only occurs in the New Testament in this passage and the parallel passage in Luke 13:21. However, its Old Testament use implies a meal of considerable importance. When the Spirit of God visited Abraham and Sarah in the form of "three men" and revealed that a son would be born to them despite their old age, Abraham instructed Sarah to "make ready three measures of fine meal; knead it and make cakes." The meal, which included a freshly slaughtered calf, butter, milk, and bread made from the three measures of meal, was a celebratory meal with God (Gen. 18:1-8).

When Hannah brought her child, Samuel, to the Lord to be dedicated to His service, she also took "…three bulls, one ephah of flour, and a skin of wine, and brought him to the house of the Lord in Shiloh…" (I Sam. 1:24). The ephah of flour was the equivalent of three measures. There, she dedicated her son to God:

"For this child I have prayed, and the Lord has granted me my petition which I asked of Him. Therefore, I also have lent him to the Lord; as long as he lives he shall be lent to the Lord.' So they worshipped the Lord there" (vv. 27-28).

The three measures of meal would have been sufficient for a large meal of dedication and celebration with the priests of God.

The religious law stipulated in Leviticus 2:1-3 that "when anyone offers a grain offering to the Lord, his offering shall be of fine flour. And he shall pour oil on it and put frankincense on it…It is most holy of the offerings to the Lord made by fire." Thus, fine flour, and especially three measure of flour, was indicative of an offering to God or a large celebratory communion meal with the Spirit of God. However, under the law, no leavening was placed in the flour of an offering to God (Lev. 2:11).

Therefore, through this parable, Jesus projected a fascinating and unprecedented possibility: What would happen if leaven were added to three measures of flour prepared as a communion meal with God? What would happen if something were added to the cold, flat, unresponsive constraints of religious law and tradition that enabled it to be totally transformed?

As the parable unfolds, new truths are revealed. Jesus stated that the woman "took" the leaven. That is an intriguing description of her action. It was not a routine, methodical action, as one would normally add an ingredient to bread dough mixture. Instead, she intentionally added the leaven. It was a premeditated, volitional act outside the norm of her activities and contrary to her routine. Obviously, she intended to produce something totally different and even shocking to those accustomed to eating unleavened bread in a religious observance. She purposefully intended to change long-standing traditions.

But she acted in a surreptitious manner: She hid the leaven in the three measures of meal. Her actions are fascinating, if not somewhat amusing. She told no one and did nothing to reveal her action. "Hid" *(enekrypsen)* describes an act in which something is intentionally hidden or buried in another substance and is the basis of our modern concept of encryption. The leaven was purposefully mixed with and buried in the meal in a manner that concealed its presence, but not its effect.

It was a mystery to an observer looking at the traditional three measures of meal. It looked the same, but something was inexplicably happening within the dough that was radically transforming it internally and changing its very nature. Soon, its appearance and action would also change. That, said Jesus, is how the kingdom of heaven works inside an individual's heart.

It is instructive that in all three of these parables there is an intentional act that begins the process of spiritual transformation: The one who found the treasure in the field reburied the treasure and then sold all that he had to acquire the field; the merchant sold all that he had in order to acquire the pearl of great price; and the woman intentionally added the leaven to the three measures of meal. If the kingdom of heaven is "like that," then Christian discipleship does not accidentally occur. It demands an intentional act of repentance and commitment to Christ. One does not ease into dynamic Christian living; rather, it is entered by making all else in life secondary in importance and taking up one's cross and following Jesus. It is only then the dynamic internal spiritual transformation brought about by the Holy Spirit begins to change the heart of an individual.

How, then, may the change in the three measures of meal be compared to Christian life? In a broad, spiritually interpretative sense, if one views the meal as the traditional demands of religious law dispassionately and methodically dictating how one is to worship God, what does adding leavening to the law produce?

Religious law becomes transformed from a set of principles to the life of Christ. Jesus specifically stated that He did not come to destroy the law and the prophets, but rather to fulfill them. Fulfill means to complete the purpose of something. Thus, Christ breathes compassionate, merciful life into the cold dictates of religious law.

Religious law is given a capacity to forgive, to reveal mercy, to pardon the wrongs of human sin, to become compassion written on a forgiving heart rather than condemnation etched in stone. The motive of religious law is no longer to shun sinners, but rather to save them.

When the leavening of the Holy Spirit is hidden in the law, the Spirit begins to change its purpose. Religion moves from one's head to his heart, and legal precepts become transformed into a new spiritual purpose in one's life. Worship no longer is a weekly hour-long service, but rather a daily walk of sanctification, praise, and thanksgiving. Limitations imposed by the law are cast off and replaced by opportunities of discipleship directed by the Spirit. The definition of neighbor is transformed, and the pride and arrogance of legal compliance give way to humility.

Further, when the leavening of the Holy Spirit is hidden in the heart of a church, it, too, becomes transformed. Members no longer half-heartedly go to church, as if it were a building and a destination, but instead see themselves as the church of Jesus Christ. They are healed of spiritual blindness and begin to view themselves as the *ekklesia*—the called out of Christ. They get a deeper vision of themselves as the ambassadors of Christ in the community in which they live. They faithfully involve themselves in the ministry of reconciliation, as if He were personally calling out to others through them, "Be reconciled to God."

The Holy Spirit begins to expand their vision, melt their hearts, and open the doors of the church to all who reverently come into the family of God to worship. The church becomes living proof of the brotherhood of believers and the fatherhood of God. All who are a part of the covenant community of believers see themselves as children of God who each has the right to call God "Father." They see themselves as brothers and sisters in Christ and joyfully rejoice in the bond of redeeming love that binds them together without consideration of race, creed, color, physical disability, or emotional orientation in life. All are equal at the foot of the cross of Christ, and all equally receive God's mercy and grace.

Worship becomes a sincere, reverent expression of praise and gratitude for God's mercy and saving grace, rather than a weekly religious entertainment session filled with shallow preaching and false promises from the pulpit. The church collectively sees itself as the body of Christ alive and reaching out to all with the redeeming love of Christ. The church no longer is concerned with the pride of preachers or the false promises of politicians who use the church to proclaim condemnation of others or to propose more laws of judgmental exclusion. Instead, the church community becomes friends with sinners and brings them into the warmth of Christian acceptance and forgiveness. The church body becomes a nonjudgmental sanctuary of compassion and understanding, a place of encouragement, hope, inspiration, and a place where lives are redeemed with love, not ruined by rejection.

In a personal sense, what happens when the leavening of the Holy Spirit is hidden in the heart of an individual? Jesus provided some amazing answers:

(1). "the Spirit of truth…dwells with you and will be in you…" (John 14:17).

The abode—the dwelling place—of the Holy Spirt becomes the heart of a repentant sinner. It is a continuous experience, for once He abides in one's heart, He will not depart. The fundamental work of the Holy Spirit is transforming the thoughts of one's heart through repentance and making them consistent with the thoughts of Jesus, thus strengthening the covenant bond between Christ and every Christian. Like the leavening, His presence cannot be seen, and He works mysteriously to accomplish God's purpose in every believer's life. Worship moves from outward religious ritual to the most interpersonal relationship that one may have with Him. Because of the indwelling of the Spirit of God, one lives in constant communion with God, regardless of the circumstances of everyday life.

(2). "…when He, the Spirit of truth, has come, He will guide you into all truth…" (John 16:13).

The Holy Spirit works unseen within our heart to guide, lead, and instruct us in all truth. It will not be a human empirical truth, or some philosophical truth, but the deepest spiritual truth revealed by God. It is the life of divine truth that has been with God since the beginning of time, and the specific work of the Holy Spirit is revealing the depth and magnitude of that truth to us. Our understanding of and spiritual growth in God's revealed truth never ceases. As a result, every Christian experiences a release from human efforts of self-righteous work and our bonds to the law are broken. We shall know the truth, and the truth will make us free to live gloriously for Christ in spiritual freedom to be all that the Spirit will lead us to be.

(3). "He will glorify Me, for He will take of what is Mine and declare it you" (John 16:14).

Through His abiding presence in us, the Holy Spirit will lead us into the closest possible covenant relationship with Christ. A covenant relationship is one in which two people become so united in heart, mind, and spirit that they become one. That is the essence of Jesus' promise when He said, "This is the new covenant in my blood" (Luke 22:20). In effect, Jesus promised that He was establishing a new eternal, perfect covenant union with God through faith in Him that fulfilled the ancient law of the old covenant.

As the Holy Spirit intensifies that spiritual bond, He will glorify and magnify every spiritual characteristic of Jesus in the human life of each Christian. The life of Jesus does not bring glory to the Christian; rather, the Christian's life brings glory to Christ through the inner spiritual work of the Holy Spirit changing him inwardly and revealing the love of Christ through him.

The Holy Spirit works to produce spiritual maturity in a truly amazing manner. The Spirit will take the truth of Jesus and "declare" that both to a Christian and through a Christian. A declaration is a public pronouncement that has been thoroughly examined and is free from error, making it acceptable as unquestioned truth. The Holy Spirit takes all of the divine truth of God revealed in the life of Jesus and makes that so reliable, trustworthy, and believable that there is no need to look further. It is like the treasure in the field and the pearl of great price. When we find God's eternal truth in Christ, the search is over. We have found the treasure, we hide it in our heart, and we are transformed by it.

But the Spirit's work does not stop there. He takes the truth of Jesus and openly declares it through our life of discipleship. Jesus said, "But you shall receive power when the Holy Spirit has come upon you; and you shall be witnesses to me..." (Acts 1:8). The Holy Spirit takes the life of a devoted Christian and makes a public declaration of Christian truth in his everyday life though how he lives and loves others. Jesus stated, "By this all will know that you are My disciples, if you have love for one another" (John 13:35). The work of the Holy Spirit is transforming cold religious law into compassionate redeeming love for all others.

In His prayer in the Garden of Gethsemane before His arrest, Jesus prayed an amazing prayer that every Christian should study. Regarding each Christian's ministry, Jesus prayed:

"I do not pray for these alone, but also for those who will believe in Me through their word; that they all may be one, as You, Father, are in Me, and I in You; that they may also be one in Us, that the world may believe that you sent Me. And the glory which You gave Me I have given them, that they may be one just as we are one: I in them, and You in Me, that they may be made perfect in one, and that the world may know that You have sent Me and have loved them as You have loved Me" (John 17:20-23).

The Holy Spirit works in the heart of each Christian to answer Jesus' prayer. That is an astounding concept. How many Christians view themselves as the answer to one of Jesus' most passionate prayers? Yet, that is what the Spirit of truth desires to bring about in each of us. The Holy Spirit works through us to declare Christ to the world.

Consider the dedication, sacrifice, and courage of the signers of the Declaration of Independence. Relying upon the blessings of God, they committed their lives, their fortunes, and their sacred honor to underwrite a public declaration of their right to be a free and independent nation. All else in their life was made secondary to that cause. What if every Christian made a similar commitment of their life, their fortune, and their sacred honor to God in order for the Holy Spirit to publicly declare the life of Jesus through them? The answer defies comprehension.

But this I know: If one does so, just like leaven in bread dough, through repentance and faith in Jesus, he will rise and be inwardly transformed in the power of the resurrection to experience spiritual truth, accomplish godly work, and live a dynamically powerful Christian life that bears true witness to the world that God sent Jesus to be Lord and Savior.

Counting the Cost of Discipleship

The Parable of the Tower Builder

> *"For which of you, intending to build a tower, does not sit down first and count the cost, whether he has enough to finish it—lest, after he has laid the foundation, and is not able to finish, all who see it begin to mock him, saying, 'This man began to build and was not able to finish'"* (Luke 14:28-30).

Christianity is not simply a religious belief system, nor is it solely a philosophy based on the teaching of a renowned spiritual leader. Uniquely, Christianity is based on one life, an individual's faith in the power of that life, and his commitment to make that life his own. Christianity is the life of Jesus. It is not a life that came into existence through normal biological conception, nor did it end with the cessation of life-sustaining breath. Jesus' life is God's life manifested in a man, and it neither began with His human birth nor ended with His death on the cross.

Jesus' life is the one eternal life divinely ordained to victoriously overcome every force and foe that is contrary to both God's plan for creation and redemption. It is a priceless treasure of everlasting, sinless life that has been laid up in heaven for Christians since before the foundation of the world was put in place. This life is the Alpha and the Omega, the Beginning, and the End (Rev. 1:8), and this life was with God in the beginning, and it was God (John 1:1).

Because this life is God's life, it is a pure, perfect, powerful, and sinless life. It is an unassailable sanctuary of spiritual security, and no force of man or Satan can minimize, limit, or destroy it. It is a life of divine truth, perfect redeeming love, limitless mercy, and boundless grace.

This divine life of Jesus cannot be earned through religious works, nor is it given for meritorious behavior in life. It can be received only as a free gift of grace. Christianity is not limited to just believing in Jesus. Christian discipleship demands an unconditional, unwavering commitment to this life—the life of Christ. His selfless divine life is the opposite of selfish human life and is the light of the world (John 8:12). Christianity is a commitment to allowing the Holy Spirit to transform us spiritually to be like Christ as much as possible. The life of Jesus must become our prime desire, and commitment to Christ must exceed our commitment to everything else, including human relationships.

The life of Jesus becomes our own treasure that renders all else secondary in importance. It is the pearl of great price that compels us to do all that is necessary to acquire the blessing of this eternal life. It is the leavening in the dough that transforms us internally and grows our capacity to serve Him to greater levels than we dreamed possible.

Once this life is given to a Christian, they become a steward of Christ's life through discipleship. They are transformed spiritually and, through their covenant with Jesus, become the "salt of the earth," or the evidence of a new covenant with God. They also become the "light of the world' (Matt. 5:13-14), living openly and dynamically in total contrast to the sinful darkness of the world. The stewardship over Jesus' life is demanding and is one of the greatest challenges a Christian faces.

The Holy Spirit works to glorify the life of Jesus in a disciple. He does not work to glorify man or to puff up inflated religious egos. Therefore, discipleship is not a joint venture based on a common consensus over the direction and purpose of one's life. Discipleship is the work of a humble servant—a bond servant of Christ—who only seeks to please his master, do His work, accomplish His will, and bring honor and glory to Him, and not to oneself.

In order to receive the life of Jesus, a disciple must first die to himself and be crucified with Christ (Luke 9:23) so that Christ may fully live within him. Christian life is not a timeshare arrangement in which a disciple lives for Christ one day and for himself the next. It is the life of Christ alone every day.

The dynamic declaration of Christ's life by the Holy Spirit cannot be effectively accomplished in a disciple who is indecisive, wish-washy, and who vacillates between attraction to the world and commitment to Christ. Jesus said, "No one, having put his hand to the plow, and looking back, is fit for the kingdom of God" (Luke 9:62).

Therefore, discipleship is unequivocal, uncompromised, and irreversible, and it takes priority over all other desires, dreams, and relationships. Unlike the Israelites who moaned and grumbled during their sojourn in the desert yearning to return to the physical abundance of food in Egypt, for a committed disciple, there is no turning back.

Importantly, prior to stating these two parables, Jesus described the demands of discipleship in very personal terms often misinterpreted. Scripture meaning is occasionally a victim of translation, and this statement by Jesus is an example:

> *"Now great multitudes went with Him. And He turned and said to them, 'If anyone comes to Me and does not hate his father and mother, wife and children, brothers, and sisters, yes, and his own life also, he cannot be My disciple. And whoever does not bear his cross and come after Me cannot be My disciple'"* (Luke 14:25-27).

Although *miseo* is expressed as "hate" in many translations, it more accurately describes a preferential choice between two opportunities, or two people in this case, that emphasizes the moral or spiritual value of one above the other. One's emotions toward the one he chooses will be far more positive than toward the unchosen one. Jesus did not condone hatred, as we understand the word. Instead, He established a discipleship standard that places commitment to Christ above all else, including oneself.

Jesus made a similar statement in the Sermon of the Mount regarding a choice between two masters:

> *"No one can serve two masters; for either he will hate the one and love the other, or else he will be loyal to the one and despise the other. You cannot serve God and mammon"* (Matt. 6:24).

It is interesting to note a couple of examples of this level of commitment in the Gospels. When Jesus began calling His disciples, the following occurred:

> *"Going on from there, He saw two other brothers, James the son of Zebedee, and John his brother, in the boat with Zebedee their father, mending their nets. He called them, and immediately they left the boat and their father, and followed Him"* (Matt. 4:21).

It is easy to marvel at their response without considering the deeply personal choice they made. In Israel's patriarchal society, James and John's father had great influence over their vocational decisions. A man essentially dictated and dominated his children's decisions for as long as he lived. For these men to leave their father and the fishing business he established for them—while they were mending nets—would have been unusual and contrary to social and religious norms.

But, they understood a choice had to be made regarding their priorities and personal commitment. In response to Jesus' invitation, they obviously did not stop loving their father and begin hating him. Instead, they personally and purposefully placed their commitment to Jesus above their commitment to him and the obligations of their fishing business.

The Apostle Peter was married because Jesus healed Peter's sick mother-in-law of a fever (Matt. 8:14-15). However, there is no indication in the Gospels that Peter failed in his commitment to Jesus because of obligations to his wife and family.

When twelve-year-old Jesus asked Mary and Joseph, "...Did you not know that I must be about My father's business?" (Luke 2:49), He was not being disobedient, and He did not stop loving them and begin to hate them. He simply placed His commitment to God on a higher plane.

Discipleship is based on difficult choices. Jesus cannot be Lord part of the time; He must be Lord all of time. Discipleship is not an investment plan with options for investment in earthly treasures and heavenly treasures. Christianity does not demand personal poverty; but Christianity demands devotion to Christ first and foremost and the pursuit of other interests secondarily.

Jesus knew that the ministry of discipleship would be difficult and challenging, and He never told His disciples otherwise. He was keenly aware of the human tendency to make promises that are not kept. The history of repentance in Israel is filled with examples. In fact, several of Jesus' followers turned away from their commitment to Him when they realized the difficult challenges involved (John 6:66).

But, if disciples are to be the "light of the world," their light cannot be connected to a timer controlled by circumstances that flashes on and off between commitment and compromise. The darkness of sin will not be illuminated by the light of discipleship flickering from a candle of commitment covered over by a basket of burdens (Matt. 5:15). The world will not be changed by disciples who let the world change them.

Thus, Jesus stated that unless an individual's commitment to Him exceeds all else, there would be no spiritual success in life. To emphasize this point, Jesus spoke two important parables that focus on the cost of discipleship and the determination to succeed.

The parable of the tower builder is a powerful portrayal of commitment. Again, a parable uses a parallel physical truth to make an equally significant spiritual truth. Therefore, the parable is not about building a tower; rather, it is about the cost of discipleship. But why use the construction of a tower to make this strategic point?

Visualizing the purpose of a tower, the cost, and the difficulty of construction helps one better understand the parable's meaning. A tower was a tall, well-constructed structure that was both a fortification and an observation tower from which to search for an approaching enemy. Often a tower became a centralized gathering place or the center of a village.

Interestingly, centuries later the idea of a fortified village surrounding a tower became known as a "burg" or "burgh" in both early English and German dialects. The names of cities and towns in both countries ending in "burg" or "burgh" can be traced back to the concept of a fortified city or a fortified tower.

There are biblical examples that provide greater insight into the significance of the tower. For example, Isaiah spoke of God's relationship with Israel by stating:

> "...*My well-beloved has a vineyard on a very fruitful hill. He dug it up and cleared out its stones and planted it with the choicest vine. He built a tower in its midst, and also made a winepress in it...*" (Isa. 5:1-2).

In Jesus' parable about the wicked vinedressers, the owner of the vineyard built a tower for protection of the vineyard before leaving it to the vinedressers (Mark 12:1). One would assume the vineyard was sizable and required an equally sizeable investment in the construction of a tower for protection.

Jesus once discussed the misfortune of eighteen men who were killed when the Tower of Siloam collapsed on them. Some had speculated that the tower collapse was punishment for their sin, but Jesus negated that idea (Luke 13:4-5). However, it was obviously a major endeavor for several men to be involved in its construction.

In a broader sense, building a tower reflects an individual's determination to erect an edifice both for his own protection and the safety of others. It may also be construed as the dreams of an individual desiring to build a city that bears his name. However one views the concept, building a tower was not a modest undertaking.

Under no circumstances would a reasonable man undertake such a project on the spur of the moment, or as a whim, without calculating the cost in order to assure that adequate means were available to complete the construction. Building a tower would have been one of the most demanding decisions one could have made both in terms of cost, personal sacrifice, and placing the project's completion ahead of all other interests and endeavors.

Interestingly, the parable is based on two cost factors—the cost of construction and the cost of failure. Each is crucially important to the parable's meaning, and Jesus emphasized both. What would be the negative reaction if one committed himself to building a tower and then gave up shortly after the foundation was laid? Jesus compared that to failing as a disciple.

Jesus used the term "finish" three times in the parable. It is a word implying the successful completion of a work. In its truest sense, it describes perfection that requires no further effort. In terms of building a tower, one can imagine a tower so complete that not one additional stone needs to be added. It is a perfect structure that will fully accomplish its purpose.

In terms of discipleship, Jesus established the standard for His followers to emulate. In the Garden of Gethsemane, Jesus prayed to His Father in heaven, "I have glorified You on the earth. I have finished the work which You have given Me to do" (John 17:4). He had fully and perfectly revealed the redeeming love of God to the world, and there was nothing more to do except offer His life on the cross. A short time later, before He died, Jesus again said, "It is finished" (John 19:30). Having given His life as the final and complete atonement for sin, there was nothing more that could be done. The work of redemption was complete.

The Apostle Paul used the same concept when he stated to Timothy, "I have fought the good fight, I have finished the race, I have kept the faith" (2 Tim. 4:7). Sadly, not every Christian can say that. What happens when one loses the fight, does not finish the race, and lives unfaithfully? The consequences are not positive for one individually or for the cause of Christ, and Jesus urged His disciples to live victoriously in order to avoid that pain.

One of the fascinating aspects about Jesus' life was His ability not to be demoralized by rejection and ridicule. He faced it throughout His ministry from His friends, family, and the religious leadership of Israel. In the parable, Jesus spoke of laying the tower foundation and then being unable to finish. He said, "...all who see it begin to mock..." (v. 29). The tower builder's failed efforts would produce scoffing, ridicule, and jeering. People do not treat failure kindly.

Jesus knew His disciples would experience a similar response if they made a public declaration of intent to follow Him and then failed. He knew the mockery of the Pharisees and others who ridiculed His claims, denounced His teaching as the babbling of a demon-possessed mad-man, and even the pain of his family coming to take Him because they thought He was insane. Jesus also knew He would eventually be mocked by the rejection of those He came to save, and that is what happened.

Following His arrest, the men who seized Jesus mocked and blindfolded Him and then struck Him on the face. Some of His tormentors jeered, "Prophesy! Who is the one who struck You?" (Luke 22:63-64). Later, as He was dying on the cross:

> "...the people stood looking on. But even the rulers with them sneered, saying 'He saved others; let Him save Himself if He is the Christ, the chosen of God.' The soldiers also mocked Him, coming and offering Him sour wine, and saying, 'If You are the King of the Jews, save Yourself'" (Luke 23:35-36).

It is just part of human nature, but scoffers, cynics, and doubters abound. Commitment to Christ is seldom fully supported by encouragement, prayer, and support even from one's family and friends. Gossip feeds on failure, not success; condemnation flows more freely than commendation; and poison pours easier than praise from the sour lips of a naysayer. Twisted human ego finds it more enjoyable to point a finger of criticism at the scattered stones of failure than to lift a hand of praise to the edifice of achievement. Jesus wants to enable His disciples to rise above the riffraff of ridicule and to triumphantly look out from atop the tower of success in their work for Him.

The Parable of the Warrior King

> *"Or what king, going to make war against another king, does not sit down first and consider whether he is able with ten thousand to meet him who comes against him with twenty thousand? Or else, while the other is still a great way off, he sends a delegation and asks conditions for peace. So likewise, whoever of you does not forsake all that he has cannot be My disciple"* (Luke 14:31-33).

Borrowing from Israel's history of turf battles and feudal rivalries, Jesus stated a second parable about a warrior king who struggled with his courage. The king had an army of ten thousand soldiers and decided to attack another king who commanded twenty thousand. Apparently, there was no strategy, no forethought, no logistical support, and no plan of war. He foolishly committed himself and his men without careful consideration of his chance of success. Then, reality set in. He was ill-equipped, outmanned, and unprepared for the task he had undertaken. He froze with the fear of failure.

His actions reveal his collapse of confidence. While the other king was a great way off, he began to look for a way out. The warrior king was under no immediate threat at this point because the king he was attacking was still a long distance away. Fear became his worst enemy. Refusing to expose himself to danger, he sent a delegation to the second king requesting conditions of peace.

That is fascinating. The war had not started, but he asked the enemy king to stipulate the conditions of peace. Out of fear, he gave up without a fight. It was unconditional surrender before the battle even began. His bravado and boasting turned into humiliation and defeat because he allowed fear to determine the outcome of his commitment. In many instances, it is the same with discipleship.

Fear is a powerful force in determining a disciple's destiny. Alone on a mountain, Jesus prayed as He watched a midnight storm developing on the Sea of Galilee. During the fourth watch of the night, sometime between 3:00 a.m. and 6:00 a.m., as the boat bearing the disciples was being tossed about by the wind and waves, Jesus walked across the water toward them. Thinking He was a ghost, they cried out in fear, but Jesus reassured them saying, "Be of good cheer! It is I; do not be afraid." Peter, however, was unsure and challenged Jesus by saying, "Lord, if it is You, command me to come to you on the water" (Matt. 14:23-29).

Consider what Peter really said: "I don't believe You. If it is really You, make me do the most unbelievable, unthinkable, impossible thing I can imagine. Make me walk on water, too." Jesus responded, "Come." Jesus beckoned Peter to accomplish the impossible and to achieve unimaginable success. Accepting the challenge, Peter began a journey he never dreamed possible. What he was doing violated all human logic, transcended the laws of nature, and allowed him to rise above every physical limitation that would have denied him success. Peter, like Jesus, was walking on water!

Peter was an ordinary fisherman, and he had spent years on the Sea of Galilee. But, he had never walked on it! Never before had he felt such a divine, supernatural power. It was the most amazing, indescribable accomplishment he had ever experienced.

But, then he saw the wind. He did not look at the waves and become afraid. He allowed the invisible wind to defeat him. Like the warrior king, Peter failed in the greatest accomplishment of his life out of fear of a force he could not see. One may feel the wind, but one cannot see the wind. His imagination took over, filling his heart with fear, and he began sinking while probably saying to himself, "This is not possible. There is no way I can do this. I cannot keep going on like this much longer. I know what's going to happen: I am going to sink and drown in this storm." He allowed something that he could not see to pull him down, and he began crying out to Jesus to save him. No doubt, when he was safely in the boat, Peter mumbled to himself, "I will not try that again." Other Christians have said the same in the midst of failure.

What might have happened if fear had not defeated Peter? Surely, walking on water would have encouraged, inspired, and emboldened him. He might have looked back at the other terrified disciples and said, "If I can do this, you can, too!" What if all of the disciples had walked on the water that night? Would they have become more determined and courageous? In the moment of confrontation with Roman authorities that tested their commitment to Christ the greatest, would they have stood strong and unwavering or run away in fear as they did? Would the history of Christianity and the world have been different if Peter had not become fearful of the unseen wind that night?

Walking on water is not just a physical feat. It is a spiritual experience in which a disciple of Jesus walks above the storm-tossed sea of life in a dramatic, dynamic victory march over the forces of fear and failure. Jesus established a benchmark for service to God that should be followed by every disciple: "Let your light so shine before men, that they may see your good works and glorify your Father in heaven" (Matt. 5:16). In like manner, building a great tower may bring glory to one on earth; but being a good disciple brings glory to God in heaven. The praise of angels rings richer and louder in the heart of a devoted disciple than the praise of men.

Random phrases expressing the ordinary wisdom of commitment sum up these two parables: Plan your work and work your plan. Do not look for a way out while looking for a way in. Succeeding is more rewarding than conceding. Do not start a race without knowing where the finish line is. All of these shed light on the parables' meanings.

However, the greatest reward of discipleship is saying about one's own efforts what Jesus said about His: "I have finished the work which You gave me to do." There is no joy in unfinished labor; there is no reward in failure; and there is no victory in vacillation. Therefore, Jesus urged His disciples to follow a simple yet challenging standard in their commitment to Him: be certain and sure, committed and confident, devoted and determined, sacrificial and successful, and count the cost up front and see it through to the end. For the glory of God and the furtherance of the kingdom of heaven, finish what you start!

The Power of Persistence

The Parable of a Friend at Midnight

> *"Which of you shall have a friend, and go to him at midnight and say to him, 'Friend, lend me three loaves; for a friend of mine has come to me on his journey, and I have nothing to set before him'; and he will answer from within and say, 'Do not trouble me; the door is now shut, and my children are with me in bed; I cannot rise and give to you'? I say to you, though he will not rise and give to him because he is his friend, yet because of his persistence he will rise and give him as many as he needs"* (Luke 11:5-8).

Christianity is not what it used to be. Today, the Christian faith is one of the world's prominent religions with millions of followers. It has transformed cultures and is the religious cornerstone of Western civilization. However, it was the exact opposite two millennia ago.

Christianity began exceedingly small with only Jesus and His immediate disciples. Although multitudes followed Him at times, it is impossible to know how many truly believed Him, or whether they only followed Him for the immediate physical benefits, such as food and healing. Interestingly, Jesus specifically accused many of that shallow level of interest and commitment (John 6:26). In the end, the multitudes cried out for Him to be crucified, and His disciples deserted Him, leaving Him to die alone.

Jesus' messianic claims about being the Son of God were rejected by Jewish religious authorities as the ranting of a demon-possessed heretic (John 8:52). Even His disciples had difficulty understanding the depth of His teaching, especially the nature of the kingdom of heaven. What Jesus taught so transformed the meaning of ancient Jewish law that it was rejected outright by Israeli leadership, who sought to condemn and crucify Him rather than believe Him (John 11:53).

In the first few years after Jesus' death and resurrection, the Christian faith was referred to as "The Way" (Acts 9:2), and it was not until some years later in Antioch, Syria that followers of Jesus were first called "Christians" (Acts 11:26). Organizationally, the church was fragmented, and small groups of believers met in homes. There was no uniform standard of belief, no plan of worship or ministry, no literary basis for the faith other than a few emerging letters of encouragement that were sent among individuals and churches, and only a limited number of recognized men who served as church leaders.

Historians postulate that perhaps twenty to thirty years elapsed before the gospels were written and the letters of the Apostle Paul began circulating among various churches. The writings were slowly recognized as the literary basis of a new covenant, or the New Testament. However, for the first few decades, principles of faith were orally passed on to others based on personal memory of what Jesus had said and done.

The process in which church leaders studied early documents and determined whether each was true or false doctrine is a fascinating aspect of Christian history. Slowly, as a result of various conferences, a consensus developed regarding which letters and writings were acceptable as divinely inspired and which were to be rejected as false doctrine. The accepted documents formed the canon of belief, and the New Testament slowly began to form as a recognized and accepted body of divine scriptural truth, but it took hundreds of years for that to fully develop.

Even as the early apostles began preaching the gospel, many were imprisoned, such as Paul and Silas (Acts 16:22-24), and the gospel message was scornfully rejected by most Jewish leaders. Even early Christians struggled to understand the relationship between Judaism and Christianity, and the church in Jerusalem, for example, debated for years whether a Christian must also comply with certain demands and traditions of Jewish law and ritual.

As Christian beliefs spread into the Greco-Roman world, Greek scholars either dismissed Christianity as foolish or demanded that Greek ideas of wisdom and knowledge be incorporated into Christian beliefs. The Apostle Paul struggled to ensure the purity of Christian doctrine while incurring the derision and condescension of Greek scholars. Thus, he proclaimed his willingness to be considered a fool (*moros*) for Christ's sake—literally to be viewed as a moron for his beliefs (1 Cor. 4:10).

The physical obstacles were also daunting. Paul wrote to the Corinthian church about the adversities he had encountered because of his faith:

> *"From the Jews five times I received forty stripes minus one. Three times I was beaten with rods; once I was stoned; three times I was shipwrecked; a night and a day I have been in the deep; in journeys often, in perils of waters, in perils of robbers, in perils of my own countrymen, in perils of the Gentiles, in perils in the city, in perils in the wilderness, in perils in the sea, and in perils among false brethren; in weariness and toil, in sleeplessness often, in hunger and thirst, in fasting often, in cold and nakedness—"* (2 Cor. 11:24-27).

Many others shared in his suffering. But Paul persevered and his letters constitute a significant portion of the New Testament.

As Christianity spread into the Roman Empire, persecutions began because Christians proclaimed Jesus as Lord rather than the Roman emperor. During the reigns of Nero and Domitian in particular, thousands of Christians were savagely tortured and killed for their steadfast refusal to abandon their religious beliefs.

In many other ways and in many other countries, this pattern of religious persecution has continued. It has never been easy to be a devoted Christian. Jesus knew that would happen to His disciples, and He warned them in advance:

> *"Behold, I send you out as sheep in the midst of wolves. Therefore be wise as serpents and harmless as doves. But beware of men, for they will deliver you up to councils and scourge you in their synagogues. You will be brought before governors and kings for My sake, as a testimony to them and to the Gentiles...Now brother will deliver up brother to death, and a father his child; and children will rise up against parents and cause them to be put to death. And you will be hated by all for My name's sake. But he who endures to the end will be saved* (Matt. 10:16-22).

Given all of the adversity, how did Christianity survive? First and foremost, Christianity has prevailed by the power of God because it is God's eternal truth and cannot be defeated or destroyed by the actions of man. Secondly, Christianity prevailed against all odds because of the sheer persistence of early Christians and others throughout the centuries. That level of determined, dogged persistence is what Jesus sought to inspire.

The parable of the friend at midnight is couched in terms of simple yet significant everyday aspects of Jewish life. Hospitality shown to family and friends was a basic feature of Jewish social life and being a gracious host to a visitor was of great importance. The parable contrasts the urgent need of an ill-prepared host with the attitude of his friend to whom he went for help, who did not wish to be disturbed.

The factual scenario of the parable is interesting. A man was awakened around midnight by a friend who stopped by his house on a journey, apparently without advance notice. He felt obligated to welcome the visitor and provide him with food and rest, but he had nothing to serve him. He was no doubt embarrassed and totally caught off guard. Whether he had no meal with which to bake bread or found it impractical to bake bread in the middle of the night is unknown, but, in either case, he had no food to serve his guest. In Jewish society, that was unthinkable, and in desperation the host went to another friend's house in the middle of the night seeking help.

The parable provides revealing insight into Jewish home-life practices. Most homes were simple one-room structures, and the door was often left open for ventilation. If the door was closed, it was a clear "Do Not Disturb" message, and one did not bother a homeowner once the door was shut at night. Interestingly, a family often slept together on mats on the dirt floor, and this man and his children were all sleeping on their beds, and the door had been securely shut.

Suddenly, the homeowner heard someone loudly knocking on his door. "Who is it, and what do you want?" he no doubt called out. The embarrassed host pleaded, "I need help. A friend on a journey has come to my house, and I have nothing to feed him. Can you lend me three loaves of bread?"

The request was unusual and immediately caused the homeowner to question his motives. Why would two men need three loaves of bread for a midnight meal? If three loaves were prepared for three meals during the day, was the host seeking food for all the next day rather than just a midnight snack? Bread was normally eaten soon after being baked so that it would not get stale. If the sleeping homeowner had three loaves, he would have prepared them late in the day for the next day's meal. If he gave them to the empty-handed host, he would then have no bread for his children or himself the next morning.

So, in response, he told the pleading host not to bother him because the door was shut, the children were asleep, and he could not rise and help him. It is important to realize that the homeowner said this to a friend and not to a neighbor or a stranger in the night. A friend was someone with whom one had the closest relationship. It was the deepest bond of affection and affinity, even exceeding familial ties. Thus, the old proverb states "there is a friend that sticks closer than a brother" (Prov. 18:24). But, in this case, the homeowner initially refused to help even his closest friend in a time of need. His refusal to help is a surprising and shocking departure from the normal custom of that day.

However, shortly afterward, he did get up and answer the host's demands. He did so not because of their friendship, but because of the needy host's persistence, and that is the underlying message of this parable. Oftentimes, persistence can be viewed either negatively or positively. Determined efforts can be praised by expressing "persistence pays off." On the other hand, persistence can be viewed as annoying when one refuses to take "no" for an answer.

In studying the parable, it is important that neither of these ordinary views about persistence is intended. *Anaideian* is best understood as "shameless determination and boldness." It conveys the idea of being unreservedly bold and determined both in one's thoughts and desires and in the manner in which they are conveyed to others. It is the image of one who not only is determinedly insistent, but also one who has no qualms or reservations about his ideas, his beliefs, or the nature of his position on a subject. Regardless of how unusual his ideas might be to others; he boldly and repeatedly proclaims them. He does not let a negative response, indifference, or even persecution from others silence him.

It is interesting, and even slightly amusing, that because of the desperate host's persistence, his friend got out of bed—perhaps awakening his entire household—and answered the man's request. Even though the host had asked for three loaves, the friend's response implied that he essentially threw up his hands and said, "Here, take as much as you need!"

Both this parable and the parable of the persistent widow are stated as an encouragement for prayer and as a guarantee of God's benevolent desire to bless His children. Jesus queried His listeners:

> *"If a son asks for bread from any father among you, will he give him a stone? Or if he asks for a fish, will he give him a serpent instead of a fish?*

> *Or if he asks for an egg, will he offer him a scorpion? If you then, being evil, know how to give good gifts to your children, how much more will your heavenly Father give the Holy Spirit to those who ask Him!"* (Luke 11:11-13).

Thus, Jesus encouraged His disciples to be persistent in prayer: "So I say to you, ask, and it will be given to you; seek, and you will find; knock; and it will be opened to you" (v. 9). The nature of God's promised response is found in these words, "how much more." The focus is not on quantitative values, such as more versus less. Instead, the focus is on good versus better. Therefore, if an earthly father knows how to give good things to his children, consider *how much more* God will give things to His children that are immeasurably better, namely the things of heaven which are far more important than the less important things of earth.

Sadly, few Christians approach prayer in that manner. We often implore and beg God with great persistence to improve our lot on earth, but not often does one pray with the same persistent intensity for God to give them even greater spiritual blessings. Most prayers focus on asking for good things on earth and not the better things of heaven. One of the challenging lessons of this parable is envisioning what might happen if all Christians prayed with the same shameless, bold insistence for God to make them more loving, forgiving, compassionate, devoted, and dedicated. Surely in response to those persistent prayers, our Father in heaven would reply, as did the friend at midnight, "I will give you as much as you need."

The Parable of the Persistent Widow

> *"There was in a certain city a judge who did not fear God nor regard man. Now there was a widow in that city; and she came to him, saying, 'Get justice for me from my adversary.' And he would not for a while; but afterward he said within himself, 'Though I do not fear God nor regard man, yet because this widow troubles me I will avenge her, lest by her continual coming she weary me'"* (Luke 18:2-5).

Again, the parable is couched in terms of prayer commitment, but its emphasis on persistence has a broad application to the challenges of discipleship. Jesus shared the parable about the persistent widow to encourage His followers and teach them "that men always ought to pray and not lose heart" (Luke 18:1).

One's outward actions can be negatively impacted by inner weariness. It is often heard in the expression "I just don't have the heart to do that." Thus, one becomes faint-hearted, spiritually and physically weak, and loses the will to act strongly and decisively. Jesus realized that, in the face of difficulty and persecution, His disciples could easily lose heart and become defeated and demoralized by the numerous challenges they would encounter.

In order to encourage the disciples not only in their prayers but also in their discipleship work, Jesus shared this parable about a persistent widow confronting a merciless judge. It is a challenging and unusual parable filled with significant meaning.

The widow faced obstacles that were insurmountable under ordinary circumstances in her personal quest for justice. Her determination, boldness, and never-say-die attitude are an inspiration to anyone facing unanswerable challenges in life. The widow only wanted someone to avenge her and provide her justice to overcome a wrong she had suffered. With dogged determination and persistence, she would not accept defeat until she was vindicated. Her persistent determination is the lesson of this parable.

The biblical role of an avenger is instructive in understanding both this woman's plight and the power of this parable. In the Old Testament, one's avenger was most often associated with a blood avenger, or a close relative who avenged the wrongful death of another. However, in the New Testament, the avenger is described as one who seeks justice, equity, and fairness for another who has been wronged.

A woman's avenger would be her husband, since a woman had very few vested legal rights of her own. She belonged to her husband, and any wrongs she experienced were extended to him also. However, the woman in the parable was widowed; she had no relative to act as her avenger; and she possessed no rights to act on her own. This woman had no legal or equitable remedy and no other recourse to protect her rights. There was nothing she could do except begrudgingly accept the wrong inflicted on her—until she decided to take matters into her own hands and find someone to avenge her!

She also faced another impossible obstacle—the legal system. Even though she had no remedy, she nevertheless appealed to a judge to avenge her. Unfortunately, she could not have found a judge more hostile to her plea for help. Jesus described the judge as one "who did not fear God nor have regard for man" (v. 11).

It would be difficult to imagine a more merciless individual to serve in the judge's capacity. Not fearing God conveys the image of an irreverent, sinful man who had no regard for religious values or divine truth. He did not fear God because he did not revere God, and he dismissed the whole idea of God's existence and moral superiority over him.

Neither did he have any regard for man. He took no recognition of any person's value or any person's rights. He had no concern or sympathy for their needs or any desire to address wrongs they had experienced. He simply did not care about the needs of others, nor was he worried that such lack of empathy and compassion was a sin against God. He was merciless, cold-hearted, and indifferent. Simply stated, he could not have cared less about the plight of a widow who turned to him for help. She was a nuisance and nothing more, and he wished that she would simply be quiet and go away. But she would not.

In order to grasp the meaning of persistence, one must imagine the widow's desperate, pitiful circumstance and what she did. Undaunted, she made up her mind to proceed in the face of extreme adversity; not to be intimidated by the callous indifference of others; to powerfully proclaim what she personally felt was truth; and she absolutely refused to be denied or to be intimidated and silenced. She set out to gain justice where none existed; to fight for right in the face of overbearing wrong; and to chart a course to correct evil, even when she had to walk that path alone.

She demanded that the merciless judge show mercy and understanding, and against all odds and precedent, avenge her and grant justice. Her actions were unprecedented and shocking. In a society where custom dictated that a widow should remain quiet, she cried out for justice. Against an uncaring, pitiless judge, she demanded that he personally serve as her avenger and obtain justice for her, even though he had no regard for her or her needs whatsoever.

At first the judge paid little attention to her pleas. But she would not relent. She was shamelessly bold in her demands and unstoppable in her persistent pleas for justice. Finally, the judge yielded to her insistent request while grumbling, "…because this widow troubles me, I will avenge her." That is a fascinating reaction. How did she "trouble" the judge?

Literally, she got in his face and would not be quiet. She invaded his space and got up close and personal in a demanding way. The intensity of her actions is described by the judge's explanation of why he answered her demands: "Though I do not fear God nor regard man, yet because this widow troubles me I will avenge her, lest by her continual coming she weary me."

Weary has a very interesting original meaning in this parable because it actually means to "strike under the eye." The judge was no doubt getting tired of her constant demands, but two other possibilities come to mind: The judge became so exasperated and weary of hearing her demands that his face was getting puffy, and he was getting bags under his eyes, or the widow got so in his face with her demands that the judge was afraid she was going to give him a black eye!

Jesus compared the action of God to the action of the judge: "And shall God not avenge His own elect who cry out day and night to Him, though He bears long with them? I tell you that He will avenge them speedily" (vv. 7-8). It is similar to His response about "how much more" God will bless His children than will an earthly father.

What lessons can one learn from these two parables? First, they teach the necessity of bold, persistent prayer. The writer of Proverbs states that God hears the prayers of the righteous (Prov. 15:29). James, the brother of Jesus, states with assurance, "The effective, fervent prayer of a righteous man avails much" (James 5:16). Jesus instructed His followers not to engage in vain, meaningless repetition (Matt. 6:7) when they prayed, but we are instead encouraged to "…come boldly to the throne of grace, that we may obtain mercy and find grace to help in time of need" (Heb. 4:16).

God does not have to be badgered into blessing us. He is not like the merciless judge who has no regard for our needs. Conversely, He knows our needs before we even pray to Him and ask for answers (Matt. 6:8). But prayer is the most effective barometer of our Christian commitment. We pray for what we want the most, and often our prayers reflect misplaced priorities. James further commented about the manner in which many Christians pray, "…you do not have, because you do not ask. You ask and do not receive, because you ask amiss, that you may spend it on your pleasures" (James 4:2-3).

How then can we change the thoughts of our heart about prayer? These parables compel a Christian to examine their attitude toward both prayer and discipleship. There cannot be a severed connection between what one prays for and what one works for as a disciple.

Jesus often prayed, and one can only assume that He prayed for the ability to accomplish the work He had been given to do. Jesus' disciples must do the same. The priority of a disciple's prayers should be the treasures of heaven and not the pleasures of earth. They should not be shallow, repetitive, ritualistic utterings, but rather bold, dynamic requests for greater understanding of Christian truth and a greater capacity to personally reflect Christ in our daily life. Our Christian life would be dramatically changed if we asked God to bless us with the gifts of the Holy Spirit with the same intensity with which the man pleaded for bread at midnight and the persistent widow prayed to the merciless judge for help.

But, if we pray that boldly are we then ready to live that boldly for Christ? The Apostle Paul declared emphatically, "I am not ashamed of the gospel of Christ" (Rom. 1:16). Yet, many professing Christians never mention His name to others out of fear of social ostracism. These parables challenge us to do otherwise and to boldly and unashamedly confess our faith in Christ to the world. We do not have to corner every person we meet and share our Christian testimony, but we are encouraged to be persistent in our personal proclamation of our faith.

Christians are stewards and messengers of the greatest and most joyous truth ever revealed to mankind. The gospel is God's good news to man! There should be no hesitation in sharing that truth. Christian disciples should remember that persistence means shameless determination and boldness in living the truth of our faith without compromise.

Christianity prevailed because ordinary men and women committed themselves to Jesus and did just as the persistent widow did. Her actions bear repeating as a description of their actions: Christian disciples made up their mind to proceed in the face of extreme adversity; not to be intimidated by the callous indifference of others; to powerfully proclaim what they personally knew was truth; and they absolutely refused to be denied or to be intimidated and silenced. They sought justice for the oppressed where none existed;

they fought for right in the face of overbearing wrong; and they charted a course to correct evil even when they had to walk that path alone and die for their beliefs.

If these parables could change the thoughts of our hearts to do the same, our personal Christian life would be dynamically emboldened, our nation would be changed, and the gospel would be more powerfully proclaimed. Persistence is an indispensable aspect of both prayer and discipleship.

The Stewardship of Discipleship

Jesus spiritually challenged His disciples in many different ways. Specifically, their individual stewardship over heavenly spiritual treasures became very important. Jesus knew once He ascended back to the Father in heaven, the success, vitality, and world-wide impact of Christianity would be entrusted to His disciples, both collectively and individually. The future of evangelical Christianity depended on their stewardship of discipleship.

Jesus adequately prepared His disciples to shoulder their responsibility. He promised to send them a "Helper" who is the Holy Spirit (John 14:16). Further, Jesus assured His disciples that He would not leave them as orphans (John 14:18), and He would be with them until the end of the age (Matt. 28:20). As they went through Jerusalem, Judea, Samaria, and the remaining nations of the world, the Holy Spirit would fill them with divine power and give them words to say (Luke 12:12). These ordinary men, and eventually women, would become true witnesses of the transforming power of Christianity and personally validate its truth. That crucial role and responsibility is vested in us today.

Unquestionably, serving as an ambassador for Christ is an intensely personal responsibility. We are stewards of Christian discipleship. For many, it is an entirely new spiritual concept, and Jesus' parables help us better understand the stewardship involved.

Christianity is not just a belief system. It is a unique form of human life that combines the divine nature of God with the human nature of man in the form of a covenant relationship. Through this covenant, one gives his physical life to Jesus, and Jesus gives His spiritual life to each Christian. They enter into a covenant bond and become one. The Holy Spirit grows and matures the nature of Christ's life in each believer, enabling every Christian to become more like Jesus in both word and deed. Obviously, this process imposes a pronounced sense of responsibility on every Christian for the manner in which they live and reveal to others the divine life of Jesus within them. Once each Christian receives by faith the eternal life of Jesus, they immediately become a steward of that life, with the attendant responsibility not only for how Christ's life grows and matures spiritually within them but also how it impacts others.

Very few Christians see themselves in this stewardship role, and the disciples surely did not, for they knew nothing about spiritual stewardship. The disciples lived under the weight of the religious law of Israel, and they knew nothing else. Therefore, they had no understanding or appreciation of spiritual stewardship. Yet their understanding of this vital component of discipleship would determine the success of the evangelical mission of Christianity to the world. Thus, Jesus used these crucially important parables to reveal the importance of stewardship, and this fundamental truth remains vitally important to all Christians today.

Spiritual stewardship is challenging for one with a legalistic mindset because religious law does not require stewardship, only compliance. One is given nothing under the law other than guidelines and mandates for action. Compliance with law is limited to the thoughts of one's head; law does not change the thoughts of one's heart. A religious legalist does not improve the law by obsessive compliance. He may diminish it by non-compliance, but he does not enhance nor improve its meaning in the life of others by unwavering adherence. Religious law does not grow into something better. It remains static and unyielding and compels its adherents to become intractable, uncompromising, and unwilling to consider any other viewpoint. Law does not make a spiritually mature disciple; rather, it often converts him into a judgmental, merciless zealot. Regardless of how devotedly one lives by the law, his moral and spiritual compass remains cold, indifferent, unyielding legalism, and he reflects those spiritual values in life.

In contrast, through the new covenant, Jesus' perfect, sinless, eternal life is freely given to every Christian based on their faith in Him. Christians are not just given His thoughts through His teaching. Christians are given the one eternal life that God ordained from the beginning of the world that alone has the power to atone for sin, redeem mankind back to God, and serve as the light of the world. Jesus stated, "I am the way, the truth, and the life. No one comes to the Father except through Me" (John 14:6). Jesus was the embodiment of this eternal, divine life, which is given to all Christians through faith in Him.

One must realize when reading this verse that each Christian is individually vested with the way of God, the truth of God, and the life of God. Discipleship imposes personal stewardship on every Christian for each aspect of the heavenly treasures entrusted to them. The spiritual magnitude of these truths elevates Christian discipleship to the highest level of trust and stewardship. One cannot envision a greater responsibility in life.

Stewardship is best understood as a concept rooted in legal principles of trust. A few key definitions will not only help define stewardship and its responsibilities but also better demonstrate its role in Christian discipleship:

- A trustee is a person, or entity, in whom the title or managing control to real or personal property is legally placed in trust for the benefit of other specific individuals or a group. An example would be church trustees who hold the title to church property for the benefit of the church and its members.
- A steward is one who manages the property or funds of another in a trust position without holding title. An example would be a church treasurer who is responsible for the financial affairs of the church.
- A fiduciary may be either, or the role is based on a trust relationship. A fiduciary role is a trust relationship between the trustee and his principal, or the beneficiary of the trust, and is premised on absolute confidence in the ability and responsibility of the trustee to act solely for the beneficiary and not further the trustee's own interests in administering that which has been entrusted to him. Within the realm of trust, it is the highest level of care and duty owed to another.

Stewardship is the act of serving in a capacity of trust over a thing of value that has been entrusted to one's care and safekeeping. A trustee never uses what has been entrusted to him for his own benefit. Rather, he always acts with reasonable care in the best interest of the trustor. His decisions must always be prudent and aimed at improving, increasing, and enhancing the value of what has been entrusted. The goal should always be to return a greater value and worth than what was entrusted, but certainly never allow a decrease in value.

Although these definitions may seem technical and legalistic, they offer an important insight into the stewardship of discipleship and the meaning of these parables. It is fairly simple to see how these roles apply in financial situations. However, when these same concepts are applied spiritually to one's Christian life, they compel a deeply introspective evaluation of one's commitment to Christ. This level of personal responsibility for stewardship of divine truth and treasures was unknown under the religious laws of Judaism. But it was essential for the evangelical spread of the gospel throughout the world in fulfillment of Jesus' commission to His disciples, and it remains so today.

How could Jesus clearly and effectively impart an understanding of the stewardship inherent in discipleship? How could He open the disciples' minds to visualize a duty unknown to them? As a strategic method of instruction, Jesus shared two parables focusing on the responsibility of stewardship. The physical truth of these parables focuses on both faithful and unfaithful servants and their use of valuables entrusted to them. The spiritual application of these parables focuses on the faithfulness of every Christian over the priceless spiritual treasures that have been entrusted to each of us. If prayerfully examined, these parables will change the thoughts of every Christian's heart about their own stewardship of discipleship.

The Parable of Three Servants Given Talents

> *"For the kingdom of heaven is like a man traveling to a far country, who called his own servants and delivered his goods to them. And to one he gave five talents, to another two, and to another one, to each according to his own ability; and immediately went on a journey. Then he who had received the five talents went and traded with them and made another five talents. And likewise he who had received two gained two more also. But he who had received one went and dug in the ground and hid his lord's money. After a long time the lord of those servants came and settled accounts with them. So he who had received five talents came and brought five other talents, saying, 'Lord, you delivered to me five talents; look, I have gained five more talents besides them.' His lord said to him, 'Well done, good and faithful servant; you were faithful over a few things, I will make you ruler over many things.*

Enter into the joy of your lord.' He also who had received two talents came and said, 'Lord, you delivered to me two talents; look, I have gained two more talents besides them.' His lord said to him, 'Well done, good and faithful servant; you have been faithful over a few things, I will make you ruler over many things. Enter into the joy of your lord.' Then he who had received the one talent came and said, 'Lord, I knew you to be a hard man, reaping where you have not sown, and gathering where you have not scattered seed. I was afraid and went and hid your talent in the ground. Look, there you have what is yours.' But his lord answered and said to him, 'You wicked and lazy servant, you knew that I reap where I have not sown and gather where I have not scattered seed. Therefore, you ought to have deposited my money with the bankers, and at my coming I would have received back my own with interest. Therefore take the talent from him and give it to him who has ten talents. For to everyone who has, more will be given, and he will have abundance, but from him who does not have, even what he has will be taken away. And cast the unprofitable servant into the outer darkness. There will be weeping and gnashing of teeth'" (Matt. 25:14-30).

The parable is a powerfully challenging strategic story whose meaning unfolds differently than expected. Rather than portraying a mean-spirited master taking aim at an untalented servant, the parable accurately portrays the attitudes and actions of a large number of Christians. When carefully examined, the parable about these three servants, whose actions reveal life within the kingdom of heaven, is an eye-opener.

The parable revolves around the reaction of three servants who are entrusted by their master with "talents" of some kind. Two respond positively, yet the third, who receives the least, responds negatively. His reasons for inaction are noteworthy.

The parable focuses on different amounts of talents that each receives. However, our contemporary use of "talent" immediately takes one in a direction not intended by the parable. A talent today is not what it was at the time Jesus stated this parable. The parable does not focus on one being talented; it focuses on one faithfully bearing the burden of stewardship.

A talent was primarily a measure of weight. It was used in different countries that set an attached weight value based on each country's standards. Generally speaking, a talent in New Testament usage was seventy-five pounds. If it described a valuable metal, a talent was usually cast as a large ingot with a handle or grip enabling one to more easily move and carry the weight.

From a monetary value, a talent was the equivalent of the weight of six thousand denarii. A denarius was a coin—worth about twenty cents by today's standards—which was the ordinary daily pay for a worker. Therefore, a talent would equate to the salary value of sixteen- and one-half years of labor, without a day off. Using this scale, five talents would equal income for over eighty-two years and two talents would equal thirty-three years of wages.

However, there is a crucial piece of information missing in the parable: It does not state the nature of the material weighed by the talent. Since the talent was a weight measurement, each talent was seventy-five pounds of something, but we do not know what. Obviously, the value involved could vary drastically depending on the material, such as the difference between gold and copper. Whatever its nature, it was merchantable, valuable, and afforded each servant an opportunity to increase its value and to increase the weight of stewardship over his master's estate.

In truth, perhaps weight is the crucial concept in the parable and not value. At seventy-five pounds each, five talents would have weighed three hundred seventy-five pounds. Two talents would have weighed one hundred fifty pounds. Moving and transferring these heavy weights, or manipulating them for investment, would have been a chore. Two would have been obviously less, but one should note that all three of these servants had the same chore of moving one seventy-five-pound talent at the time. The first two had the burden intensified by multiple talents and increased stewardship, but they were not asked to do a task beyond their ability. How the first two servants moved and stored the heavy talents is not stated. But they did, and they used them to the eventual pleasure and blessing of the master. The third servant did not.

It is important to note the master's attitude toward each servant. He knew each one personally and had watched each of them work. He knew their abilities and limitations, their temperament, and their physical and emotional strengths and weaknesses. Thus, his entrustment of talents to them was carefully decided, and he gave talents to each servant "according to their ability." That is a fascinating and revealing standard of individual assessment by the master. One might read the parable and conclude that he was hard, demanding, and showed favoritism. That is incorrect: The master was the opposite.

The talent was a heavy weight, regardless of its substance. Each seventy-five-pound talent would have to be moved, protected, and manipulated for investment or trade. Not every servant could bear the weight of a talent easily, and especially if several heavy talents were entrusted to him. Some would be better than others dealing with the weight and burden of faithful stewardship. Therefore, the master carefully evaluated the ability of each servant and allocated talents to each based on their individual ability to bear the weight and responsibility given to them. No servant was given the weight of a talent that the master deemed him ill-equipped physically or emotionally to bear. In reality, the master made a compassionate assessment and treated each servant fairly and equitably. That truth is crucial to this parable.

The servants' reactions are a picture of the history of Christian discipleship. The servant who was given the heaviest load did exceedingly well. He handled the weight of five talents and used them judiciously and faithfully. He never complained about the burden of stewardship and used the talents for the best interests of his master, doubling the five talents to ten. In doing so, he also doubled the burden he was under and doubled the weight of stewardship. Through his faithfulness, he multiplied what had been entrusted to him one hundred percent.

The servant given two talents did equally well bearing the lesser load of responsibility for his master. Even though he could not bear the load of the first servant, he nevertheless used his lesser ability to the maximum and did the best he could. He doubled his two talents to four. Interestingly, his strength grew to the point that he was nearly as capable as was the first servant when they were originally entrusted with the weight of stewardship.

Both servants worked with their weight of stewardship, and, true to the master's assessment, did their best "according to their ability." They moved the heavy talents, protected them, invested their worth, and doubled their value. They willingly assumed the greater tasks of stewardship as the weight of their burden gradually increased.

When the master returned and asked for an accounting from each servant, he evaluated each one based on how they had handled the weight of stewardship. The first and second servants, although given different weights and different burdens to bear, both reported they had done well under the weight of their talents, and each had doubled what had been entrusted to him.

They were rewarded for their stewardship in two meaningful ways: First, the master's approval of their efforts was premised on his assessment of their inherent moral and spiritual character combined with their faithfulness and devotion to him. Each of the first two servants was described as a "good and faithful servant." "Goodness" defines a unique form of inner goodness that manifests itself outwardly in acts of grace and benevolence, and one possessing this goodness is incapable of any other action or behavior.

Jesus described this level of goodness through an analogy about a plant. Regarding faithful discipleship, He stated:

> *"You will know them by their fruits. Do men gather grapes from thorn bushes or figs from thistles? Even so, every good tree bears good fruit, but a bad tree bears bad fruit. A good tree cannot bear bad fruit, nor can a bad tree bear good fruit. Every tree that does not bear good fruit is cut down and thrown into the fire. Therefore, by their fruits you will know them"* (Matt. 7:16-20).

Consequently, the servants' stewardship over their talents was a consequence of their spiritual goodness that naturally led to a whole-hearted commitment to their master. They could have done nothing else.

The master also described each of them as faithful, which defines a trust relationship and bears a unique relationship to "good." Once a servant becomes totally persuaded that his master is true and just with him, he unconditionally and uncompromisingly commitments himself to his master to such a degree that he is incapable of dealing falsely with his master or with that which the master entrusts to him. He is totally loyal, and thus his master finds him completely trustworthy. No thought of infidelity enters the servant's mind, and no thought of doubt enters the master's mind. Because of the servant's inner goodness and his total loyalty, the master has complete trust in him. There is no higher level of stewardship.

Therefore, "faithful" describes the characteristics of a relationship premised on the highest order of loyalty and duty. It more appropriately describes the emotional commitment of one to another. The master hoped for the highest level of commitment from his servants when he entrusted the talents to them, and the evidence which he saw of that commitment was their doubling the talents through stewardship. These two servants were so committed to their master that he could have total reliance and confidence in their inner goodness and their desire to serve him only and advance his interests, and not their own. Thus, he found them faithful.

Their reward was an experience of joy that transcended their status as a servant. It is difficult to imagine life as a servant being joyful. However, as a reward for their goodness and faithfulness, the master bestowed his joy on them—his personal joy and the abundant, joyful life he knew within his kingdom.

The concept of joy expressed in this parable is important, for the good and faithful servants were invited to "enter into the joy of your lord." There is a spiritual difference between experiencing joy and entering the joy of another. One may personally have a joyous experience resulting from a personal act. It is his alone, and he alone knows the reasons for and depth of his joy. His joyous moment is private and personal, until his joy is shared with others. The master's joy will always be greater than the servants' joy. As the servants' stewardship increases, the master's kingdom increases, and so does the master's joy. It is a never-ending process of joyous spiritual increase for both master and servants. That is the nature of the kingdom of heaven.

The master's joy was not a giddy, euphoric joy, but rather a deep, joyous contentment based on the nature of his realm and the grace he expressed in bestowing blessings on his servants. One must understand that the master never expected more than a servant could do, he never gave a servant an impossible mission, and all he bestowed on each servant was carefully calculated to grow them in stewardship and in their appreciation of the value of the riches of the master's kingdom.

In response, their stewardship was not a labor of obligation under law, but rather an experience of personal opportunity under grace. Thus, the master viewed the efforts of the first two as "well done," and invited them to enter into the abundant joy of his kingdom. The master did not have to reward them. It was not their joy of achievement based on works; it was the joy of the master's love based on grace. They did not earn their master's joy; they entered into the pre-existing joy of their master that was graciously given to them.

The master then provided them with a way to increase their joy—he increased the burden of stewardship, their responsibilities to him, and their personal role in the advancement of their master's kingdom. It was an increasing joy and reward based on faithful stewardship over a constantly increasing kingdom. As their stewardship increased, the kingdom increased. As the kingdom increased because of their faithfulness, their joy increased, as did the master's. There was no limit to any of these. Thus, because they had been faithful with a few things, the master entrusted greater things to them. It was not a physical reward but rather increased responsibility and stewardship. The servant owned nothing. All with which he was entrusted belonged to his master. But, as the responsibility increased, so did the joy of service and the satisfaction of furthering the master's interests.

This parable contains a significant phrase relevant to Christian discipleship. Before departing, the master assembled his servants and "delivered his goods to them." The phrase denotes far more than simply distributing talents to his servants. The concept of goods not only describes possessions that are immediately identifiable, but it also encompasses possession of valuables and treasures that have long pre-existed and been under one's control and possession and that are now "at hand." These possessions are now ready for one's use or to be assigned and given to another for immediate use. The pre-existing treasures, when entrusted to another, provide a new beginning through goods, valuables, and treasures that one had no hope or expectation of possessing. These long-existing treasures, which are so valuable to the owner, are entrusted, committed to, and handed over to another to exercise stewardship over them.

Two important concepts are evident: Jesus declared the kingdom of heaven and all of its spiritual treasure was "at hand" and could become the possession of any disciple through repentance. Thus, the heavenly treasure, which God has possessed since the beginning of time, is ready to be used and enjoyed by all Christians. When a disciple receives these blessings through faith, he enters into a new relationship with God and experiences a new beginning—"old things have passed away; behold, all things have become new" (2 Cor. 5:17).

Jesus told His disciples, "It is to your advantage that I go away" (John 16:7). It is through Jesus' ascension back to the Father that the goods and treasures of the kingdom of heaven are entrusted to His disciples for their benefit and spiritual growth through the power of the Holy Spirit. Through entrusting the riches of the kingdom to them, Jesus will find whether or not each disciple is a good and faithful servant.

The reward experience for faithful stewardship is incalculable. Though entrusted with a "few things," the faithful servants were made rulers over "many things." These words describe treasures, possessions, and blessings that are vast, plenteous, and so exceedingly high in number they cannot be accurately counted. To "rule over" these blessings means that the faithful steward is put in charge and given standing authority over them for his use and blessing. These spiritual possessions and blessings are firmly set and established for every Christian disciple. How firmly are they set and established? The Apostle Pau described the security of God's love for all believers in this manner:

> *"For I am persuaded that neither death nor life, nor angels nor principalities nor powers, nor things present nor things to come, nor height nor depth, nor any other created thing, shall be able to separate us from the love of God which is in Christ Jesus our Lord"* (Rom. 8:38-39).

The same sense of security applies to all spiritual blessings of the kingdom of heaven. They are forever set in place for all faithful Christians. In the case of the servants in the parable, the master had given one servant five talents, another two talents, and the third servant received one. But there was no limit to what these could grow into as they continued to increase the talents. One never reaches the maximum limit of discipleship and stewardship in Jesus' work, and one never reaches the maximum experience of spiritual joy experienced through faithful discipleship.

Christian joy is a divine, heavenly joy not derived from any earthly experience or possession. It is spiritual and emotional, not physical. It is the joy of God that has existed from the foundation of the world based on His desire to give, bestow, and bless those who faithfully believe Him with all the blessings of the heavenly kingdom. Jesus said, "Do not fear, little flock, for it is the Father's good pleasure to give you the kingdom" (Luke 12:32). Simply stated, it is God's eternal plan and purpose to give all that He has to His spiritual children because of His limitless grace and through their faith in Christ. This divine pleasure and joy has always existed with God because it has always been His desire to share this joy. Thus, the angelic proclamation of Jesus' birth was declared to the entire world with "good tidings of great joy which will be to all people" (Luke 2:10).

The joy of delivering and sharing the redemption plan of God was known by Jesus—despite all of His earthly persecutions—and He specifically encouraged His disciples to "make My joy complete." Therefore, as a Christian, by faith and through repentance, we enter into and experience the joy of Christ—which is the pre-existent joy of redeemer God. The disciple's joy is not his own; he enters into the joyous purpose of God.

The joy of the kingdom is a new and everlasting life, free and forgiven, empowered by the Holy Spirit, and blessed with all the spiritual treasures of the kingdom of heaven. Our personal efforts have nothing to do with it; it is not earned. This experience of joy is a gift that our heavenly Father has been waiting to bestow on us since the beginning of time. When we enter into His redemptive purpose for our life through faith in Jesus, we make God—along with all the angels in heaven—exceedingly joyful, and we enter into and share that divine joy with Him.

In stark contrast, the servant given one talent experienced none of his master's joy. His fear cost him everything. Fear is toxic to faith. Fear never produces joy. Fear is reactionary, not visionary. Fear paralyzes, it does not energize. Fear is a curse, not a blessing. Fear is the opposite of faith. The servant given one talent immediately froze with fear. There is no indication that he attempted to do anything with the talent entrusted to him. He could not have been overwhelmed by the weight of stewardship entrusted to him because the master gave to each servant "according to his ability." He was not overloaded by the burden of stewardship; rather, he was overcome by both his fear of failure and his fear of change.

The reason for his inaction merits close study, for it reveals a similar reticence in many Christians to fully commit themselves to a life of dynamic discipleship. When later questioned about his opinion of his master, the servant with one talent stated, "Lord, I knew you to be a hard man, reaping where you have not sown, and gathering where you have not scattered seed." What does this mean? What did the scared servant truly feel about his master?

One word in his statement is very revealing. "Hard" describes something that is unyielding and stern. Considering that was his opinion of his master, his motivation for service was fear rather than love and devotion, and thus it was a joyless relationship. It was pure obligation with no sense of personal desire or achievement. "Reaping where you have not sown" is a proverbial expression meaning that one does all the work while another gets all the credit. Thus, the servant was filled with resentment because the master got all the praise and reward for the servant's work.

No doubt he often asked himself, "What do I get out of this? It's all the master's, and I get nothing. All of my efforts go to making him look better and making him richer. There is nothing in this for me except hard work and sacrifice, and I get nothing in return." His service was a boring, burdensome obligation and he did only what was minimally required, and he resented having to do even that.

Neither Jesus nor any of the disciples received any personal earthly reward for their service. In fact, Jesus specifically stated, "For I have come down from heaven, not to do My own will, but the will of Him who sent Me" (John 6:39). In stark contrast, the scribes and Pharisees were primarily motivated by their hypocritical desire for public recognition for their prayers, charitable giving, and fasting (Matt. 6:5). They loved being seen wearing their purple linen robes of apparent wealth, and they coveted the choice seats of highest recognition at public gatherings. The Gospel of John notes that while many of the religious rulers believed in Jesus, the Pharisees did not, "…lest they should be put out of the synagogue; for they loved the praise of men more than the praise of God" (John 12:42-43).

Consider the following aspects about the servant's attitude:

- He was unwilling to commit himself to endless hours of labor for the master's benefit, knowing he would receive no earthly reward or recognition.
- He had no concept of his master being loving, compassionate, and gracious. Instead, he saw him as stern, demanding, and unyielding.

- He had no realization of his personal stewardship to advance and expand the interests and realm of his master.
- He was more focused on himself than his master.
- He only desired to maintain the status quo; he made no changes in what was given to him and took no chances with it.
- He was a legalist; law and tradition were his only talents. He viewed his only obligation to his master as simply preserving what had been entrusted to him intact and unchanged.
- He wanted the glory for his preservative work. Hearing that his master "reaped where he did not show," he was unwilling to do the work of stewardship so that his master would receive the benefit and credit. He was, as Jesus referred to the Pharisees, one who enjoyed the praise of men more than the praise of God.

Thus, the servant did nothing. His greatest desire was to keep things just as they were, make no change, follow tradition, habit, and custom, and condemn those who did otherwise. He felt his greatest duty was to preserve and protect his one talent and simply return to the master what had been entrusted to him, unscathed, unchanged, and unused. In response to the trust placed in him, the servant buried his one talent in a hole and made no effort to do anything except preserve and protect it so that no change or loss would occur. That is the attitude of a religious legalist.

But that was not what the master desired, and that was not the purpose of the test of stewardship. The master knew that his kingdom would never increase if his servants did nothing with the talents entrusted to them. Digging a hole, burying the talent, and preserving it unchanged were the opposite of the master's desire. He wanted to see his realm grow and increase, and that could occur only through the devoted work and stewardship of his servants who were focused on their master and his glory, and not themselves.

Thus, unlike the other good and faithful servants who entered into the dynamic joy of their master, the unfaithful servant experienced no blessing or reward from his master and had no sense of the master's good pleasure. His conservative, fundamentalist attitude left him joyless, frustrated, suspicious, and jealous of the blessings bestowed by the master on those who were different. The master, unimpressed and angry, referred to the servant as "wicked and lazy." Because of his reluctance to advance and enhance the master's kingdom in any manner, the master condemned him as evil—the exact opposite of good and faithful.

There is a somber element in this parable that must be considered. The master viewed the first two servants as "good and faithful" and the third as "wicked and lazy." Those are not casual descriptive words because they determine both reward and judgment. Disciples who are good and faithful enter into the master's joy and grace and are abundantly blessed with greater treasures within the master's realm.

Those who are wicked and lazy are deemed by their master as disinterested in his kingdom, reluctant to do his work, and unready to be entrusted with his treasure. Understandably, the master takes from them any talent of stewardship and entrusts his work to those who are good and faithful. A wicked and lazy servant is left with nothing except the darkness of despair and the "weeping and gnashing of teeth" that results from divine judgment on evil.

One of the sad realities of contemporary Christianity is the number of frustrated, indifferent, lazy church members who view their Christian life as nothing more than a religious obligation to be relatively good and moral and occasionally attend church. They have no desire to do more than that for Christ.

A parable portrays two parallel truths, and one must look for the spiritual truth within the related physical account of the parable's story. Consequently, if the spiritual weight of Christian discipleship entrusted to us is symbolically comparable to the physical weight of the talents entrusted to the servants, we begin to find the parable's spiritual meaning and its application to our life today. Christian discipleship involves more than just going to church and being a good person. If we could see the covenant life of Jesus as the pearl of great price, or the treasure buried in the field, that we are willing to give up all else in order to acquire, and God graciously entrusted it to us by faith, how do we see our stewardship over the incalculable value of that heavenly treasure?

If we were one of the servants and the master gave us one million dollars in talents to invest and expand his kingdom, how would we have responded to the burden of that responsibility? Similarly, how are we responding to the weight of responsibility for expanding the kingdom of heaven through the life of Christ? How heavily does the weight of stewardship over Jesus' life burden us? Do we strive to enhance the richness and meaning of His life within our own earthly experience and the lives of others? How are we investing His life in the world around us? Do we have a personal plan and purpose for sharing the gospel in a way that expands Jesus' kingdom? Do you see yourself as an individual trustee over the value of His life and take great responsibility for using the talent given to you in order to increase His heavenly kingdom? How are you bearing up under the weight and burden of the stewardship of discipleship?

These parables are direct challenges to change indifferent attitudes about stewardship through repentance and view commitment to Christ as the greatest and most joyous opportunity afforded in life. We are blessed with differing gifts, and God wishes to use us according to our individual ability. One should shun the comfort zone of tradition and habit and boldly allow the Holy Spirit to multiply one's talents and abilities to serve Christ greater than ever imagined. Do not be afraid to let God change the thoughts of your heart, the attitudes of your mind, and the abilities and work of your hands and thus mold you into a good and faithful servant.

The Parable of the Minas

> *"A certain nobleman went into a far country to receive for himself a kingdom and to return. So he called ten of his servants, delivered to them ten minas, and said to them, 'Do business till I come.' But his citizens hated him, and sent a delegation after him, saying, 'We will not have this man to reign over us.' And so it was that when he returned, having received the kingdom, he then commanded these servants, to whom he had given the money, to be called to him, that he might know how much every man had gained by trading. Then came the first, saying, 'Master your mina has earned ten minas.' And he said to him, 'Well done, good servant, because you were faithful in a very little, have authority over ten cities.' And the second came, saying, 'Master, your mina has earned five minas.' Likewise he said to him, 'You also be over five cities.' Then another came, saying, 'Master, here is your mina, which I have kept put away in a handkerchief. For I feared you because you are an austere man. You collect what you did*

not deposit and reap what you did not sow.' And he said to him, 'Out of your own mouth I will judge you, you wicked servant. You knew that I was an austere man, collecting what I did not deposit and reaping what I did not sow. Why then did you not put my money in the bank that at my coming I might have collected it with interest?' And he said to those who stood by, 'Take the mina from him, and give it to him who has ten minas.' (But they said to him, 'Master he has ten minas.') For I say to you, that to everyone who has will be given; and from him who does not have, even what he has will be taken away from him" (Luke 19:12-26).

The parable of the ten servants given minas, while similar to the parable of the three servants given talents, is in many ways a prophetic assessment of contemporary discipleship. The parable's setting is during a time in which the master is gone away, and the servants are left to their own abilities to advance the master's kingdom through the minas entrusted to them.

In the parable of the three servants given talents, each one is entrusted with differing amounts, possibly of great value. In contrast, the servants in this parable are each treated equally, with each one receiving a single mina. None are given a mina "according to his ability" as were the three with talents. Thus, all ten servants were equally blessed, equally called to be a good servant, and equally gifted to do the master's work.

The master's instruction and the gift of the mina are important. A mina was a monetary measure (it could also apply to weight) equivalent of one hundred denarii. A denarius was a coin used for one day's pay for a laborer. Therefore, the master gave each servant one hundred days wages and instructed them to "do business till I come." In essence, the master told each servant to live, trade, carry on with your life, and do my work while I am away, and the mina will supply your needs while I am apart from you. There is no reason why each of the ten servants could not have been productive in their master's work while he was gone, and certainly that is what he expected. But that is not what occurred.

One of the most noticeable aspects of this parable is the small number of faithful, productive servants. Although ten were given minas, only two increased their master's work while he was separated from them. Seven of the ten are not mentioned again, and the reason is unknown. They do not give an accounting, and no description of their stewardship is given. One is left to wonder if they squandered the blessing of the mina on themselves and abandoned their master never to be seen again. Thus, only two out of ten were faithful.

The Old Testament provides an interesting comparison. When Gideon assembled an army to fight the Midianites, he began with thirty-two thousand men, but after excluding those unwilling or unable to fight, he was left with only three hundred men—about one percent of his original number (Judges 7:1-7). Yet God granted him and his faithful few a great victory.

Of the original twelve disciples, and removing unfaithful Judas from the number, several are not mentioned again. They were all equally called, but not all equally served. The application of that truth to modern Christian discipleship is obvious.

The parable's setting provides insight into its purpose. Jesus was passing through Jericho, only a few miles from Jerusalem. In recording the parable, Luke stated, "He spoke another parable because He was near Jerusalem and because they thought the kingdom of God would appear immediately" (Luke 19:11).

It was believed the Messiah would suddenly appear in Jerusalem, manifested by amazing signs and wonders and cataclysmic upheavals of nature, especially cosmic phenomena. That is why Satan tempted Jesus to turn stones into bread and to leap from the highest pinnacle of the Temple without injuring Himself as a sign of His messianic nature. Jesus knew His kingdom was spiritual and not of this world physically, and He refused Satan's temptation. Rejecting the belief that His kingdom would immediately appear, as was expected, Jesus stated, "The kingdom of God does come with observation; nor will they say, 'See here!' or 'See there!' For indeed, the kingdom of God is within you" (Luke 17: 20-21).

Thus, Jesus explained that the revelation of God's kingdom would not be sudden and physical, but instead would be a gradually increasing spiritual reality manifested to the world through the redeemed lives of faithful stewards who, through repentance, would advance His work and His kingdom after He ascended back to His Father. However, a significant percentage of Jesus' followers do not become personally involved in His work. It is the age-old story of God's people: Most are waiting for Jesus to make things right for them, and He is waiting for us to make things right for Him. He has called and gifted every Christian to engage in His redemptive work, but most do not.

The parable of the minas represents a time when all of the master's servants are equally called and gifted, but only a small percentage is actually good and faithful. Why? Some are too lazy, indifferent, and unconcerned, and some waste their master's mina on blessings for themselves and the fruitless pursuit of earthly riches and pleasure. Others are reluctant and will not become involved and leave their personal comfort zone. They prefer not to be seen as overly religious and incur the skepticism of family and friends. They never speak out nor stand out and are indistinguishable from others. They provide no outward indication of their covenant life with Christ, and that is sad.

There is, however, another reason for the failure of stewardship over the master's business, and it is represented by the servant who hid his mina in a handkerchief—fear. As did the servant with one talent, this servant feared his master because he was an "austere" man. His attitude was similar to the servant with one talent who viewed his master as a "hard" man. Whereas the one-talent servant considered his master to be hard and unyielding, this servant viewed his master as a grim, strict, and severe taskmaster who exacted every ounce of toil and sweat from his servants without any expression of gratitude or reward.

In offering an excuse to his master for his inactivity, he stated, "You collect what you did not deposit, and reap what you did not sow." Again, as in the case of the one-talent servant, this phrase implies that one gets all the credit for work done by another. Thus, because of his consuming fear of his master, he was afraid to do anything with the mina and afraid to involve himself in his master's work.

He realized the master expected his servants to expand his kingdom and do business while he was absent, yet he had no idea what to do. Rather than being a visionary steward, he resorted to the traditional confines of the past. To alleviate his fear of the future, he tried to find security and comfort in the cultural and religious traditions instilled in him. He rejected the challenge of dynamic stewardship and instead chose the confines of the law.

Not being able to visualize anything else to do with the mina, he wrapped it in a handkerchief and put it away, keeping it stored unchanged and unused until the master returned. All he was requested to do, so he thought, was keep the mina just as it had been entrusted to him. His attitude was to take no action, take no risk, make no changes, do not disturb the past, leave things just as they are and maintain the status quo.

His action clearly reveals his attitude. Interestingly, the handkerchief in this parable was a cloth much different to a modern handkerchief. It could indeed be used to wipe perspiration from one's face, but its more formal use involved bathing the face of the dead and being placed over the deceased's face in burial. Because of its presumed contact with a dead body, the handkerchief in the parable would have been considered religiously unclean, and no one would have touched it—a perfect place to hide the mina. The servant wrapped his mina in the legal ritual of death, rendering him unable to serve his master in any capacity while he was away, and he defiantly did nothing.

The problem remains with us today. Many Christians are scared and reluctant to become involved in a life of dynamic discipleship and do nothing with the treasures of the kingdom entrusted to them. They, too, have wrapped their mina in the facecloth of spiritual death.

The servants who wisely and effectively used their mina were abundantly blessed, but the master took the mina from the unfaithful servant and gave it to the one who had ten minas. Is there a lesson we can learn from the master's actions? Maybe the truth is a bit broader than we think. Christian servants who devotedly use their heavenly blessings to expand and increase their Master's kingdom will experience continued blessings, giving them an ever-increasing capacity to serve Him.

Conversely, servants who are more focused on the past than on the future, who wrap their blessings in past habits that appeal to no one, and who are content to see their spiritual life slowly die wrapped in a death cloth of spiritual indifference will eventually lose what level of interest and commitment they might have had. They exemplify a spiritual life that has no vision, no purpose, no joy, no passion, and no reward. They make no difference for Christ in the world and are useless to their Master in advancing His kingdom.

Surveys show increasing disinterest in Christianity and church attendance. It is easy and simplistic to dismiss this trend as just a sign of the times. Using the ten servants as a model, perhaps the key to spiritual revival lies not with the small percentage of Christians who are faithful and devoted, but rather with the large percentage who take the blessings of God and disappear into the mass of humanity around them, never to be seen or heard again.

Repentance involves a spiritual and moral reversal from a self-centered life of indifference to the work of a devoted servant of Christ. It involves nothing less than one's total transformation from a lazy and wicked servant to a good and faithful servant unwaveringly committed to increasing his Master's kingdom. That was Jesus' strategic purpose in sharing these parables.

The Parable of the Unproductive Fig Tree

"A certain man had a fig tree planted in his vineyard, and he came seeking fruit on it and found none. Then he said to the keeper of the vineyard, 'Look, for three years I have come seeking fruit on this fig tree and find none. Cut it down; why does it use up the ground?' But he answered and said to him, 'Sir, let it alone this year also, until I dig around it and fertilize it. And if it bears fruit, well. But if not, after that you can cut it down'" (Luke 13:6-9).

There are two fig trees in my enclosed backyard that were once in a pasture area. For years, their low-hanging limbs were a convenient back scratcher for cattle grazing in the pasture, providing an easy way to get rid of bothersome insects. The animals made so many circular, back-rubbing trips around the trees they wore out large ruts in the ground, leaving the soil packed so hard it held water for days after a rain. The trees were bushy, undergrown with weeds and briars, and seldom produced an abundant crop. Now their condition is much different, and their use has greatly changed. Once they became part of the expanded yard, I cleaned around them and filled the ruts with soil and compost, allowing the top roots to grow into soft, fertile soil. The change in their appearance and productivity was remarkable.

The transformation exemplifies a parable Jesus told about a fig tree that had not produced figs for three years, and the owner was ready to cut it down. However, the keeper of the vineyard requested the owner to give the tree one more year, during which the keeper would dig around it, loosen the soil, and apply fertilizer (animal waste), thus transforming the hard ground into good soil. If it did not then respond, the owner could cut it down. We are not told if he did so. That is not the intent of the parable.

There are important lessons about our spiritual life that can be learned from this unique parable. The fig tree is one of the historic symbols for Israel. For example, Micah the prophet spoke of a future day of peace for Israel:

> *"They shall beat their swords into plowshares, and their spears into pruning hooks; nation shall not lift up sword against nation, neither shall they learn war anymore. But everyone shall sit under his vine and under his fig tree, and no one shall make them afraid"* (Micah 4:3-4).

Thus, one may say the fig tree in this parable represents Israel and Jesus' teaching new truths for three years, which the defiant religious conservatives rejected.

Even though Jesus clearly warned Israel about God's judgment for denying the gospel, nevertheless there was an additional period of time granted to them. Following Jesus' crucifixion and resurrection, the gospel spread throughout the Roman Empire for the next four decades, but the defiant and headstrong Jews of Israel continued to deny its truth. In A.D. 70, the Romans completely destroyed Jerusalem, and Israel ceased to exist as a nation until 1948. However, the gospel continued to spread and ultimately became the official religion of the Roman Empire. The Christian nations of Western Europe later emerged, generating America's religious and political origins.

Regardless of this historical narrative, maybe there is another truth in this parable that speaks more directly to the issue of Christian discipleship. If animals trodded out a packed, rock-hard rut around my trees, could they not have done the same to the tree in the parable? Could the hardness of the soil around the tree be the key to understanding the parable? Maybe its truth focuses on how hard and resistant people can be to new ideas and deeper concepts about God's redeeming love for all people.

In the parable of the soils, Jesus spoke of the gospel seed falling on an area packed hard by human traffic. The seed never had a chance, immediately died, and was eaten by birds. Some seed also fell on rocky soil that appeared good and fertile on the surface, but was solid as a rock underneath, causing the seed to wither and never mature. The seed that fell in good soil, however, produced an amazingly abundant crop, far exceeding expectation (Matt. 13:18-23). Thus, the focus of this parable is the transition of the soil around the fig tree from impenetrably hard to soft and fertile.

Jesus spoke to a nation that revered religious tradition above all else. In that kind of environment, this parable recognizes that repetitive, meaningless, ritualistic religion will so harden one's heart and mind that new understanding about God will never sink in. Consider, for example, Jesus' statement "Do not think that I came to destroy the Law or the Prophets...." The phrase means when any new idea was introduced, the immediate reaction was a defensive refusal to even hear it (Matt. 5:17). When Stephen, an early follower of Jesus, was stoned to death for his faith, his accusers placed their hands over their ears to avoid hearing his testimony about Jesus (Acts 7:57).

Some people are like that today. They adamantly refuse to consider new truth or new ideas that may alter their lifelong way of understanding God. That kind of mental reluctance is exactly what Jesus struggled against in revealing the gospel. He tried to break through the hardened religious mentality of a society in which it was unlawful to think any new thoughts about God, other than those approved by the rabbis and High Council.

Therefore, Jesus recognized that time is necessary for the nurturing of new ideas. That is why He used so many parables to stimulate thought. Consequently, in this parable, the vineyard keeper was mercifully given more time to loosen and fertilize the hard, compacted soil and allow the new truths of the gospel to germinate in good soil and grow. Maybe the fact we are not told that the tree was later cut down indicates that it did.

The enormous challenge Jesus faced in transforming religious thought is largely unappreciated by most Christians. Israel was founded on concepts of religious law that had expanded over centuries into a voluminous legal code defining virtually every aspect of religious and social life. The outspoken religious conservatives considered any violation of the law as sinful and demanded strict adherence to its every facet. Anyone who advocated any other interpretation of the religious law or departure from the traditions of the elders of Israel was branded as a heretic worthy of death.

Consequently, Jesus knew when He began teaching a new understanding of the law that He was putting His life on the line and would ultimately be condemned and crucified. Likewise, the disciples individually understood that association with Jesus would likely result in their arrest and condemnation, which helps explain Peter's denial of Jesus and the other disciples' consuming fear after Jesus' arrest and crucifixion.

Jesus fully understood the difficulty of transforming thought that was otherwise chiseled in the rock-hard stone of religious tradition. The people had known no other religious concepts for generations and were strangled by fear in considering any other ideas. Thus, the gospels record the gripping portrayal of Nicodemus, a respected religious leader who desired further explanation of His teaching, coming to Jesus at night under the cover of darkness because of his fear of being seen talking to Him (John 3:1-2).

One must comprehend the mental hardness of religious thought and understanding that Jesus had to penetrate in order to plant the seed of the gospel. He fully knew the truth of Christianity would not be eagerly and immediately embraced by God's covenant people because of the hardness of their heart and their reluctance to consider new ideas. And, quite honestly, it never changed. Christianity's greatest growth was in the Greco-Roman world outside of Israel.

The new covenant of grace through faith in Jesus is a means of extending the promises of God to a new covenant community throughout the world not bound by the shackles of Jewish religious law. Despite the size of Christianity worldwide, Israel still has not accepted the teaching of Jesus. Indeed, the soil around the fig tree of Israel remains packed so hard it will not allow the living water of divine truth to penetrate.

In many ways, the same issue applies today, even within the church. The Christian heritage for many is rooted in a deeply conservative and fundamentalist interpretation of scripture, premised on a strict legalistic interpretation of the Bible. With this mindset, it is easy to condemn others for violation of some religious legal standard or to shun others who are different physically or racially. The transition to a deeper Christian attitude of love and acceptance of others, as taught by Jesus, is not easy for many and often takes years, or even a lifetime. Loosening the soil under our own fig tree and making it fertile for the seed of the gospel to grow is one of the greatest challenges of discipleship, and it only occurs through repentance and the work of the Holy Spirit transforming us spiritually into the image of Christ.

The word of God is a living word, going to the very core of our heart and mind and revealing new, amazing truth about Jesus and God's love for us. God gave us a brain to use for a greater purpose than keeping our ears from rubbing together. Do not be afraid to use it. An open mind is good, fertile soil in which the seed of new thoughts can germinate. Grow in the word and allow your heart to become softened. Allow the Holy Spirit to fill your mind with fresh new thoughts, insight, and understanding about God's love for you and for others. The fruit you bear will multiply greater than you can imagine.

The Parable of the Unjust Steward

> *"…There was a certain rich man who had a steward, and an accusation was brought to him that this man was wasting his goods. So he called him and said to him, 'What is this I hear about you? Give an account of your stewardship, for you can no longer be steward.' Then the servant said within himself, 'What shall I do? For my master is taking the stewardship away from me. I cannot dig; I am ashamed to beg. I have resolved what to do, that when I am put out of the stewardship, they may receive me into their houses.' So he called every one of his master's debtors to him, and said to the first, 'How much do you owe my master?' And he said, 'A hundred measures of oil.' So he said to him, 'Take you bill, and sit down quickly and write fifty.' Then he said to another, 'And how much do you owe?' So he said, 'A hundred measures of wheat.' And he said to him, 'Take your bill, and write eighty. 'So the master commended the unjust steward because he had dealt shrewdly. For the sons of this world are more shrewd in their generation that the sons of light. And I say to you, make friends for ourselves by unrighteous mammon, that when you fail, they may receive you into everlasting habitations"* (Luke 16:1-9).

A man once said of a prominent, successful acquaintance, "He is a good Christian man, but you better watch him." His sage advice simply meant one could freely worship with him on Sunday but be careful doing business with him on Monday. What a sad and troubling observation to make about another individual, but unfortunately it applies to many Christians. Interestingly, however, there is an element of truth in that statement worthy of consideration. The individual was no doubt a Christian, but he had a keen eye and sharp mind bent on protecting, preserving, and advancing his personal interests and holdings. That was his foremost interest. His devotion and dedication to advancing the work of Christ was secondary.

Yet Jesus specifically told His disciples not to lay up treasures on earth that are easily lost or destroyed, but rather to layup treasures in heaven that are eternally safe, secure, guaranteed, and protected by the power of God. Very few Christians follow His advice. But, what if we did? What changes would occur in our personal spiritual life, the life of our church, and the life of our nation if Christians committed themselves to the work of Christ with the same fervor they possess in pursuing their own interests?

Stewardship applies to both the treasure of the kingdom of heaven and the treasure of a good and godly life on earth. Living life in a manner that glorifies Christ is not reserved for Sunday. One of the sad realities of Christianity is the failure of Jesus' disciples to live by the beliefs they advance. Generally, we do not adhere to the tenets of our faith. We can boldly proclaim them and encourage others to believe them, but we do not consistently practice them ourselves, and that is hypocritically sad.

One of the fundamental principles of the Christian faith is one's covenant promise to Jesus to place His spiritual kingdom of heaven above and beyond our own earthly interests and desires. We cease living exclusively for ourselves, and we live for Him alone as our Lord and Master. Thus, His work and the advancement of His kingdom should be our greatest priority in life, but generally it is not.

This parable employs a fascinating and peculiar twist of logic. One should not read the parable as a divine endorsement of duplicity and unfaithfulness. However, the parable poses an interesting contrast between the commitments of Christian servants to advancing their own interests versus their commitment to advancing the work of Christ.

As an example, consider Jesus' relationship with Judas. Why did Jesus not immediately dismiss Judas as one of the twelve disciples because of his thievery and under-handed dealings with others? Judas was responsible for stewardship over offerings and contributions given to Jesus and the disciples for their ministry, yet he routinely took money from the treasury box for his own use (John 12:6). Surely, Jesus knew this, yet there is no record that Jesus confronted or reprimanded Judas for his thievery and embezzlement. Could it be that Jesus often pondered about Judas' stewardship in his earthly business dealings compared to his indifference to the work of Christ's kingdom and wondered how He could get equal commitment and determination from him?

Is it possible Judas wanted to be treasurer of a political government he hoped Jesus would establish? Unquestionably, Jesus sensed Judas' obsession with money, but Jesus also noticed something else about this disciple. Judas was also hedging against the possibility that all his dreams about position, prestige, and power would come to naught, and he was embezzling money and hiding it for his own future use and protection. Is that why he ultimately betrayed Jesus for thirty pieces of silver? He placed his own interests ahead of his master and decided he would reap as much financial gain as he could in order to protect himself. Was there a time when Jesus looked at Judas and thought to Himself, "I do not appreciate him taking money from Me, but I have to admire his shrewd determination to take care of himself in the future. I only wish he was as devoted to Me as he is to his own self."

One must remember the disciples did not fully understand that Jesus spoke of a heavenly kingdom within them spiritually compared to a physical, political kingdom in Israel, which all the disciples longed for. In fact, they openly discussed who among them would have the greatest role in the kingdom they believed Jesus would establish (Luke 9:46), and even the mother of James and John pleaded with Jesus to allow her sons to sit at His left hand and right hand in the new government (Matt. 20:20-28). Interestingly, immediately prior to Jesus' ascension back to heaven, the disciples asked Him, "Lord, will You at this time restore the kingdom to Israel?" (Acts 1:6). Clearly, Jesus saw this obsession with personal gain and advancement and their posturing for prized political positions as exceeding their commitment to the work of His spiritual kingdom.

Is it possible this parable grows out of Jesus watching His disciples dreaming and fantasizing about how rich, powerful, and influential each would be in the new kingdom and arguing about which of them would be greatest (Luke 9:46)? Did He ponder within His own mind how he could get equal or greater commitment and devotion from them to their spiritual work as His disciples? If Jesus looked at the actions and attitudes of His first disciples in that questioning manner, does He still look at our actions and attitudes in the same way today?

In many ways, this parable may be viewed as a hypothetical "what if" parable. "What if" Christians were as equally devoted to furthering the work of Christ as they are their own interests? What if all Christians yearned for spiritual possessions as much as they desire physical possessions? What if our shrewd, calculating desire and ability to enhance our earthly physical life were applied with equal fervor to enhancing our Christian spiritual life? What if every Christian understood that stewardship over physical possessions entrusted to us by our Master also applies to spiritual dimensions of life?

How could Jesus change the thoughts of His disciples' hearts and generate a profound new level of spiritual stewardship akin to their own stewardship over earthly blessings? He told them a parable about a shrewd servant, and He followed the parable with critically important statements every Christian should examine.

True to the parallel concept of a parable, the scenario involved facts that occasionally happened. A wealthy man heard an accusation that one of his servants was "wasting his goods." It is unknown whether the steward's actions were intentional or unintentional. However, the master called the servant before him for an accounting, "for you can no longer be steward."

Fearfully realizing he now faced a quandary—for he could not dig and do manual labor and he was ashamed to beg—the steward betrayed his loyalty and stewardship to his master even greater. He cunningly and shrewdly decided to convert obligations others had to his master into obligations to himself by telling each of his master's debtors to significantly reduce their debt to his master. In effect, he said to them, "I am taking care of you and helping you, and if and when I need it, I expect you to help and take care of me. You don't owe my master what you thought you did; now you owe me!"

The master learned of the servant's duplicity and commended him for his shrewd tactics, rather than condemning him. "Shrewdly" describes an action that is sensible, prudent, and wise from the perspective of the one taking the action, regardless of whether others agree or disagree. Despite his irritation with the servant, the master nevertheless saw a level of determination and self-preservation in him that was commendable and noteworthy.

Reflecting on the actions and attitudes of His disciples, Jesus made a sobering assessment about people's decision-making strategy, "For the sons of this world are shrewder in their generation that the sons of light." Jesus simply, yet profoundly, observed that most people are far more sensible and prudent about taking care of themselves in the world than they are in taking care of themselves in the heavenly realm, and He was right.

A simple comparison of the strategy, planning, and work that one does in seeking earthly treasure compared to one's effort of seeking heavenly treasure is shocking. Those pursuing the treasures of earth are far more adept and capable in their persistent strategies than are those seeking the treasures of heaven. That truth is evident today, and the disparity is steadily increasing.

Jesus' comment at the conclusion of this parable reveals His sobering foresight regarding His disciples' commitment level: "And I say to you, make friends for yourselves by unrighteous mammon, that when you fail, they may receive you into everlasting habitations" (v. 9). He had watched these men closely, and He had heard them discussing their desire for prominent positions within an earthly kingdom. Jesus knew that some would fail in their discipleship efforts within the kingdom of heaven once they understood its true spiritual nature. They were not going to be rich and famous; rather, they were destined to poverty, hard work, and physical and emotional sacrifice in their service to Him, and some would not be willing to endure the pain and hardship. What were they to do when they failed?

In a statement revealing an unusual element of acceptance, understanding, and compassion, Jesus told them to make friends with those in the world so that if and when their courage failed, or the earthly things on which they placed greater value were lost, they would at least have some level of personal security. Jesus' statement is quite personal.

Jesus then stated a revealing assessment of Christian discipleship commitment: "He who is faithful in what is least is faithful also in much; and he who is unjust in what is least is unjust also in much" (v. 10). Jesus fundamentally believed that a true disciple—one who is a good and faithful servant—does not live by dual standards of commitment and reliability. The faithful way in which he handles the little things in life is the same standard by which he handles the larger and more meaningful responsibilities in life. He does not need to be second-guessed or watched over because his master finds his spiritual goodness and faithfulness unwavering and trustworthy.

Thus, Jesus carefully watched His disciples and silently evaluated both their commitment level and their believability and reliability. He evaluated them not on the larger level of commitment to the broad nature of His heavenly kingdom, but rather on the small issues of everyday life. If they were faithful in the little things that seemed relatively unimportant, then He could count on them to be faithful in their higher commitment to His heavenly kingdom. For example, in the case of Judas, Jesus evaluated Judas' ability to be a good and faithful servant not on his work as a disciple or in his ministry to others, but rather on what Judas did with a single coin entrusted to him to place in the collection box. When Jesus saw Judas steal one coin, He knew Judas would steal all the coins.

It was this dichotomy and duality in commitment Jesus observed in His disciples that prompted His profound statement, "No servant can serve two masters; for either he will hate the one and love the other, or else he will be loyal to the one and despise the other. You cannot serve God and mammon" (v. 13). Why did Jesus say that? Because He had observed the human struggle between physical and spiritual desires in His disciples, and He knew they could not give equal devotion to Him and to their earthly dreams. If one is to be a good and faithful servant, a crucial life-changing decision must ultimately be made between the two. They cannot be simultaneously served.

This parable is deeply challenging because it compels every Christian to determine one's ultimate priority in life—the kingdom of heaven or the kingdom of this world. Once that decision is firmly and unconditionally made and the kingdom of heaven becomes one's greatest priority, then the personal spiritual and physical qualities of a good and faithful servant appear in that Christian's life as naturally as good fruit abundantly grows on a good tree, and the servant of Christ will be known by the fruit he bears (Matt. 7:16-17).

A New Definition of Duty

Parable of the Master and Servant

> *"And which of you, having a servant plowing or tending sheep, will say to him when has come in from the field, 'Come at once and sit down to eat?' But will he not rather say to him, 'Prepare something for my supper, and gird yourself and serve me till I have eaten and drunk, and afterward you will eat and drink?' Does he thank that servant because he did the things that were commanded him? I think not. So likewise you, when you have done all those things which you are commanded, say, 'We are unprofitable servants. We have done what was our duty to do'"* (Luke 17:7-10).

Beginning with his bar mitzvah at age thirteen, every Jewish male assumed a duty to the law of Israel. The duty was not primarily viewed as a personal duty to worship and serve God, but rather a duty of fidelity to the ancient religious laws of Israel and to the customs and traditions of the elders of the nation. Every male had a duty to obey the law, comply with all Jewish religious ritual, observe and celebrate religious feasts and holy days, and maintain an attitude of reverence and loyalty to the tenants of Judaism. Failure in the performance of these basic religious obligations cast one as a sinner.

Many individuals, especially the scribes and Pharisees, sought to create a public persona of righteousness and favor with God through public prayers, charitable actions, and fasting. These ritual obligations were done as openly as possible, such as standing on the street corners to pray, so others could observe and admire. A direct correlation existed between performance of religious duty and the expectation of public reward and recognition for being a devoted "son of the law."

However, as often occurs when the experience of worship shifts from spiritual to physical, religious duty produced personal pride and a judgmental condemnation of those less devoted to those religious standards. Jesus condemned these public prayers and charitable acts, saying they were done only to be seen by others and not out of devotion to God, and He accused those flaunting their religious practices of seeking the commendation of man rather than the approval of God (Matt. 6:5).

The religious legalist, such as a scribe or Pharisee, not only views duty and loyalty to religious ritual as the foundation of his religion, but he also considers his personal fulfillment of religious ritual as essential to his religion's character and continuation. Thus, his duty to the law and to the traditions of the faith is needed by God for continuation of the faith, or so he thinks. He does not depend on God to perform religious ritual, but rather believes God is dependent on him. In his heart, He sees himself as an indispensable asset to God, and he condemns others who are not as equally committed to his narrow, traditional view.

The haughty attitude of those committed to religious duty is seen in the anger of the older son upon the return of his prodigal brother (Luke 15:28) and in the resentment of the workers in the vineyard who had worked all day but received no more than those who had worked only one hour (Matt. 20:11-12). In both cases, there was an expectation of greater reward than others received because of their work and commitment. Legalists have no concept of grace, unmerited reward for duty not performed, and divine blessings not personally earned.

Inherent in this religious mindset is an overriding expectation of reward. It is not a monetary reward, but rather the reward of public recognition as a godly person, respect, and deference from others, holding positions of authority and influence, and expectation that one's decisions and desires will be respected and granted because of his work record. Quite often, when these are not received, the legalist will become angry and intolerant of others not sharing his views. In his opinion, he has earned the respect he is due by faithful performance of his religious duties, and he feels everyone should recognize that. However, in this parable, Jesus described an entirely different view of duty completely opposite to this traditional attitude.

There are several reasons why a moral or religious duty arises in relationship to another:

- A duty arises from a natural or assumed relationship. For example, a father has a duty to his children and to his wife to provide love, protection, and sustenance.
- A duty arises from a responsibility. An employer has a responsibility to his employees, a doctor to his patients, a

lawyer to his clients, and a teacher to their students. The examples are numerous.

- A duty arises from a trust. There is a legal and ethical duty to do one's best to preserve and protect something that has been entrusted.
- A duty arises from a commitment. If one commits himself to a task, he has a duty to faithfully complete the work.
- A duty arises from identity. A citizen identifies themselves as an American and they have a duty to uphold American values, principles, and beliefs. The same is true for Christians.
- A duty arises from a calling. If one is divinely called to perform a specific work, there is a duty to perform the task with utmost competence and fidelity.
- A duty arises from a gift. If one is uniquely gifted with a talent—especially one that benefits his fellowman or glorifies God—there is a duty to faithfully use the gift to the fullest extent.

Interestingly, many gifted people expect praise and adoration for the performance of their duty, especially those gifted with a recognized talent. Every singer expects applause at the conclusion of a performance. But, in truth, should the performance or completion of work that one is duty-bound to perform be rewarded by human standards? Should a father expect his children to praise him for being a good dad? Should a husband expect praise from his wife for his duty to care and provide for her? Should a citizen expect public recognition for regularly voting?

Jesus shocked His listeners by implying that it is wrong to expect commendation or reward for the performance of an ethical or religious duty. In doing so, He sought to change the thoughts of those who served God in order to receive the compliments of man.

This parable is premised on the relationship of a master and his servant. A servant was under the total control and direction of his master, and his duty arose from that relationship and the work that he dutifully performed with no expectation of reward. In the parable, a master has a servant working in a field. According to Jesus, when the servant returned from the field, he would not expect his master to serve him a meal. Instead, it was his duty as a servant to prepare his master a meal and then he would eat afterward. The servant would have no expectation of reward for the performance of his fundamental duties because it was expected of him. It would be inconceivable that the servant would say to his master, "I have plowed your field and tended your sheep. Now, prepare me a meal as my reward and you can eat after I do." Rather, the servant would have continued serving his master and performing the minimum expected from him. He would not have been offended, felt anger, or thought he was abused. It was his basic duty.

Applying the strategic reasoning of the parable, Jesus said to His listeners, "So likewise you...." In surprising, if not shocking, contrast to the expected reward for duty, especially religious duty, Jesus employed two phrases as an eternal redefinition of ethical and religious obligation:

(1). "We are unprofitable servants..." established a completely opposite standard to the attitudes and expectations of the religious legalists of Jesus' day. Whereas many thought that the continuation of Judaism was indispensably dependent on them and their adherence to the law and tradition of the elders, Jesus stressed that one's true attitude in the performance of an obligation to God should be viewing oneself as an unprofitable servant.

According to Jesus, duty is not motivated by reward, but rather by devotion, loyalty, and stewardship. A good soldier does not fight a battle in order to get a medal; rather, he fights because it is his duty. One's attitude should remain unchanged by faithful performance of a basic obligation, and their faithful efforts should not produce pride, expectation of reward, a demand for recognition, or a feeling of judgmental superiority toward others.

In the parable, the servant saw himself as unprofitable to his master—literally of no personal value—and unworthy of reward or commendation. In his humility as a humble servant, he neither considered himself as personally possessing nor contributing anything of enhanced value to his master. If the concept of "worth" is viewed as a measurable standard of value, then the servant saw himself as "worth-less," because in the performance of his basic duty as a servant, he added no additional value to his master's estate. His attitude was the complete opposite of arrogant religious pride and the accepted definition of duty and reward.

(2). "We have done what was our duty to do." "Duty" describes a moral duty that is the highest level of ethical responsibility, either to God or one's fellowman. Borne out of the deepest concepts of one's essential morality and fundamental ethical goodness, this level of duty is work and service that must be done for God or others as an expression and extension of one's basic goodness and responsibility. It is what one cannot restrain himself from doing as an expression of his moral and ethical nature with no thought of reward or commendation. In reality, he views his duty as the least he can do for God or others, and he is burdened by the reality that he has not done more.

In the parable, the servant realized he was morally, legally, and ethically obligated to his master, and his duty was undiminished by personal attitudes or wavering emotions. He did not allow his circumstances to define his duty; instead, he allowed his duty to transform his circumstances.

This parable demands personal spiritual introspection and answers to the following questions:

- What is my true relationship to Jesus? Is He Lord and Master in my life and am I His humble servant? If so, what is my duty to Him?
- What is my Christian responsibility to the church and to the work of the heavenly kingdom? Am I fulfilling that duty?
- If Jesus entrusted His eternal life to me in a covenant relationship, how am I fulfilling my duty to live His life?
- Am I totally committed to Jesus above and beyond all else in life? Do I see fulfillment of that responsibility as my greatest moral and spiritual duty?
- Do I unashamedly identify myself as a Christian, regardless of what others may think or how they may react? Am I fulfilling my duty to live my Christian faith openly and gloriously?
- What is my Christian calling? Am I fulfilling that duty to the fullest extent?
- What spiritual or physical gifts has God uniquely given to me that I can use in His service? What is the nature of my spiritual duty to use those gifts for His glory?

Finally, there is another question about duty that every Christian must ask, and it is of foremost importance: When our life is over and we face the Lord, do we expect reward or commendation from Him, or do we simply want to hear Him say, "Well done, good and faithful servant; you have fulfilled your duty to Me"?

The Fallacy of Bigger is Better

The Parable of the Rich Man and His Barns

"The ground of a certain rich man yielded plentifully. And he thought within himself, saying, 'What shall I do, since I have no room to store my crops?' So he said, 'I will do this: I will pull down my barns and build greater, and there I will store all my crops and my goods.' And I will say to my soul, 'Soul, you have many goods laid up for many years; take your ease; eat, drink, and be merry.' But God said to him, 'You fool! This night your soul will be required of you; then whose will those things be which you have provided?' So is he who lays up treasure to himself and is not rich toward God" (Luke 12: 16-21).

Religious legalism lends itself to a spiritually destructive trap of self-reliance. Essentially, the focus is not on faith for one's righteous relationship with God, but rather reliance on one's own efforts and works. Personal compliance with religious law does not make one spiritually consecrated to God. Mechanical robots programmed to perform a function do not have emotion and feelings about the impact of their actions on others, and neither do zealous religious legalists. Religious ritual does not produce spiritual righteousness. One of Jesus' great challenges was injecting emotion—love, compassion, mercy, and forgiveness—into the mechanical ritual of religious law. In order to accomplish that, He had to move the focus of religious endeavor away from the individual and redirect it toward God.

The Jewish preoccupation with personal wealth and status was one of the major stumbling blocks in this spiritual transition. Presumably, obedience to the religious laws of Israel and to the traditions of the elders produced favor with God, who then abundantly blessed one with material wealth, status, and recognition as a righteous and godly person. That was the life focus of most traditionalists, especially the scribes and Pharisees. Jesus countered this concept by personally owning nothing and by having no interest in worldly possessions. As an example, He once said, "Foxes have holes and birds of the air have nests, but the Son of Man has nowhere to lay His head" (Matt. 8:20).

Some of Jesus' most specific statements and parables pointed out the fallacy of relying on wealth and material blessings as evidence of one's righteous relationship with God. Among those is His parable about the rich man and Lazarus; His statement that it is easier for a camel to go through the eye of a needle than for a rich man to enter the kingdom of heaven; His question, "What does it profit a man if he gains the whole world but loses his soul?; and His litany of charges against the scribes and Pharisees for their devious ploys in gaining wealth and property by cheating others (Matt. 23:1-39). This parable is directly aimed at the foolish attitude of self-reliance versus reliance on God.

The concept of a "storehouse" is at the heart of Jesus' statement. In the Sermon on the Mount, Jesus warned against laying up treasure on earth versus laying up treasure in heaven. The terms for treasure and storehouse are virtually identical and inseparable. It is not like a modern version of money and a bank, which are separate entities and concepts. In Jesus' day, one's storehouse (depository) was his treasure, and his treasure was his storehouse. Stated differently, everything that one relied on for sustenance, safety, and security was kept in one's storehouse; thus, one's storehouse was the greatest treasure of his life and was the focus of his life and his labor.

In this parable, the rich man's barns were his storehouse. Whatever treasure they contained was there only because he had earned it without reliance on another or reliance on God, or so he thought. The accumulated earthly treasure belonged only to him, and he owed no one an expression of gratitude, even God. His only expression was self-congratulation. This was a prevalent attitude, especially among the Pharisees who were "lovers of money" (Luke 16:14).

However, Jesus countered the fallacy of dependence on earthly treasure with this powerful parable. It would have been shocking and deeply troubling to those who first heard it, even as it is too many today. The parable actually focuses on attitude because the rich man did not build the bigger barns. Rather, the parable is about his inner thought process and what he considered doing to assure himself greater security, safety, comfort, and peace in life. His answer was to acquire more earthly treasure and take no thought about spiritual values. What a vivid portrayal of life both then and now.

The man was already rich, but he wanted more. He had no inner peace, no contentment, and no gratitude for his present possessions. Enough is never enough; there had to be more. The god of greed is never placated.

As a wealthy man in Jewish society, he possessed more than many others could imagine. He had social status and acceptability; he was deemed in favor with God and abundantly blessed because of his wealth; and he was considered a righteous man. But, with all his earthly riches, he was not rich with God. Just as Jesus compared the Pharisees to white-washed tombs full of dead men's bones (Matt. 23:27), this man may have been rich on the outside, but he was spiritually impoverished on the inside. In all of his planning, he never thought about God, prayed for divine guidance, or expressed gratitude for divine blessings. As he "thought within himself," he thought only of himself. He was self-centered, self-absorbed, and self-glorifying. His attitude is very alive today.

This rich man is an example of greed and self-aggrandizement. In his desire to show his success and wealth, foster his pride, prove his right relationship with God, and provide visible evidence of God's blessings, he boastfully thought within his sanctimonious and self-confident self, thusly:

- "I seemingly can do no wrong. I am a living example of how God blesses good people."
- "I am successful at every level, and there is no apparent end to the success of my efforts."
- "Everything I touch turns into additional wealth, and I desire to increase my earthly wealth to the maximum extent."
- "I not only want more, but I also want all I can get. My desire for wealth and status is limitless."
- "God must be pleased with me because of the earthly treasure I have accumulated."
- "I am successful, recognized, admired, and respected. I want more so that my status as a good, godly, and righteous man will only increase."
- "How can I accomplish this goal? My barns are my storehouse, so I will build bigger barns to hold more

goods—more earthly treasure—to further my sense of success, safety, and security."
- "All that I desire in life will come from bigger barns filled with more goods and earthly treasure."

Sadly, in all of his planning and evaluation of the future, he never thought of God. He envisioned only continued success and a good, happy life. He spoke boastfully and confidently to himself about the result of his labor and efforts, "I will say to my soul, 'Soul, you have many goods laid up for many years; take your ease, eat, drink, and be merry.'" He saw nothing ahead, but a long, successful life based solely on his own efforts. Life was good, and it would continue to be as far as he could visualize.

But Jesus concluded the parable with a shocking twist: What if that very night that man's soul—the one to which he boasted about his success—is required of him? Jesus could not have asked a question more contrary to the parable's premise of wealth and happiness. The traditional Jewish concept of an after-life did not encompass the blessed, eternal life in heaven with God that Jesus promised. Death involved descending into Sheol—the abode of the dead—and its dark, uncertain nature was essentially the opposite of the bright happiness the rich man enjoyed in life.

"Required" is a sobering concept. It is the reality that one's soul (his life) is given to him by God and now God demands it back, and in doing so, exacts what is due Him for the use of the life He has given. One might think of it as the action of the master in the parables of the servants given talents and those given minas when their master demands an accounting of their stewardship. Because the rich man had only laid up treasure on earth for himself and had never laid up treasure in heaven for God, he had nothing to spiritually show for his use of the divine treasure of life.

Thus, he went from abundant earthly wealth to eternal spiritual nothingness in the blink of an eye. He had it all, and he lost it all. Jesus extended these dire consequences to all who possess this prevalent attitude by stating, "So is he who lays up treasure to himself and is not rich toward God." This rich man, dreaming of bigger barns, is the prime example of Jesus' question, "What does it profit a man if he gains the whole world and loses his soul?"

Jesus said that any person willing to take that risk is a fool. The concept describes an individual who does not possess a perspective of the future consequence of his present action, especially the relationship between how his actions and attitudes in his physical life impact his eternal life. He has no understanding of cause and effect and willfully and imprudently ignores the reality of how his actions today determine the nature of his life tomorrow. He is foolishly short-sighted, focuses only on the present, and possesses no overall perspective of life. Just as the rich man said to himself, if he can eat, drink, and be merry today, why worry about tomorrow?

Sadly, in spite of Jesus' specific admonition in the parable, this attitude still exists today. People obsessed with wealth and status have not changed, and Jesus' opinion about their foolhardy actions has not changed. Parables are strategic stories that can change the thoughts of our heart through repentance. Anyone who foolishly thinks that the ultimate meaning of life is found in building bigger barns should prayerfully consider this powerful parable of divine truth.

The Fallacy of Riches Versus Righteousness

Parable of the Rich Man and Lazarus

> *"There was a certain rich man who was clothed in purple and fine linen and fared sumptuously every day. But there was a certain beggar named Lazarus, full of sores, who was laid at his gate, desiring to be fed with the crumbs which fell from the rich man's table. Moreover the dogs came and licked his sores. So it was that the beggar died and was carried by the angels to Abraham's bosom. The rich man also died and was buried. And being in torment in Hades, he lifted up his eyes and saw Abraham afar off, and Lazarus in his bosom. Then he cried and said, 'Father Abraham, have mercy on me, and send Lazarus that he may dip the tip of his finger in water and cool my tongue; for I am tormented in this flame.' But Abraham said, 'Son, remember that in your lifetime you received your good things, and likewise Lazarus evil things, but now he is comforted, and you are tormented. And besides all this, between us and you there is a great gulf fixed, so that those who want to pass from here to you cannot, nor can those from there pass to us.' Then he said, 'I beg you therefore, father, that you would send him to my father's house, for I have five brothers, that he may testify to them, lest they also come to this place of torment.' Abraham said to him, 'They have Moses and the prophets, let them hear them.' And he said, 'No, Father Abraham, but if one goes to them from the dead, they will repent.' But he said to him, 'If they do not hear Moses and the prophets, neither will they be persuaded though one rise from the dead'"* (Luke 16:19-31).

The parable is not a condemnation of wealth; rather, it is a condemnation of unmerciful spiritual coldness, which was rampant. As Jesus journeyed around Israel, the gospels reveal numerous times when the blind, crippled, and those with various diseases begged Him to mercifully heal them. Multitudes of sick people came to Him seeking help and healing. One is left with the conclusion that very little was done to assist the sick and destitute, except for that given by family and friends.

For many, this parable is simply about a rich man who went to Hades, while a poor beggar went to heaven, and, in reality, that is the bottom-line result. But the reason this occurred is far more important and is seldom seriously studied.

The ancient Jewish view of God's kingdom focused on a physical, earthly realm. Thus, divine blessings likewise were viewed physically, such as good health, wealth, and a large, respected family with many offspring, especially sons. Material possessions and personal riches were the most obvious measurement of divine blessings for those with this viewpoint. Many today still employ the same standard.

To better understand how deeply this belief was entrenched in the ordinary understanding of many, consider the disciples shocked inquiry when Jesus said it was easier for a camel to go through the eye of a needle than for a rich man to enter heaven. They quickly asked, "Who then can be saved?" (Mark 10:26). The predisposed attitude was that all wealthy individuals were in favor with God, regardless of how spiritually cold, arrogant, and unmerciful they might be.

After Jesus had spoken about the impossibility of serving both God and mammon (wealth), the Pharisees, "who were lovers of money, also heard all these things, and they derided Him" (Luke 16:14). Literally, they arrogantly turned their nose up at Him. One can imagine them asking in a huff, "Who do you think you are, and what gives you the authority to advise us about our wealth?" This was a pervasive attitude that Jesus set out to change, and He told this parable to change the thoughts of their hearts.

The rich man was extravagantly wealthy. His beautiful robes were fashioned from a very expensive and highly sought-after linen made from costly Egyptian flax or cotton that was elegant, delicate, and difficult to obtain. These exquisite robes were accentuated with fabric dyed a luxurious purple that highlighted his extreme wealth and symbolized he was among the elite culturally and economically. Publicly wearing such finery and hearing the jealous comments and audible gasps of envy would have been the ultimate ego trip for him.

The rich man's house would surely have been large and elaborately decorated. Every aspect of his personal appearance, his home, and his lifestyle was magnificent. He lived splendidly, was the epitome of wealth and success, and he wanted everyone to know it and admire him as a righteous man greatly blessed by God with earthly treasures, which he valued above all else. Surely, his earthly blessings would continue in perpetuity within the heavenly realm when he died, and no one doubted that.

But, inwardly, he was a cold, cruel, merciless shell of a man who cared not one bit about the plight of the poor and the indescribable suffering around him. He was unfazed by pleas for mercy, unmoved by obvious hunger and suffering, and totally devoid of the slightest desire to help the suffering poor around him.

A starving beggar named Lazarus was laid at his front gate by someone hoping the rich man would help him. Lazarus was emaciated and covered in open sores that the mongrel street dogs licked. That was his only source of a soothing balm for his festered skin lesions, but it helped. The rich man ignored him and turned a deaf ear and a cold heart to his pitiful pleas for mercy.

It has been said that people in that day, especially those whose every meal was a feast, often used stale, day-old bread to wipe their cooking utensils and even the food residue from their hands. The bread scraps were dropped to the floor and later thrown to the hungry dogs wandering the streets. Lazarus begged the rich man for pieces of this bread, but his pleas were ignored. The rich man had more compassion for a hungry dog than he did for a starving human.

At death, he found himself tormented in Hades and begging for Lazarus, who was in Abraham's bosom, to bring water for his scorched tongue. His eternal fate was the exact opposite of his beliefs about what his wealth, power, and luxurious life would gain him. With all his personal wisdom about making money, he foolishly deluded himself into a spiritual catastrophe and carried many, who so deeply admired him, to a similar fate. How tragic.

It is fascinating that even in torment, which he never expected, the rich man clung to his cherished religious traditions. He did not ask God for mercy; rather, he asked "Father Abraham." Abraham was greatly revered as the father of Judaism, and he was widely referred to as Father Abraham. But, rather than finding mercy, Abraham not only denied his plea for help, but instead reminded him just how wrong his attitude in life had been. Abraham said to the tormented rich man, "Son, remember that in your lifetime you received your good things, and likewise Lazarus evil things, but now he is comforted, and you are tormented" (v. 25).

One should note in his statement the complete reversal of the expected reward for good and evil. It would have been a shocking aspect of this parable to those first listeners, and also for many today. The rich man would have certainly expected his blessings to continue into his afterlife, but they did not. His life focused only on physical blessings and not spiritual, and his eternal reward reflected that. He is a classic example of one who laid up treasures on earth and not in heaven—in direct contrast to Jesus' admonition (Matt. 6:19-20). Thus, at death his earthly treasure turned into a spiritual curse.

In contrast, the poor beggar, upon whom society and the rich man had dumped evil things, found spiritual comfort because he had laid up treasure in heaven. He was not only poor physically, but he was also poor in spirit, which allowed him to inherit the kingdom of heaven (Matt. 5:3). The idea of such a spiritual inheritance based on spiritual poverty and not spiritual arrogance and entitlement would have been inconceivable to the rich man.

The rich man had the lowest possible view of Lazarus as a human because of his poverty. He considered him to be evil in God's sight, and in his sight, also. Broadly interpreted, the word for evil also means inwardly rotten, poisoned, and foul, and that adequately describes how the rich man viewed Lazarus, especially with his open sores. It was personal: He could clearly see Lazarus, smell his reeking body, and clearly hear his pleas, yet he callously ignored him. For him, that justified passing by Lazarus, even though close enough to touch him.

Lazarus was the opposite of the rich man in every conceivable measurement, except one—the status of his soul. In death, their roles became reversed. The rich man was now suffering and tormented by the consequences of his cold, merciless indifference. Whereas, he once stood close beside Lazarus and could have personally brought him comfort, now he pleaded for Lazarus to come stand beside him in torment and provide him with similar relief. The word for comfort in the parable describes physically coming to and standing beside another, calling out to them, and providing comfort and relief.

Abraham told the rich man that was now impossible. Because of his attitude in life, he could not experience Lazarus' eternal comfort in death, and neither could Lazarus experience his eternal anguish. The gulf between the spiritual blessings of those who lay up treasure in heaven and those who only layup treasure on earth is so vast that it cannot be crossed. In effect, Abraham told the rich man, "He cannot enter your torment, even to comfort you, and you cannot enter into his blessings. In life, you refused to enter into his suffering and show him compassion, because of the great religious gulf between the rich and the poor, and now there is an equally wide spiritual gulf that prevents him from entering into your suffering and bringing you the same comfort in death that you denied him in life."

The tormented man then made another unusual request, because he realized how wrong he had been, but it was too late. The rich man begged Abraham to send Lazarus to his father's house and warn his five brothers, "lest they also come to this place of torment." But Abraham also had an interesting response for that request, "They have Moses and the prophets; let them hear them" (v. 29). Abraham thus stated that, if his brothers followed the true spiritual intent of the law and obeyed the prophetic calls for mercy, obedience, and repentance, they would not suffer the rich man's fate, because they would fulfill the law's purpose. By implication, Abraham likewise told the rich man he would not be in torment either, if he had lived by the spiritual tenets of the law, rather than interpreting it to fit his preconceived prejudices and purposes.

The rich man persisted, however. He pleaded, "No, Father Abraham; but if one goes to them from the dead, they will repent." It is a fascinating statement. He in effect stated, "My brothers may not respond by spiritual faith; but they will respond to physical facts. They may believe if they see a powerful physical sign. Please send them physical proof by allowing a dead man to live again and tell my brothers this is true." Abraham said, "If they do not hear the law and the prophets, neither will they be persuaded though one rise from the dead" (v. 31).

Is this the reality of the great gulf—the broad chasm—between heaven and hell? Is it the gulf between faith and fact? Does it describe the eternal consequences of those who steadfastly refuse to respond in faith through a personal commitment to the spiritual truth of God's word? Numerous times the Pharisees and scribes demanded of Jesus, "What sign will You perform then, that we may see it and believe You? What work will You do?" (John 6:30). The essence of Satan's temptation of Jesus was to make Him do just that—make believers through inspiring them with some great, amazing physical act. Law focuses on facts; faith focuses on belief.

When Jesus raised Lazarus (the brother of Martha and Mary, not the Lazarus of this parable) from the dead, what greater sign of

His divine power could He have given? Instead, the religious leaders immediately began plotting how they could kill Him. Indeed, if they would not believe Moses and the prophets, neither would they believe one alive from the dead. Jesus' resurrection is God's greatest proof of the truth of the words spoken by Jesus, but those who refuse to accept the spiritual demands of God's word and instead live by their cold, dogmatic adherence to religious law do not accept the power of His resurrected life either.

Indeed, there is a gulf between those who live by rigid, religious law and unmercifully apply it to others and those who live by faith. The difference is as distinctive as the difference between the torment of Hades and the comfort of heaven. If one will not cross over the chasm between merciless law and redeeming love in life, neither can he go from the torment of Hades to the comfort of heaven in death.

For those who adhere to the principles of cold, religious law in their relationship with others, and who believe that God's blessings can be calculated and measured as if they were printed out on a ledger sheet, the parable of the rich man and Lazarus is Jesus' effort to change the thoughts of their heart.

The Rewards of Preparation

Parable of the Wise and Watchful Servants

> *"Blessed are those servants whom the master, when he comes, will find watching. Assuredly, I say to you that he will gird himself and have them sit down to eat and will come and serve them. And if he should come in the second watch, or come in the third watch, and find them so, blessed are those servants. But know this, that if the master of the house had known what hour the thief would come, he would have watched and not allowed his house to be broken into. Therefore, you also be ready, for the Son of Man is coming at an hour you do not expect." (Luke 12:37-40).*

This parable is filled with a degree of mystery and also an abundance of amazing, divine blessings. In its broadest depiction, the servants are watching for the return of their master, who was attending a wedding feast, and they were uncertain about the time of his return. Because the duration of wedding celebrations was unpredictable—often spanning days in length—the master could return unannounced at any time. His servants would be expected to welcome him home, wash his feet, provide clean clothing, and prepare him a meal. Thus, they should be alert and ready any time of the day or night to gird themselves in their servant's clothing at the sound of the master's voice, or his knock on the door, and faithfully serve him. That was their fundamental responsibility.

Jesus drew on this basic duty of servants, who were essentially personal slaves, to convey an amazing spiritual promise to Christian servants who are ready to dutifully serve their master at any time. The manner in which Jesus changed the role of the master and servants in the parable would have been shockingly unbelievable to His followers, and it continues to be for many Christians today.

Equally shocking is the underlying concept of the master for whom the servants were watching. This parable is not necessarily about the second coming of Jesus, although that certainly can be an interpretation. It is deeper, broader, and more personal than our anticipation of a future event. Rather, it is about Christianity today and how faithful, watchful servants of Christ live.

For centuries, Israel struggled with the concept of the messiah and when he would appear, the physical manifestations of his power, and the nature of his messianic reign on Earth. It was universally believed the messiah would suddenly appear amidst cataclysmic upheavals of nature and the cosmos, often referred as "The Day of the Lord" (Joel 2:31; Acts 2:20). The true messiah would prove his authenticity through miraculous signs and wonders, defying human ability and understanding. In keeping with this belief, skeptics once asked Jesus, "What sign will You perform then, that we may see it and believe You? What work will You do?" (John 6:30). And, of central importance, through his messianic work, the messiah would rid Israel of her enemies through military force and power, ushering in a golden age of peace and prosperity. The whole Jewish messianic concept was physical in nature.

But Jesus' kingdom is spiritual, and it is the opposite of popular messianic concepts, both then and now. Jesus specifically stated, "My kingdom is not of this world" (John 18:36). Further, in contrast to the belief that the messianic kingdom would be physically visible around them, Jesus declared that His kingdom is spiritually invisible, and He emphatically stated, "…the kingdom of God is within you" (Luke 17:21). Most important to this parable's meaning, Jesus told His disciples that He did not come to destroy the religious law, but rather to fulfill its purpose and meaning within them spiritually, and that would occur through the changed attitudes of their heart and the resulting change in their actions.

If one is to understand the magnitude of Jesus' struggle in changing the disciples' understanding of the nature of the kingdom of heaven from physical to spiritual, ponder the disciples' question to Jesus immediately prior to His ascension back to heaven, "Lord, will You at this time restore the kingdom to Israel?" (Acts 1:6). Having followed Him for the duration of His ministry and having heard His truths and observed His miraculous works, the disciples still did not comprehend the true nature of the kingdom of heaven, which Jesus said was "at hand" and readily available to them (Matt. 4:17). Instead, they continued desiring the establishment of a political kingdom of power that would impose the rigid demands of religious law on others by force. Many Christians today are no different.

In order to address this entrenched religious attitude, what strategy could Jesus have employed that would have impacted and potentially changed the thoughts of His disciples' hearts? Jesus thus told this parable focusing on the spiritual rewards of those servants who vigilantly watch for the master (the true messiah) to appear and reveal the ultimate spiritual meaning, purpose, and power of His heavenly kingdom. The parable paints a powerful contrast between the reward of those who just methodically go through the mundane ritual of messianic expectations and watchfulness compared to those who are vigilantly seeking and waiting for the ultimate truth of God's word to be revealed, and their vigilance is constant, uninterrupted, and focused on the true messiah and not themselves.

Many contemporary Christians do not possess this watchful mindset. They fundamentally believe Jesus will physically return a second time and do exactly what the Jews anticipated the messiah would do: rid the country of sin and corruption, impose religious-based law and order, and validate His power through amazing signs and wonders. Their singular focus is on Jesus eventually correcting all of the wrong around them when He returns, and they essentially do nothing to address the sin and spiritual coldness and corruption of the world themselves. With fervent expectation, many wait for Jesus to appear and change the world for them through His physical kingdom. Jesus, on the other hand, waits for them to change the world for Him through the power of His kingdom within them, as they faithfully serve as His true witnesses in the world.

In delving into the background of this parable, consider how Jesus clearly spoke of His kingdom in a shocking and surprising manner, one that even today most Christians struggle to comprehend. Rather than being an earthly political and military dynasty based on the imposition of force, Jesus described the kingdom of heaven as a transforming spiritual experience uniquely personal to each believer and premised on compassion and love for others. Therefore, the methods and means of advancing the kingdom of heaven on earth cannot follow traditional religious ritual or the traditional means of establishing an earthly kingdom.

The fundamental characteristics of Christ's heavenly kingdom are unconditional love for God and unconditional redeeming love for all others, including one's worst enemy and those physically, economically, and socially different. It is impossible to impose redeeming love through force, yet for 2100 years Christians have tried to force others to believe and behave as they do. It does not work, yet we remain obsessed with the concept. Religious law does not define redeeming love.

Jesus also added an equally shocking dimension to the nature of the heavenly kingdom by stating that instead of being a visible political kingdom throughout the nation, the kingdom of heaven was instead an invisible spiritual experience within the heart and soul of each individual. It would not be experienced by rebellion against one's enemies, but rather though repentance and a profound change of personal attitudes and actions that glorified God rather than gratifying one's sense of revenge and retribution. Nothing of this nature had ever been spoken in Israel.

Here is the central issue of modern evangelical Christianity in relation to this parable: How many Christians today personally seek the true spiritual meaning of God's word through intense prayer and in-depth Bible study and dutifully live those concepts as a living witness of Christian truth? The focus of evangelical Christianity has become far too political, far too packaged, and far too professionalized with involved plans, fancy promotional programs, and over-paid preachers and promoters. How many Christians see through the fakery of all that and instead truly seek to discover, understand, and quietly and reverently make the spiritual principles of the kingdom of heaven, as taught by Jesus, the foundation of their life's work? Not many. Thus, in order to encourage the Christian faithful to be constantly vigilant and watchful for the truth of Christian ideals, Jesus strategically told this parable in order to stress the amazing spiritual blessings received by those who faithfully seek spiritual understanding and commitment and who never waiver in their desire and persistence.

A startling truth underlies the parable's broader meaning and interpretation: If one visualizes the faithful servants described herein as those who earnestly seek the true meaning of their master's kingdom and who deeply desire the most faithful relationship with their master, without regard for personal reward, then, because the nature of what these faithful servants were watching for was totally different to what was expected of them, the rewards they experienced were also totally opposite to the traditional relationship between a servant and his master. Astonishingly, the parable portrays a complete reversal of roles. Very few Christians ever think about Jesus serving them and instead focus on their service to Him. But that is the reward depicted in the parable.

The concept of "watching" denotes remaining awake, clear-headed, and not going to sleep during one's watch, thereby shirking a personal duty to their master. The parable states that all who are watchful are blessed, but special blessings are reserved for those who remain watchful during the second and third watches of the night. The second watch extended from 9:00 a.m. until midnight, and the third watch from midnight until 3:00 a.m. Thus, even in the dead of night, the watchful servants remained alert, vigilant, and responsible. They did this not to impress their master and garner favor, or to posture themselves in contrast to other servants who went to sleep on the job, but rather because personal zeal for their responsibilities and their devotion to their master kept them clear-minded and focused.

It is crucial to note that this watchfulness was the faithful servants' attitude in the middle of the night, when no one else was observing them and when there was no benefit or reward for their faithfulness, except their own sense of responsibility to their master. Unlike hypocritical Pharisees who were condemned by Jesus for exercising religious duties in order to be "seen by men" (Matt. 6:5), these faithful servants dutifully performed their responsibilities when seen by no one and their actions were unknown to others.

But who are they vigilantly watching and waiting for? If the servants responded to only a knock on the door, it would be easy to grant entrance to a thief or a stranger, especially for those servants who were disinterested, unfaithful, and not watchful. That portrays numerous times in Israel's history when false prophets appeared claiming to be the messiah and deluded many with false hope and expectation. It is akin to Jesus' statements about sheep hearing only their master's voice, and not the voice of a stranger, and following only him (John 10:5).

The watchful servant thus becomes adept at separating truth from untruth, the deceptive promises of a false teacher and preacher from the true proclamation of the gospel, and he wisely opens the door to his heart and soul only to the voice and knock of his true master. He is a faithful servant, not a foolish servant easily led astray and entrapped by the false promises of a cunning deceiver.

Thus, because of their faithful actions, the watchful servants' reward becomes manifestly important and is the primary focus of the parable. Under no circumstances in ordinary Jewish life would servants be treated by their master in the manner Jesus described. However, because of the faithfulness of the watchful servants, in a complete reversal of roles, the master girds himself in the servants' clothing, prepares a meal for them, makes them recline in the most comfortable dining position, and he serves them! The master's actions reveal Jesus' attitude in saying that "...I am among You as the One who serves" (Luke 22:27). The master's actions also no doubt inspired the stanza from the hymn "Brethren, We Have Met to Worship," written by George Askins, which proclaims, "...Then He'll call us home to heaven, at His table we'll sit down; Christ will gird Himself and serve us with sweet manna all around."

It must be noted that the servants did not help their master prepare the meal, but instead enjoyed it as a special gift of grace from him. It is a vivid picture of the heavenly blessings experienced by faithful, watchful servants singularly devoted to their master, compared to the experience of those who care less about spiritual values and look only to advancing their own interests through the forceful application of cold religious law on others or the manipulation of others in the name of Christ for personal gain. Today's Christian church is plagued with those professing to be servants, yet possessed with this demeaning, deceptive, and harmful attitude.

In a race, a horse is often fitted with blinders that restrict his view to the side and to the rear. He is able to see only what is in front of his nose, so to speak. In many ways, Israel wore spiritual blinders that did the same. She was singularly focused on a specific concept of the messiah—one possessing miraculous powers who would restore the power, prestige, and wealth of the ancient kingdom of David—and she adamantly refused to visualize either the messiah or his kingdom in any other way.

Jesus was totally different to this historic messianic concept. He eschewed political power; He sought no earthly wealth or prestige; He stressed the importance of understanding the spiritual meaning of Israel's religious law, rather than blindly following ancient concepts and ritual; He emphasized the necessity of a personal inner change, akin to a spiritual rebirth, through repentance; He focused on loving all others in a redeeming manner, rather than shunning them; He stated that the gifts of the kingdom of heaven were graciously given by God, rather than earned through man's works under the law; He emphasized that salvation was through faith in Him and the sacrifice of His life on the cross for all sinners, rather than through self-righteous effort; He stressed that the power of the kingdom of heaven was a transforming, personal inner experience that would enable His followers to go out into the world as His witnesses and change the world for Him, rather than waiting passively for Him to change the world for them; and He promised the anointing power of the Holy Spirit, who would help them and enable them to accomplish their work through individual spiritual gifts.

Jesus' message, His mission, and the messianic kingdom He proclaimed were so fundamentally different to entrenched expectations that it was virtually unbelievable, except for a faithful few who were watching for the true messiah. Thus, Jesus warned that if they had known when the true messiah would appear, they would have been ready for him, just as the master of a house would have been waiting for a thief breaking in if he had known what hour the thief would appear. But Israel was not watching for a spiritual messiah; she was not ready for Jesus and His heavenly kingdom; and she rejected Him as the messiah and crucified Him.

Most Christians today focus on the physical aspects of faith. They go to church, listen to the preacher, and return to their normal lifestyle until the next religious service. In doing so, they ignore the spiritual opportunities of Christianity. If the kingdom of heaven is within us and the power of the Holy Spirit empowers us daily, how do we respond to the countless opportunities to share Christian love and truth to those around us? In all honesty, many Christians try to act like Jesus on Sunday and live like the devil the rest of the week. Some of the most cold, cruel, and condemning actions are taken by church-going Christians against others who are different from them socially, economically, and physically.

If the Son of Man appears to them at an hour they do not expect and places a spiritual opportunity before them to faithfully serve and glorify Him to the world as His true witness, are they ready and watchful? How many Christians faithfully respond when the Holy Spirit moves within them to serve Christ as His faithful servant and witness, especially during the "second and third watches" of their day, when no one sees their service, no one pats them on their back for their effort, and no one else knows of their faithfulness and watchfulness, except Christ? Indeed, the Son of Man often appears to us at an hour we do not know, and far too often we do not recognize Him.

A parable posits a spiritual truth alongside a physical truth and uses the physical depiction to reveal a much deeper spiritual message. Here is the broader spiritual reality of this short, startling parable: The faithful servants were those who continuously and vigilantly searched for a spiritual truth they had never known; looked for a heavenly kingdom they had never experienced; and waited for the appearance of a master whose heavenly power and nature they could not truly understand. But they did so continuously, even in the darkest and quietest moments of their life, for they knew there had to be a better way to glorify God than through cold, lifeless religious ritual, and that is what made them so amazingly faithful and watchful.

The Parable of the Wise and Foolish Virgins

> *"Then the kingdom of heaven shall be likened to ten virgins who took their lamps and went out to meet the bridegroom. Now five of them were wise, and five were foolish. Those who were foolish took their lamps and took no oil with them, but the wise took oil in their vessels with their lamps. But while the bridegroom was delayed, they all slumbered and slept. And at midnight a cry was heard: 'Behold, the bridegroom is coming; go out to meet him!' Then all those virgins arose and trimmed their lamps. And the foolish said to the wise, 'Give us some of your oil, for our lamps are going out.' But the wise answered, saying, 'No, lest there should not be enough for us and you; but go rather to those who sell, and buy for yourselves.' And while they went to buy, the bridegroom came, and those who were ready went in with him to the wedding; and the door was shut. Afterward the other virgins came also, saying, 'Lord, Lord, open to us!' But he answered and said, 'Assuredly, I say to you, I do not know you.' Watch therefore, for you know neither the day nor the hour in which the Son of Man is coming"* (Matt. 25:1-13).

It is helpful to again consider the basic concept of a parable before examining this verse. A parable is a literary story involving two unfolding truths—one physical and the other spiritual—that jointly move forward along separate, parallel lines. The physical story is usually a well-known, often recurring event that is easily understood and widely accepted.

The corresponding spiritual truth is, however, not so widely known, and yet it is equally as important and true, and its literary development rides the coattail, so to speak, of the parable's physical truth. Once the physical premise is established, the parable's intent is to cause the listener to understand that the spiritual truth "is like that."

The parallel spiritual truth involves the same logic, the same development, and the same consequences. One is able to better grasp the lesser-known spiritual truth through his understanding of the better-known physical truth, for these unfolding truths are virtually the same, although one is physical and the other is spiritual. This parable is a good example. The mysterious nature of the kingdom of heaven becomes more understandable as one considers the purpose and meaning of the parable's physical story. As a result, the parable becomes an amazing instructional narrative about each Christian's spiritual life.

As a physical story, the parable describes the contrasting actions of ten young women, divided into two groups of five each and described as virgins, who were preparing to attend a wedding feast upon the bridegroom's arrival. But, the time of arrival was unknown, and it could occur any time during the day or night. How the two groups prepared for the moment is the parable's focus, and their attitude of preparation is as equally important as are their actions.

One group of five virgins is described as foolish, whereas the other five are described as wise in their preparations for the bridegroom's arrival. If one looks at the parable closely, it is apparent that there had been a period of waiting due to the preparation of those who were wise. Neither the wedding feast nor the bridegroom's arrival was a spur of the moment event. There was both planning and anticipation for the unknown moment, with adequate time for preparation. Consequently, one must explore the mindset of both groups during this waiting period in order to discover the gem of truth in the parable's narrative.

Jesus described the actions and attitudes of the first five as "foolish." As their actions are examined in light of the circumstances, one can better understand how this description becomes magnified. However, in reading this parable, the importance of their attitude can be easily overlooked, yet it is the motivational force underlying both their subsequent actions and the resulting consequences they experienced.

In Israel at that time, a young woman's status as a man's wife was very important, but her marriage in no way reflected our modern matrimonial concepts. A woman's marriage was arranged by her father through negotiation with the bridegroom. Frankly, she was considered to be the possession of her father who then gave her to the groom, and she became his. The bride had very little to say in the matter. Often a young woman became a man's wife in her early teens upon reaching child-bearing age.

But, prior to the actual marriage, if the bridegroom so requested, the bride could be physically examined to establish her virginity, and if she were not, the religious law of Israel provided she could be stoned to death (Deut. 22:20-21). It is interesting to note this was the dilemma Joseph faced in his marriage to Mary, Jesus' mother. The status as a married woman was greatly desired, and any young woman reaching adulthood as an unmarried maiden was viewed suspiciously as an unwanted individual.

A wedding feast may then be considered not only as the scene of the consummated wedding arrangement for a young woman, but also (and of importance to this parable) as a place where other young women were seen as available to the male guests. The feast was a time to dress in one's finery, laugh, eat, and engage in all the merriment of the occasion—and possibly catch the eye of a man who wanted her as his wife. It is noteworthy that Jesus' first miracle, symbolizing the new, joyous life He sought to give believers, was at a wedding feast in Cana, where he changed water into wine (John 2:1-11).

Attending a wedding feast as an attractive, available young woman could be a totally life-changing event and one for which she would carefully prepare. Thus, every young virgin would have approached a wedding feast with anticipation, preparation, and a personal determination to do all that was needed to experience the joy and happiness of the occasion.

The feast began with the arrival of the bridegroom, and that moment was the focal point of the celebration and excitement. But there were always contingencies to consider. If the bridegroom arrived during the day, it would be much easier to prepare. However, what if the bridegroom arrived at an unexpected time, such as the middle of the night? How could a young maiden personally prepare for that unexpected hour? The answer is the heart of this parable.

Let us first examine the physical story. These young women were invited to a personal meeting with the bridegroom that could potentially change their life dramatically. If he arrived at night, they each knew the necessity of having an ample supply of oil for their lamp so they could travel safely. Without the lamp oil, travel at night would have been very difficult, if not impossible.

Each young virgin had adequate time to purchase the necessary oil. But it was the attitude of gross indifference to the magnitude of the potentially life-changing moment that makes the actions of the foolish virgins so shocking. The word "foolish" is derived from *moros,* from which we get the word moron. However, its meaning and application in the parable does not imply mental impairment, but rather describes someone not mentally alert to the potential of circumstances and not grasping the meaning of a situation. Their foolish attitude is not caused by low intelligence, but rather by a lack of interest and concern. Important moments of opportunity are missed because they do not care, do not understand, and do not comprehend significance, and each day is lived without thought and preparation for tomorrow.

So, the possibility of the bridegroom arriving at night, requiring them to have oil for their lamps, did not concern the foolish virgins. If it was at night, what difference would that make? They would see him later during daylight hours. There was no need, in their estimation, to worry about stocking up on oil for lamps when it might not be needed.

One might put their foolish attitude in the same category as a present-day warning of the impending strike of a hurricane and the necessity of storing up not only food and water, but also batteries for light. The foolish response would be indifference, laziness, and lack of concern, with one saying, "I am not worried about that. I will do something later, when and if it hits." Those who foolishly respond in this manner are usually the ones frantically calling for help in the height of the storm's fury.

In contrast, the response of the five wise virgins was entirely different. They were practical, prudent, and insightful. Their understanding of the magnitude of the opportunity compelled them instinctively to prepare for each potential circumstance, including the possibility the bridegroom might arrive in the darkness of night. Thus, in advance they bought an ample supply of lamp oil, not knowing whether it would actually be needed, but nevertheless wisely preparing for any contingency so they would not miss the great feast to which they had been invited. The women evaluated each possibility and thoroughly prepared in every way they could.

If the bridegroom arrived in the middle of the night, they would be as ready as if he arrived in the middle of the day, and they would not miss one moment of the joy his arrival. Both the foolish and the wise virgins soon learned that attitudes produce actions with life-changing consequences. Indeed, the bridegroom did arrive at night, and the preparation—or the lack thereof—of both groups greatly impacted their lives.

On learning of his arrival, both the foolish and the wise virgins "went out to meet" the bridegroom. The phrase implies more than a casual meeting and indicates one's intent to meet someone for the purpose of both joining up with them and also joining into their actions. None of the ten virgins were becoming his bride, but each had been invited to become a part of the bridegroom's wedding celebration, sharing in the feast, and personally experiencing the tremendous joy of his wedding celebration. Five saw the invitation as the greatest opportunity of their life; the other five could not have cared less.

Poor choices can produce painful experiences. The bridegroom's midnight arrival caught the foolish virgins woefully unprepared. Upon hearing of his arrival, all ten virgins arose to meet him, but only then did the consequences of their indifference hit home with the foolish ones. As they trimmed their lamps to make them brighter, the foolish realized they had no oil and begged the wise to share what they had stored in preparation for this moment. As with many today, the foolish virgins thought they could enter the bridegroom's joy and festivities based on the preparation of others. But, the invitation was personal, and their obligation to prepare was personal. They could not light their way to the bridegroom's feast using the oil of others!

Understandably, the wise refused to share, lest there be insufficient oil for their own lamps, and told the foolish ones to go buy oil from the oil merchants—at midnight. In another display of ill-preparation, they actually went out frantically looking for someone to sell them lamp oil in the middle of the night.

But, to their dismay, the bridegroom arrived while they were gone, and the door to the wedding feast was closed. Upon returning, the foolish virgins begged the bridegroom to open the door and grant them entrance, but with a tone of finality, he refused. For these women, there could have been no greater sense of rejection than hearing the bridegroom's words, "Assuredly, I say to you, I do not know you." This sobering statement merits one's most intense examination.

The bridegroom's words are an emphatic, declaratory expression that has a deeper meaning than just physical recognition. "Assuredly" is a translation of "amen," and may be understood as a definite, final expression of truth. The general meaning of "amen" is "let it be so." With regard to a final pronouncement of fact, or the nature of a granted request, "amen" means "let this be the final, unalterable resolution of this matter."

The bridegroom's statement to the foolish, uncaring virgins is filled with astonishing, judgmental reality. The phrase "I do not know you" is derived from a word meaning "to see, behold, and consider." It involves an implied sequence beginning with the physical response of actually seeing someone, but then transitioning into a mental consideration of their true motives and intent, whether good or bad. Thus, one may literally see the actions and attitudes of a person and then see their motive behind those attitudes and actions. It is akin to listening to someone's explanation and then responding, "Oh, I see what you mean." Or, on another level, one may say, "I see what you did, and I also see why you did it." Of a more negative nature, one may thus see the motive behind crude remarks, indifferent attitudes, and total disregard for divine truth and reality.

Therefore, consider what the bridegroom truly meant by "I do not know you": Imagine him coolly and dispassionately uttering these words to the foolish virgins, "You had the opportunity to attend a wedding feast of joy and new life. You had ample time to prepare for the moment, regardless of the time it occurred, but you did not. I cannot see nor understand how you could be so indifferent to and unprepared for this moment. You now plead for entrance and admission to my feast, but all I truly see is laziness, indifference, and an unexplainable, indefensible lack of preparation. I do not know anyone with the audacity to ignore all preparation for this hour, and then request to enter into the joy and celebration of those who did prepare. I do not know anyone who cares so little about my invitation to this feast, and yet expects the door to swing wide for their entrance. That is not how the invitation to my wedding feast works. You made the choice of indifference, unconcern, and no preparation, and the consequences are yours alone. Most assuredly, I say to you, I do not know anyone like you." And the door closed.

How may one make a spiritual application of this parable? Jesus does not operate on the basis of a calendar or a clock, and neither does the Holy Spirit. God does not have bed-time hours, and thus His Spirit may move suddenly and mightily in one's life at any moment of the day or night. God does not wear either a Timex or a Rolex, and, as the Bible states, "His ways are not our ways" (Isa. 55:8-9). His timetable for spiritually moving in our life in a transforming manner is not according to a pre-arranged schedule for our convenience and knowledge. It can occur at any moment—just like the arrival of the bridegroom in this parable. What, then, is one's attitude of anticipation and preparation for this pivotal moment? Jesus described the attitude of the two groups of virgins as foolish and wise. Against the backdrop of the unknown time of the bridegroom's arrival, the foolish attitude and the wise attitude reveal with amazing clarity the attitude of many Christians today about the unknown movement of the Holy Spirit in their life.

The New Testament describes some of God's actions as occurring suddenly. For example, after the angel of the Lord announced the birth of Jesus to the startled shepherds, "…suddenly there was with the angel a multitude of the heavenly host…" (Luke 2:13). Jesus' call to His disciples caused them to immediately respond and follow Him (Mark 1:17-18). The Holy Spirit moved suddenly at Pentecost, filling the disciples with indescribable spiritual power (Acts 2:2).

It is true that this parable may describe one's preparation for the return of Christ, and we have all been given adequate time to prepare. But on a more personal level, the Holy Spirit may suddenly move in your life with the same transforming power as He did with others in the Bible. Whether it is the realization of one's sinful nature and the need for repentance and salvation, or God's call on your life for spiritual service, that life-changing moment may occur at any time.

On a Sunday morning in June 1975, I was attending the worship service at First Baptist Church, Jackson, Mississippi. During the Hymn of Invitation, suddenly and without any warning, the Holy Spirit called me into the ministry. The power of God's call on my life to share the gospel was so overwhelming that I almost collapsed onto the pew. It was as if ten thousand angels were shouting the word "ministry" into my spiritual ears. Almost immediately, I began preaching sermons to myself, and that continued for days, even while I worked or tried to sleep. During the past forty-six years, I have sought to know God's will and to do His work, occasionally with some degree of uncertainty. But four decades later, I have never once doubted that the sudden movement of the Holy Spirit was real and transforming, and my life has never been the same.

Are you spiritually prepared for such a moment in your life? Do you dismiss the idea of God working powerfully in your life, or have you ever considered how you would respond if He did? Have you in any manner prayerfully prepared for that unknown moment if it occurred? Maybe your study of this parable will change the thoughts of your heart and inspire you to at least consider the possibility.

Jesus' promise to "come" ends The Revelation and concludes the New Testament. The word implies rapid, direct movement from one place to another. "And behold, I am coming quickly, and My reward is with Me, to give to everyone according to his work," said the Lord (Rev.22:12). Both the Spirit and the Bride implore Him, "Come!" (v. 17). The final words of Jesus to all of us are, "Surely I am coming quickly," to which we all should equally respond, "Amen. Even so, come, Lord Jesus!" (v. 20).

The Revelation describes a beautiful and personal invitation to the redeemed of Christ to attend the marriage supper of the Lamb. That might sound a bit strange, but it describes the joyous, eternal covenant union of Jesus, the Bridegroom—the sacrificial Lamb of God—with His Bride—the redeemed, purified, sinless church. We are all invited to attend and personally participate through faith in Christ. This great wedding feast of the Bridegroom and His Bride will surely occur, but we do not know the day or the hour when the Bridegroom will appear. We have each been invited. The great test of our faith is whether we shall prepare for this divine moment foolishly or wisely.

The Judgment Parables

Judgment is not a pleasant topic, yet it is a fundamental tenant of New Testament theology. Jesus shared several parables relating to the certainty of a final judgment, plus He spoke on other occasions about a judgmental conclusion to His work as Redeemer. In fact, it may be argued that a final judgment is a basic purpose of His work. For example, Jesus said, "For judgment I have come into the world, that those who do not see may see, and that those who see may be made blind" (John 9:39). He made this statement in response to the Pharisees' disbelief about Him healing a man born blind.

In like manner, the writer of Hebrews states, "And it is appointed for men to die once, but after this the judgment" (Heb. 9:27). Unquestionably, the concept of judgment is an essential Christian doctrine, and this book would be incomplete without an in-depth examination of these judgment parables. Generating a sense of doom is not the intent. Rather, those who are wise will see these parables as both an admonition to prepare and the assurance that a faithful servant of Christ has no reason to fear. In fact, the good and faithful servant may see God's judgment as a vindication of and a reward for his faith in Christ. For the redeemed, judgment is a positive experience; for the foolishly unprepared, it is not.

Judgment should not be viewed as God arbitrarily sitting behind a divine judgment bench coldly passing sentence on our sins. One must look at judgment in a broader sense and against the divine purpose of God's new covenant with man through faith in Jesus. Establishing the new covenant of grace and faith was the fundamental work of Jesus and the basis of the New Testament. Jesus specifically stated, "This...is the new covenant in my blood (His life), which is shed for you" (Luke 22:20), and He further stated that "God so loved the world that He gave His only begotten Son that whoever believes in Him should not perish but have everlasting life" (John 3:16).

The new covenant, therefore, is based on the individual faith of anyone anywhere in the world—not just a covenant of law with Israel alone. Through covenant faith, every believer is guaranteed everlasting life, the assurance of salvation, and the promise that we have "passed from death into life" (John 5:24).

Judgment is God's determination of whether an individual has wisely committed himself to Christ in faith and entered into this covenant, or whether he has foolishly rejected the divine offer of forgiveness and eternal life from God. Judgment is simply God distinguishing between those who accepted His offer of eternal life through Christ and those who did not. It does not mean that God is harsh. Instead, judgment is God sharing the blessings of the new covenant with those who are wisely faithful and affirming the consequences of disbelief with those who are foolishly indifferent and unconcerned.

Judgment is not an arbitrary divine decision; rather, it is very personal involving the divine affirmation of our faith in Christ or the imposition of the consequences of disbelief. Judgment is God affixing the seal of finality on what we have individually chosen about Jesus. If it is not pleasant, He is not to be blamed, we are. Eternity is our choice. Judgment is God's final Amen on our life. He looks at our wise choice of belief or our foolish choice of disbelief and says, "let it be so." And it is—for all eternity.

The Parable of the Weeds among Good Plants

> *"The kingdom of heaven is like a man who sowed good seed in his field; but while he slept, his enemy came and sowed tares among the wheat and went his way. But when the grain had sprouted and produced a crop, then the tares also appeared. So the servants of the owner came and said to him, 'Sir, did you not so good seed in your field? How then does it have tares?' He said to them, 'An enemy has done this.' The servants said to him, 'Do you want us then to go and gather them up?' But he said, 'No, lest while you gather up the tares you also uproot the wheat with them. Let them both grow together until the harvest, and at the time of harvest I will say to the reapers, "First gather together the tares and bind them in bundles to burn them, but gather the wheat into my barn"'...*
>
> *He who sows the good seed is the Son of Man. The field is the world, the good seeds are the sons of the kingdom, but the tares are the sons of the wicked one. The enemy who sowed them is the devil, the harvest is the end of the age, and the reapers are the angels. Therefore, as the tares are gathered and burned in the fire, so it will be at the end of this age. The Son of Man will send out His angels, and they will gather out of His*

> *kingdom all things that offend, and those that practice lawlessness, and will cast them into the furnace of fire. There will be wailing and gnashing of teeth. Then the righteous will shine forth as the sun in the kingdom of their Father. He who has ears to hear, let him hear!"* (Matt. 13:24-3:36-43).

Christianity is premised on a contrasting concept of peace. At its core, divine peace is spiritually given to believers through faith in Jesus (John 14:27). However, this inner peace is often experienced in the midst of unpleasant circumstances and disturbing relationships with others, especially those who do not accept the gospel of Jesus and do not support its growth and expansion. Interestingly, however, the absence of physical peace can significantly contribute to the growth and maturity of one's spiritual peace. Therefore, this parable helps one better understand the spiritual purpose for "tares" in their life.

Jesus was a realist, and He caringly prepared His followers for adversity. The obstacles facing Jesus and early Christians were not just disinterest in the gospel and reluctance to embrace its truth, but also the close-minded refusal of most to even consider new religious doctrine. It was a violation of Israel's religious laws and the traditions of the elders to consider any idea not consistent with the centuries-old religious law and the writings of the prophets. A good example is the reaction to Stephen, the early martyr, who was stoned to death. As he began describing his heavenly vision of Jesus standing at the right hand of God, his accusers covered their ears while rushing toward him so they would not hear his testimony (Acts 7:55-57).

Thus, it was inevitable those sharing the new, joyous truth of the gospel would encounter entrenched opposition from the religious establishment, and Jesus vividly described this opposition:

> *"Now brother will deliver up brother to death, and a father his child; and children will rise up against parents and cause them to be put to death. And you will be hated by all for My name's sake. But he who endures to the end will be saved"* (Matt. 10:21-22).

Is this statement a picture of the tares and the good plants existing side by side? What closer proximity to opposition and intimidation could one have than one's own family?

However, in a contrasting statement, Jesus spoke about the joy of persecution, "Blessed are those who are persecuted for righteousness' sake, for theirs is the kingdom of heaven" (Matt. 5:10). His statement is broader than it seems. The blessedness that the beatitude promises stems from an inner sense of peace with God and the satisfaction and reward from doing His work. In the beatitude, the word for "persecuted" defines opposition and resistance in multiple forms and at every level, and it can come from any source, including family and friends.

Jesus faced opposition from His own brothers, as shown by their cynical comment about His work:

"'Depart from here and go into Judea, that Your disciples also may see the works that You are doing. For no one does anything in secret while he himself seeks to be known openly. If You do these things, show Yourself to the world.' For even His brothers did not believe in Him" (John 7:3-5).

This was a crude remark and not the encouragement it may seem. In effect, they told Jesus if He was such a great teacher and miracle worker, then go to Jerusalem, with its large population, and let everyone know about it. Otherwise, keep quiet. Again, the tares were growing among the wheat.

In the parable of the sower (Matt. 13:3-9), the one who is sowing casts the majority of his seed in areas where he knew they would not thrive, yet he showed them anyway without prejudice. Logically, the sower would have planted his seed only in the good soil. But he used the same amount of seed, the same effort, and the same resources to cast seed among stones, briars, and in open pathways. He fully realized the seed would produce only momentary growth among the stones, would be choked by competition with other plants among the briars, and would be stomped to death by the indifferent human traffic and worldly lifestyles of uncaring people in the pathways. Yet, he tried, and he left the good plants to struggle and grow among the tares and briars into which they fell.

Sharing the gospel of Jesus is no different. This parable not only challenges a disciple of Christ to be undefeated by failure and frustration, but also to plant the seed of the gospel in the hearts and minds of those who have no interest—those who are in fact enemies of the gospel message. When sown without judgmental discrimination, the good seed of the gospel will always fall among the tares of rejection.

But why would Jesus allow His followers to encounter such resistance, both then and now? With His divine power, why not create a clear path free of opposition, fear, and intimidation for the gospel to be shared worldwide? Is there a divine purpose for tares in our life? Is our faith made stronger by the opposition and adversity we face? Is that the reason why we are to rejoice in the face of persecution so that we may grow spiritually? This is one of Jesus' most challenging beatitude statements—one that few Christians ever do—and we deny ourselves a great spiritual blessing for failing to do so.

Interestingly, our personal values and attitudes are often formulated as a result of comparison. As an example, consider a track star. The winner of a one-hundred-yard sprint usually demonstrates very impressive speed. But we form an opinion and appreciation for his speed by comparing him to others who do not perform as well. Would there be the same appreciation for his athleticism if he ran alone? No, we know he runs fast only because others run slower.

Likewise, would we appreciate the service and sacrifice of a Christian servant if his ministry was free of challenges and opposition and his preaching resulted in thousands of believers? Perhaps, but our appreciation would be greater if this servant faithfully worked while enemies of the gospel resisted him at every opportunity. Perseverance and determination in the face of opposition produce admiration and validity of the message.

Nothing in the gospels states that being a living witness for Christ will be easy. In fact, the contrary is often true. Indeed, Jesus told His followers that He was sending them out "as sheep in the midst of wolves" (Matt. 10:16). That phrase has lost a bit of its impact through the years from being overly used. Seldom does one stop and consider the true magnitude of the literal image. There could be few creatures more frightened and burdened with an overwhelming sense of helplessness than a defenseless sheep encircled by ravenous wolves. Its only hope would be the strength and power of its shepherd interceding on its behalf.

The image is, however, a vivid picture of the bitter resistance that both Jesus and His disciples encountered as they shared the good news of the gospel. Indeed, the power of the gospel of love was contrasted against the bitterness of religious exclusion; compassion manifested itself against condemnation; unyielding law stood in contrast to redeeming love; and righteousness by faith was compared to self-righteous works. The good seed of the gospel was in daily contrast with the harsh constraints of the seed of religious law. Planting the seed of grace and love caused many disciples to be beaten, imprisoned, and humiliated, because the work of the enemy planting tares in their life was unending.

This parable, therefore, has a challenging truth: Removing the tares would do the good plants more harm than good. Both the good plants and the tares were rooted in the same soil, fed on the same nourishment, and their roots and lives were intertwined. But while one used all its resources for evil, the other used the same resources for good. In many ways, that is a picture of the contrast between the gospel of grace and the unyielding demands of religious law. Both are a product of Jewish heritage, both grew out of the concept of fulfillment of the law of Israel, both had the same cultural heritage, and both worshipped God.

But the harvest each produced was entirely different. One stressed total dedication to the traditions of the elders of Israel, obedience to the thousands of religious laws, and refused to consider any other variation of ancient interpretation of the law and the prophets. The other stressed faith in Jesus as the only begotten Son of God, salvation through faith in Him and not in self-righteous works of man, redeeming love for all mankind and not just one's Jewish neighbors, and a worldwide sense of evangelism rather than a limited divine covenant with Israel only.

The magnitude of Christianity's spiritual goodness is best measured by contrasting it with the magnitude of obstinate resistance. There is no better example than Jesus healing a woman on the Sabbath who suffered from a back deformity and been unable to stand straight for eighteen years. When Jesus miraculously healed her and she stood upright again, she began praising and glorifying God. However, the ruler of the synagogue angrily and indignantly said to the amazed observers, "There are six days on which men ought to work; therefore come and be healed on them, and not on the Sabbath day" (Luke 13:14). One can visualize this startled religious leader, who had no explanation for Jesus' miracle, loudly and pointedly trying to retain the people's commitment to the religious law which, in his opinion, had greater priority than mercy, compassion, and the miracle of healing.

The ruler of the synagogue saw the same divine miracle others saw, heard the same words from Jesus, and saw the same joy in the life of the healed woman. He had the same opportunity to believe this was a miraculous work of God, yet he steadfastly refused to accept what he saw and heard as divine truth. He alone was responsible for the consequences of his unbelief. Whatever judgment he experienced could not be blamed on God, but rather on himself. God just put a final amen on his personal choice and his personal obstinacy.

The incident is a revealing comparison between law and grace, between merciless ritual and tender compassion for one's fellow man, and between the dictates of the traditions of the elders that refused to consider any new truth and the awe and amazement of the people seeing a divine miracle before their very eyes. Again, the good seed was growing among the tares. How better to contrast the mercy of Jesus with the coldness of the synagogue ruler than to place them side by side, with one showing compassion and love and the other showing bitter condemnation.

In stating this parable, Jesus described what each element represented, and one can readily see the parable's application in Christian life. Through our faith and commitment to Christ, Jesus uses every good and faithful Christian servant to sow good seed in all kinds of circumstances in the field of the world. The good seeds are the sons of the kingdom.

However, the devil is the enemy of all who serve Jesus, and he opposes the sowing of good seed however possible. Those who do the devil's work and oppose the gospel message are the tares—the sons of the devil. Their life is fruitless, and they accomplish nothing for Christ, yet they live and prosper alongside a fruitful, devoted Christian servant, and their lives are often intertwined, just as the roots of the plants were.

Every devoted servant of Christ will encounter enemies, and they can produce some very strained and painful relationships and situations. The definition of enemy in this parable does not mean another's intent to inflict bodily harm. Instead, one's enemy is someone who is openly hostile to one's Christian life and work and who possesses a malicious intent to harm that work and reduce its impact. Yet, interestingly, this parable implies they are essential for Christian growth and maturity. Therefore, we can rejoice over the hindrance and disruption they cause in our life, otherwise the Lord would remove them and the difficulties they create for Christian servants.

No soldier shouts for joy standing in the middle of a minefield, yet that is the amazing message of this parable for a devoted servant of Christ. It is hard to do, but when we are able to see even the tares in our life as blessings and are thankful for them, we achieve a spiritual victory and spiritual peace that the world cannot provide.

Things drastically change, however, when harvest time arrives, and that is where the ultimate truth of this parable becomes magnified. From the standpoint of a final judgment, the tares—the enemies of the work of Christ—will be uprooted and separated from the servants of Christ. Their disruptive work will be bound and ended, just as Satan will be bound (Rev. 20:2-10). That is a sobering truth, but it is the promise of Jesus. The good plants, however, will be safely stored.

This parable will change the thoughts of your heart about the tares in your life. Rejoice, for the imagery of the parable assures us of one thing: Christians are headed to the barn; their enemies are headed to the burn pile.

The Parable of the Fishing Net

"Again, the kingdom of heaven is like a dragnet that was cast into the sea and gathered some of every kind, which, when it was full, they drew to shore, and they sat down and gathered the good into vessels but threw the bad away. So it will be at the end of the age. The angels will come forth, separate the wicked from among the just, and cast them into the furnace of fire. There will be wailing and gnashing of teeth" (Matt. 13:47-50).

When a parable is premised on a well-known physical experience that is a facet of daily life, the spiritual truth depicted by the parable becomes even more poignant and meaningful. The parable of the mustard seed is a good example. Probably everyone had seen a mustard seed, as well as the large plant that the seed produced. This parable comparing the kingdom of heaven to a fishing net is another example.

The Sea of Galilee, located in northeast Israel, is about twelve miles long and seven miles wide and has historically been the center of varied fishing activities. Unlike the salty Dead Sea, which has virtually no marine life because of the high saline level, the Sea of Galilee teemed with a large variety of fish that provided both food for many people and a livelihood for many fishermen. Because of their dependence on good and edible fish, fishermen understandably removed the unusable fish from their net and cast them aside, rather than returning them to the lake, thus reducing the unwanted fish population.

Several of Jesus' disciples actively worked as fishermen on the Sea of Galilee before joining in His ministry. It is interesting to note that the Gospel of John records how Jesus instructed Peter and some of the other disciples, who had fished all night and caught nothing, to cast their net on the other side of the boat. Obligingly, they did so and caught so many large fish they had to drag the net on to the shore. The net amazingly contained 153 fish (John 21:3-11), and some early church theologians, such as Jerome and Augustine, argued that the number represented the different fish species in the lake, symbolizing the capacity of the gospel to reach all races of mankind.

It is noteworthy that Jesus specifically said the kingdom of heaven was like a dragnet cast into the sea. Fishermen would most often use a casting net thrown from their boat. As it sank, fish that were directly underneath the net were caught and pulled into the boat. A dragnet worked differently and was larger and more complicated. Weights were attached, causing the net to sink and drag across the bottom, thereby dislodging fish from rocks, crevices, and other hiding places. As the dragnet was pulled along, it basically caught every fish in its path, whether good or bad. The designation of a dragnet in the parable is significant due to it denoting that God's judgment will touch every person and none will escape.

Thus, Jesus used the physical process of fishermen separating fish caught in their dragnet to make the compelling parable statement: The judgement will be much like what you see fishermen doing every day when they separate the good fish from the bad. In a similar manner, in the judgment, the angels of God will separate believers from unbelievers. Just as the bad fish flail about on the ground, so will unbelievers struggle in the pain of divine rejection knowing their fate is sealed.

If indeed there were 153 different fish species in the Sea, and the number of good, edible fish was limited, then one is faced with the sobering reality that this parable describes a judgment in which the majority of people are condemned because of their indifference and rejection of the gospel, just as the majority of fish caught on any given day were likely cast aside as no good.

By comparison, the bad fish are much like the tares. They lived in the same water as the good fish, ate the same sea life, prospered, and grew. Within that environment, they no doubt felt safe, perhaps even dominant, not realizing that they would be caught in a dragnet of judgment. Suddenly, without warning, life as they had known it was over. Thus, it shall be for all people at the end of the age.

The reality of Jesus' words is unpleasant to consider, but it is divine truth and serves as a warning to those who are without faith and commitment.

The Parable of Two Sons: One Obeys, and One Does Not

> *"But what do you think? A man had two sons, and he came to the first and said, 'Son, go, work today in my vineyard.' He answered and said, 'I will not,' but afterward he regretted it and went. Then he came to the second son and said likewise. And he answered and said, 'I go, sir,' but he did not. Which of the two did the will of his father?...Assuredly, I say to you that tax collectors and harlots enter the kingdom of God before you"* (Matt. 21:28-31).

Old Testament history is filled with examples of Israel's defiant and rebellious nature traceable back to Adam and Eve. Notable examples include the chronology of sin and repentance recorded in the Book of Judges. Some kings are described as doing good in the eyes of God, while the reign of many others is described as evil. It was an unending cycle stretching over many years.

Later, Jeremiah challenged Israel's denial of her sins and compared the nation to a wild donkey in her mating season, sniffing the wind in search of one who might satisfy her carnal cravings:

> *"How can you say, 'I am not polluted, I have not gone after the Baals'? See your way in the valley; know what you have done: You are a swift dromedary breaking loose in her ways, a wild donkey used to the wilderness, that sniffs at the wind in her desire; in her time of mating, who can turn her away? All those who seek her will not weary themselves; in her month they will find her"* (Jer. 2:13-24).

The last Old Testament prophet, Malachi, listed at least six examples of how Israel had rejected God's love and defiled the act of worship. Rather than repenting, Malachi further described their arrogant denial of sin:

"'Your words have been harsh against Me,' says the Word, 'yet you say, What have we spoken against You?' You have said, 'It is useless to serve God; what profit is it that we have kept His ordinance, and that we have walked as mourners before the Lord of hosts?'" (Mal. 3:13-14).

Jesus pointedly described how Israel had not only disobeyed prophetic voices in her past, but also had killed the prophets in order to silence their call for repentance:

"Woe to you, scribes and Pharisees, hypocrites! Because you build the tombs of the prophets and adorn the monuments of the righteous, and say, 'If we had lived in the days of our fathers, we would not have been partakers with them in the blood of the prophets.' Therefore you are witnesses against yourselves that you are the sons of those who murdered the prophets. Fill up then the measure of your fathers' guilt" (Matt. 23:29-32).

Jesus knew the same would happen to Him.
Given Israel's history, this parable focuses on the issue of faith and obedience to God, and Jesus used it to paint a fascinating contrast. The Jews, particularly the scribes and Pharisees, prided themselves on fanatical obedience to the law, and piously condemned others they considered as sinners. In this parable setting, Jesus addressed "the chief priests and elders of the people" (v. 23), which no doubt contained members of both groups.

Certainly, harlots and tax collectors headed their list of the condemned. Interestingly, however, a despised tax collector, Matthew, became a disciple of Jesus and wrote the Gospel of Matthew. A demon-possessed woman named Mary Magdalene, who most likely survived financially by selling her favors to men, became one of Jesus' most devoted followers after He cast seven demons from her (Luke 8:2). However, the legalistic Jews, who prided themselves as God's elect, neither believed Jesus nor followed Him.

Using the language of the parable, the basic question must then be asked: Who did God's will—the religious zealots who rejected Jesus' teaching or the harlots and tax collectors who accepted it? Those who the priests considered the most sinful—tax collectors and harlots—had a deeper and more life-transforming understanding of the kingdom of heaven than did the chief priests and elders who prided themselves in their compliance with the religious laws of Israel. With amazing clarity, this parable sets forth the answer.

According to the parable narrative, a man had two sons, and he asked each of them to go work in his vineyard. The first son initially refused, but later changed his mind out of regret. The second son said he would, but did not do so, apparently lying to his father. Jesus asked which of the two sons did their father's will. The priests and elders responded that the first son did, even though he initially refused and then changed his mind. Jesus did not agree with them.

Jesus' response would have both startled and infuriated his listeners. By telling them that "tax collectors and harlots enter the kingdom of God before you," Jesus said that individuals, who the self-righteous zealots considered the lowest form of humanity, would inherit the kingdom of God first because of their faith rather than those who viewed themselves as entitled to the blessings of God's kingdom because of their works. Jesus could not have said anything more shocking to them.

Thus, Jesus occasionally described this spiritual reality in reverse order—those who firmly believe they have earned God's favor will have the least understanding of the unmerited gift of grace. Conversely, those who view themselves as the least worthy, but who profess faith in Christ alone, will have the greatest understanding of grace. Jesus described this spiritual truth by stating, "the last will be first, and the first last" (Matt. 20:16).

Realistically, these two sons had no real interest in their father's work. There was no commitment to his purpose or an appreciation for the goal of his labors. The first son was unmotivated to work for his father, and he ultimately did so only out of regret or fear. In his heart, he was completely disinterested and really did not want to do the work. The second son was even more brazen in his refusal. He told his father he would, but did not do so, and he lied to his father without remorse.

The priests and elders believed the first son did his father's will since he did reluctantly go, but Jesus neither agreed nor disagreed.

Surprisingly, He gave them an entirely different and quite shocking answer.

Jesus said that all the law and the wisdom of the prophets could be summarized in two spiritual concepts—loving God with all your heart, with all your soul, and with all your mind and loving your neighbor as yourself (Matt. 22:36-40). If that is the summation of the law of God, this parable reveals that neither of these two sons of the law was willing to do that.

How could it be said that one who initially had no interest in his father's work, and later did so only reluctantly, truly loved his father with all his heart and soul? He did not. He saw only a legal obligation for which he had no personal interest.

Likewise, how could anyone who outwardly said all the right religious things about his father's will and work, but who secretly had no intention of actually doing the work be regarded as committed to his father's purpose of loving others as much as he did his own self? His outward religious commitment was nothing but shameful pretense. He was a liar and a tool of Satan.

The scribes and Pharisees were the two most outwardly religious groups in Israel. Scribes were responsible for recording and transmitting copies of the law, along with any new interpretations, and were considered as the most knowledgeable about the detailed content of the multiple volumes of religious law. The Pharisees were the most conservative religious group and openly boasted that their name meant "the separated ones," because it was through their rigid adherence to the exact meaning of the law that they distinguished themselves.

But, both groups were unyielding in their contempt for all others, especially Gentiles. Any concept they had of a loving God was premised on unwavering obedience to and performance of the religious laws and rituals in which they yearned for self-righteous glory rather than glorifying God. They were the ones Jesus condemned for openly praying and doing charitable deeds "in order to be seen by men" (Matt. 6:5). And it was a Pharisee in Jesus' example who prayed in the Temple, "God, I thank you that I am not like other men—extortioners, unjust, adulterers, or even as this tax collector. I fast twice a week; I give tithes of all that I possess," while a tax collector stood afar off praying, "God, be merciful to me a sinner." As Jesus said, "I tell you, this man went down to his house justified rather than the other, for everyone who exalts himself will be abased, and he who humbles himself will be exalted" (Luke 18:11-14).

Yet, despite all their self-glorifying obedience to the law, the obedience of the scribes and Pharisees to the true work of God was nonexistent. There was no love or compassion for anyone outside their own belief and there was no desire to reach out to others. Their concept of God's kingdom applied only to Israel, with no interest in the rest of the world. Regardless of their religious talk, they steadfastly refused to do their father's true work.

Compare that to the attitude of Matthew, who abandoned a lucrative position as a Roman tax collector and immediately followed the call of Jesus to work in the sharing of the gospel to everyone. A tax collector was under contract to Rome to produce a certain level of tax income from his assigned district, and any amount that he collected over that levy was kept as his fee. Thus, many tax collectors were heartless, brutal, greedy individuals who were considered traitors to Israel because of their commitment to Rome and its burdensome military occupation. Rome, the Roman soldiers, and those collecting taxes for Rome were passionately hated. A merciless tax collector who was willing to use force and intimidation could become very rich, such as Zacchaeus, a chief tax collector in Jericho (Luke:19:2-3). Walking away from that kind of income in order to follow the call of Christ required devotion greater than we can imagine. But despite how badly religious elitists may have hated Matthew for his tax collection work, it is his account of the life and ministry of Jesus that begins the New Testament.

Thus, there would be no doubt that Matthew's understanding of the love and grace of the kingdom of heaven far exceeded any understanding of the scribes and Pharisees, or the priests and elders. The greater one understands the gift of grace, the greater is the experience and expression of joy. For example, consider the parable of the vineyard workers. Some workers were hired at the beginning of the day, others were hired throughout the day, and some were hired just before the closing of the day, yet all received the same pay from the owner (Matt. 20:1-16). The workers hired last, who nevertheless received a full day's pay, understood the grace and charity of the owner far more than those hired first, who thought they earned their wage and were angry at the gift given to the one's hired last.

Christians often see themselves as inferior to the spiritual giants around us, such as well-known religious leaders. But, surprisingly, this parable tells us something different. It does not matter how well-known someone might be, even the pastor of a large church, if he does not personally commit himself to the work of loving all others, rather than piously condemning them for his own personal glory or the advancement of a political platform. Conversely, the worst sinner who humbly repents and, through his faith and commitment to Christ, joyously and willingly does the work of his heavenly father is greater in the kingdom of heaven.

Regardless of how lowly you may occasionally feel about yourself, the truth of this parable will change the thoughts of your heart and lead you boldly into the joy of the kingdom of heaven.

The Parable of the Wicked Tenants

"There was a certain landowner who planted a vineyard and set a hedge around it, dug a winepress in it and built a tower. And he leased it to vinedressers and went into a far country. Now when vintage-time drew near, he sent his servants to the vinedressers, that they might receive its fruit. And the vinedressers took his servants, beat one, killed one, and stoned another. Again he sent other servants, more than the first, and they did likewise to them. Then last of all he sent his son to them, saying, 'They will respect my son.' But when the vinedressers saw the son, they said among themselves, 'This is the heir. Come let us kill him and seize his inheritance.' And they caught him, and cast him out of the vineyard, and killed him. Therefore, when the owner of the vineyard comes, what will he do to those vinedressers?" (Matt. 21:23-40).

This parable is also premised on a well-known physical basis. There were numerous vineyards in Israel that produced large volumes of wine grapes. Most people had seen these vineyards, and some who heard the parable may have worked in one of them. Such a setting is also the basis for the parable of the vineyard workers.

Some vineyards were no doubt just an area planted in grapevines with no special care given to it. These would have been easily accessible by others who would have picked some of the fruit for their own use. But, this vineyard was special, and it is a picture of Israel as God's special vineyard. Isaiah described it in this manner:

> *"Now let me sing to my Well-beloved a song of My beloved regarding His vineyard: My beloved has a vineyard on a very fruitful hill. He dug it up and cleared out its stones and planted it with the choicest vine. He built a tower in its midst, and also made a winepress in it; so He expected it to bring forth good grapes, but it brought forth wild grapes. And now, O inhabitants of Jerusalem and men of Judah, judge, please, between Me and My vineyard. What more could have been done to My vineyard that I have not done in it?"* (Isaiah 5:1-4).

Similarly, in this vineyard the owner not only had labored to plant the vines, but he then planted a thick protective hedge barrier around it, much like a fence. Anticipating a good harvest, he dug a winepress where juice from the grapes could be pressed out. As a measure of security, the owner then worked to build a tower, usually made of stones, which served as an elevated observation post from which to view any intruders into the vineyard. Truthfully, there was not much more that could have been done to protect and secure the vineyard and make it productive.

Afterwards, the owner leased the vineyard to vinedressers who would care for it, trim the vines so the new growth would yield more fruit, and apply dung around the vines as fertilizer. The stewardship of the owner's work, his investment, and his anticipation of a harvest was in the vinedressers' hands. In this role, the vinedressers faced a fundamental test of stewardship. They could be faithful servants and stewards of the owner's vineyard and produce a bountiful harvest for him, reserving unto themselves the agreed value of their labor, or they could convert all that belonged to the owner and use it for their own self-glorification and enrichment, with the owner receiving nothing. It was a simple yet life-changing choice.

Since the owner was not around directing their daily activities, they had only their devotion to him, their gratitude, their sense of stewardship, and their personal integrity as moral guides in their life. Sadly, they chose to glorify themselves and betray the owner, without much thought about the long-term consequences. But there were indeed future consequences for their rebellious stewardship. At the time of harvest, the vineyard owner sent at least three servants to the vineyard to receive the fruit of the harvest. The evil vinedressers beat one, killed one, and stoned the other.

After the first three, then the owner sent "other servants, more than the first," who were also brutally treated, just as were the first ones. If the first group was three and the second group was "more than the first," then logically the second group was at least four in number, if not more, totaling a minimum of seven servants of the owner who were beaten or killed by the evil vinedressers. We do not know the precise number.

Is this a picture of the Old Testament prophets sent by God to Israel who were likewise beaten or killed? The Bible records the heart-breaking experience of rejection of prophets such as Elijah and Jeremiah, but Jesus said, "you killed the prophets," and the specific number is not stated. We do not know the number of prophets who were sent by God to Israel and were beaten or killed in order to silence them.

The parable then takes on a more personal meaning for Jesus because the focus changes from the servants to the owner's son. One would think the vinedressers would not only recognize the relationship of the son to the owner and treat him with the respect and deference the relationship merited, but they did not. Instead, they plotted how they could kill him.

The parable is not unlike the circumstances Jesus faced. The religious leadership in Israel faced a dilemma. Jesus enjoyed widespread popularity and many people thought He must be the long-awaited messiah. But His teaching was totally opposite to what the messiah was expected to say, although His words were supported by many unexplainable miracles that He performed.

If He was indeed the messiah, accepting the new spiritual truth He taught would require each of them to personally repent and experience a life-transforming spiritual conversion akin to a new birth. That would be tantamount to admitting that their historic teaching about God's covenant with Israel, along with all the cherished traditions taught by respected religious elders had not been the full revelation of God's will or His nature. Such a profound change would be difficult for most to experience.

Most of the scribes and Pharisees cherished the respected status enjoyed as righteous pillars of their community. In truth, many of them loved the praise and adulation of men more than they cherished the praise of God (John 12:42-43).

Committing themselves to accepting and following Jesus was simply more than could be done. Those who did believe Jesus was the messiah did so secretly out of fear of being put out of the synagogue by others who did not believe (v. 42). Self-preservation can be a strong motivator of decision making. Their only other option was to kill Jesus and silence Him, and that would require careful planning and coordination with both the chief priests and Roman authorities who directed military and civil control over Israel.

And then the miracle that no one could possibly explain or dismiss occurred—raising Lazarus from the dead. Lazarus was the brother of Mary and Martha, two of Jesus' closest friends. They had sent word for Jesus to come when Lazarus became ill, but Jesus waited until Lazarus died so that He could finally and fully reveal His divine power.

According to Jewish beliefs about death, the soul fully departed the body after three days, and Jesus intentionally waited until the fourth day. By that time, even Martha remarked to Jesus that the odor of bodily decay was obvious. But Jesus called Lazarus to come forth from his tomb, and he walked out alive, leaving observers gripped with amazement and fear.

Now the religious leadership had their backs to the wall—either openly confess Jesus as the messiah or kill him to prevent further belief in Him. To them, there were no other options. The chief priests and Pharisees gathered together and concluded, "If we let Him alone like this, everyone will believe in Him, and the Romans will come and take away both our place and nation" (John 11:48). Once they had agreed on a course of action, "from that day on they plotted to put Him to death" (John 11:53).

Is this the reality that Jesus wove into the parable? Jesus knew the fate that awaited Him, for He plainly said, "The Son of Man is being delivered into the hands of men. And they will kill Him. And after He is killed, He will rise the third day" (Mark 9:31).

A comparison between the attitude of the chief priests and Pharisees and the parable's wicked tenants is fascinating. The priests and Pharisees openly admitted that the best course of action to prevent the Romans from destroying their country if an insurrection occurred was to kill Jesus and silence His followers. It would be a logical strategic move to protect their interests, or so they thought. They were not concerned with His divine truth; rather, self-preservation was their only motivation.

By comparison, the wicked tenants agreed that, even though they had beat, killed, and humiliated the master's servants, now they had an opportunity to kill his son—who was heir to his father's estate—and thereby seize control of all that belonged to the master and use it for their own personal glory. It was a scheme of the devil and doomed to disaster, but they did so anyway.

And therein lies the key to this parable. Unlike many other parables, this one ends with a direct question that is a masterpiece of logic and debate. It is a loaded question, because it forces the listener into a damning corner of admission from which there is no easy escape.

After the vinedressers had killed the vineyard owner's son, Jesus posed this question: "Therefore, when the owner of the vineyard comes, what will he do to those vinedressers?" The trap was being set through sheer logic. The vineyard owner had entrusted the entirety of his vineyard to these vinedressers who callously rejected the stewardship entrusted to them and instead placed a greater priority on their personal profit and interests. Rather than change, they ultimately killed the vineyard owner's son in a cold-hearted effort to use the vineyard owner's estate for their own twisted purposes. These vinedressers betrayed the trust placed in them, killed all the messengers sent to them for correction and reproof, and finally killed the vineyard owner's son rather than humble themselves to the vineyard owner's purpose for them as vinedressers.

Jesus' question is simply this: "If you were the vineyard owner, what would you do to the wicked vinedressers?" No logical person would expect the vineyard owner to do nothing, but what action would he justifiably take? The priests and elders unhesitatingly gave the most obvious answer: "He will destroy those wicked men miserably and lease his vineyard to other vinedressers who will render to him the fruits in their seasons." The debate trap was sprung, and they fell for it.

The clear application of the parable to the actions of Jewish leaders in rejecting their stewardship over the covenant work of God, murdering and stoning prophets who were divinely sent to reprove them, and then plotting the death of Jesus is unmistakable. What, then, would be God's most reasonable and appropriate response?

Jesus answered His own question:

"Did you never read in the Scriptures: 'The stone which the builders rejected has become the chief cornerstone. This was the Lord's doing. And it is marvelous in our eyes.' Therefore, I say to you, the kingdom of God will be taken from you and given to a nation bearing the fruits of it. And whoever falls on this stone will be broken, but on whomever it falls, it will grind him to powder" (vv. 42-44).

What a powerful summation of the parable! The cornerstone is a structure's most basic foundation unit, providing it with strength and permanent stability according to the owner's design and purpose. The scriptures clearly describe Jesus as the cornerstone of God's eternal kingdom, the stability of His covenant of grace, and the purpose for which all things in heaven and on earth have been made. The Gospel of John states, "All things were made through Him, and without Him nothing was made that was made" (John 1:2).

This verse should be carefully and thoughtfully considered in its relationship to this parable, for it is profoundly powerful and all inclusive: "…without Him nothing was made that was made." Literally, everything throughout God's eternal universe was made with the intention of Jesus being the cornerstone of all creation! The sobering question raised by the parable is this: What is the most logical action that God should take toward those who knowingly and intentionally reject the cornerstone of Jesus and try to use God's creation for their own selfish, sinful purposes? What should be the eternal consequences incurred by one who rejects the most basic purpose of God's creation, rejects the promises of the gospel, rejects, and humiliates preachers and prophets sent to them with a message of forgiveness and salvation, and ultimately rejects and crucifies the Son of God?

The answer is likewise found in this verse: Their plans of profit, greed, and self-glorification will fail because of the solid, immovable nature of the cornerstone. In their journey to damnation, they will inevitably fall across the stumbling block of Jesus and His glorious gospel message of salvation through faith in Him. In the judgment of God, when they and all of their devious deeds are brought before God and the weight of the cornerstone of Jesus falls upon them, they will be crushed.

He who has eyes with which to see and ears with which to hear should ponder their individual actions in regard to the sobering promises of this parable.

The Parable of the Fig Tree

> *"Now learn this parable from the fig tree: When its branch has already become tender and puts forth leaves, you know that summer is near. So you also, when you see all these things, know that it is near—at the doors! Assuredly, I say to you, this generation will by no means pass away till all these things take place. Heaven and earth will pass away, but My words will by no means pass away" (Matt. 24:32-35).*

A prophet was given the divine visionary ability to accurately predict the immediate future (forth-tell) as well as long-term developments (foretell), sometimes many years into the future. Not only did he prophetically warn of the future consequences of present attitudes and actions, but he also spent considerable time pleading for immediate change and repentance in order to prevent those consequences from occurring, along with calling for a return to the true worship of God.

Jesus' description of the political, military, and religious climate in Israel in 33 A.D. fell into these prophetic categories. Although, traditionally, the turmoil and cataclysmic events Jesus identified have been ascribed to His second coming, it is more reasonable to view them as relating to both immediate events in Israel and to long-term manifestations of divine power, which have yet to occur.

It is illogical to conclude that the descriptions of events contained in Matthew 24:1-44 all relate to the twenty-first century or beyond. Certainly, the disciples who heard Jesus' remarks would not have assigned them to developments two thousand years in the future. Employing His prophetic gift, Jesus used existing circumstances to forth-tell immediate events and to foretell developments generations into the future.

But the overall importance of this parable focuses on the often-overlooked issue of one's preparation for God's work in both his life and in the world around him, and how keenly he looks for and discovers signs of God's unfolding plan of judgment. In both His reference to the leaves on a fig branch (v. 32) and His earlier reference to eagles soaring over a carcass (v. 28), Jesus emphasized that the watchful servant would be able to discern the meaning of unfolding events and prepare for them.

Even though God's judgment on Israel had powerfully impacted the nation in 722 B.C. when the Assyrians conquered the northern part of Israel and took ten tribal regions captive and in 587 B.C. when Babylon conquered the two southern tribes and destroyed much of Jerusalem, Jesus could foresee developments with the existing Roman occupation of Israel that would be far more disastrous than either of the prior conquests. Hatred of Roman occupiers was deep-seated. In fact, the Zealots were a political group advocating rebellion against Rome, even though the odds of success were slim, and Jesus knew it was only a matter of time until conflict between the Romans and the Zealots would occur. These passages describe Jesus' perception of the inevitable collision between the dominating military power of the Roman Empire and the defiant Jewish resistance movement.

In addition to their devotion to traditional religious ritual, the Jews took great pride in the beauty of the Temple and regarded it as a holy place. As long as the Temple stood and God's Spirit dwelt within the Holy of Holies, they would be safe and prevail, or so they believed. Thus, as Jesus departed the Temple on one occasion, His disciples pointed out the magnificent buildings and marveled at their beauty. Jesus' response shocked them:

> *"Do you not see all these things? Assuredly, I say to you, not one stone shall be left here upon another that shall not be thrown down"* (v. 2).

Jesus then retreated to the nearby Mount of Olives, and His perplexed disciples came to Him seeking an explanation. One must consider they believed that such an event would herald Jesus' manifestation of Himself as the Messiah, and all the power and glory of Israel would finally be restored. More than anything, they wanted to know what to look for so that they would be prepared for the momentous event and not miss any of the incredible developments. They wanted inside information of the time and place so they would be the first to know when the messiah would appear. So, they asked Him:

"...Tell us, when will these things be? And what will be the sign of Your coming, and of the end of the age?" (v. 3).

Jesus' answer was not what they expected. Anticipating a description of observable events that would herald the messiah's appearance, the disciples instead heard Jesus describe horrific developments unlike anything they had experienced:

"And Jesus answered and said to them: 'Take heed that no one deceives you. For many will come in My name, saying, "I am the Christ," and will deceive many. And you will hear of wars and rumors of wars. See that you are not troubled, for all these things must come to pass, but the end is not yet. For nation will rise against nation, and kingdom against kingdom. And there will be famines, pestilence, and earthquakes in various places. All these are the beginning of sorrows. Then they will deliver you up to tribulation and kill you, and you will be hated by all nations for My name's sake. And then many will be offended, will betray one another, and will hate one another. Then many false prophets will rise up and deceive many. And because lawlessness will abound, the love of many will grow cold. But he who endures to the end will be saved. And this gospel of the kingdom will be preached in all the world as a witness to all the nations, and then the end will come." (vv. 4-14).

Notably, when Jesus said, "...and then the end will come," was it more likely He was referring to events within the disciples' lifetime and experience, or to some future developments thousands of years later? Or is it possible He was referring to both? Although future prophetic promises of the Bible are true, a greater scriptural understanding can be found by looking closely at events soon to transpire at that time that provide a more logical and plausible meaning to Jesus' words.

There are some notable examples in these verses: When Jesus said, "Many will come in My name, saying 'I am the Christ,' and will spread deception, He was no doubt referring to so-called prophets who falsely claimed to be the messiah, and even dressed the part. A prophet often wore a distinctive cloak made from sheep's wool (John the Baptist wore a cloak made from camel's hair), but false prophets not only wore the distinctive cloak, but they also acted out the prophetic role only to obtain personal power, prestige, or profit. Jesus referred to them as "wolves in sheep's clothing," and they deceived many innocent people.

There were indeed "wars and rumors of wars" as nations and kingdoms occasionally tried to defy the power of Rome, only to have their efforts crushed. Israel was often the hotbed of defiance as the Zealots sought to start an armed revolt against Roman occupation.

Regarding persecution and tribulation, the disciples began to immediately experience the hostility of Jewish authorities who imprisoned and physically tortured and abused them. The Book of Acts records the imprisonment and beating of several of the apostles (Acts 5:40). In addition, Greeks did not immediately accept Christian theology, viewing the idea of Jesus being God incarnate with skepticism and disbelief. Although the Roman persecution of Christians did not begin immediately, nevertheless, Roman authorities would not have tolerated the idea of a "king" or ruler other than one they authorized. Years later, the Roman persecution of Christians became extreme, even horrendous in many instances.

But, despite all the hardships and adversity, the gospel did spread across Israel, Asia Minor, into Northern Africa, and eventually into Europe. "The gospel of the kingdom" was indeed proclaimed "in all the world as a witness to all the nations."

Jesus said when that occurred, the end would come. Was He speaking about His Second Coming and the end of the world, as we think about it, or was He speaking about events that would occur in the disciples' lifetime that many of them would witness? Jesus not only foresaw the inevitable clash between Jewish Zealots and the Roman army, but He also knew what the outcome would be, and His warning came true.

In 70 A.D., Jewish resistance fighters launched a rebellion against Roman occupation. Rome had long tolerated the peculiar nature of Judaism and allowed the continuation of Jewish religious practices and rituals, as long as they did not interfere with Roman dominance of the region. But this uprising was too much for Rome to tolerate. Not only did Roman soldiers forcefully suppress the insurrection and kill many of the insurrectionists, but in order to permanently eliminate the Jewish threat, the Roman Army destroyed the Temple in Jerusalem, literally tearing it down stone by stone, just as Jesus had predicted. All vestiges of Jewish worship were restricted, and Israel ceased to exist as a country. The end of Israel and the end of traditional Jewish life and worship had come, and the recognized existence of the nation of Israel would not occur again until 1948.

Thus, when Jesus said to them, "When you see the abomination of desolation, spoken of by Daniel the prophet, standing in the holy place...," He was not foretelling some futuristic, distant event. Instead, He was forth telling the immediate possibility of foreign individuals, such as Roman soldiers, entering the Holy of Holies, which was the most sacred place in the Temple where the Spirit of God was believed to dwell with His people, and desecrating the holy Temple.

Jesus gave them these words of warning:

"Therefore, when you see the 'abomination of desolation,' spoken of by Daniel the prophet, standing in the holy place (whoever reads, let him understand), then let those who are in Judea flee to the mountains. Let him who is on the housetop not come down to take anything out of his house. And let him who is in the field not go back to get his clothes. But woe to those who are pregnant and to those with nursing babies in those days! And pray that your flight may not be in winter or on the Sabbath. For then there will be great tribulation, such as has not been seen since the beginning of the world until this time, no, nor ever shall be" (vv. 15-21).

One should note that this warning was addressed to "those who are in Judea," which was the Roman name for the ancient tribal area of Judah around Jerusalem. Jesus admonished them not to be misled and to be prepared:

"Then if anyone says to you, 'Look, here is the Christ!' or 'There!' do not believe it. For false Christ's and false prophets will arise and show great signs and wonders, so as to deceive, if possible, even the elect. See, I have told you beforehand. Therefore, if they say to you, Look, He is in the dessert!' do not go out, or 'Look, He is in the inner rooms!' do not believe it" (vv. 23-26).

Jesus' explanation then shifts to a futuristic emphasis:

"For as the lightning comes from the east and flashes to the west, so also will be the coming of the Son of Man be. For wherever the carcass is, there

the eagles will be gathered together. Immediately after the tribulation of those days, the sun will be darkened, and the moon will not give its light; the stars will fall from heaven, and the powers of the heavens will be shaken. Then the sign of the Son of Man will appear in heaven, and then all the tribes of the earth will mourn, and they will see the Son of Man coming on the clouds of heaven with power and great glory. And He will send His angels with a great sound of a trumpet, and they will gather together His elect from the four winds, from one end of heaven to the other" (vv. 27-31).

With deference and respect to how each person interprets Bible passages, one should realize these verses typify "apocalyptic" descriptions found throughout the Bible. This form of literary expression is often equated with the great "Day of the Lord," as described in Joel 2:31 and Acts 2:20. Developments are marked by cataclysmic upheavals of nature, unexplainable cosmic phenomenon, and revelation of God's heavenly power in unimaginable ways. The imagery is intended to generate awe and wonder, resulting in personal submission and humility. Frankly, it is a style of exaggerated language that is not intended literally. One must study these passages mindful of that concept.

Therefore, if the focus of study is on what is known about Christian history, rather than on what is unknown about Christianity's future, one is able to find an interesting truth in Jesus' prophetic statement. Light is an ancient symbol of God, and that is initially revealed in Jewish history through the pillar of fire that not only guided the Israelites at night during their exodus from Egyptian captivity, but also served as a comforting reassurance of God's presence. The Menorah—the golden seven-candle lamp—in the tabernacle and then the Temple, which constantly gave off light that never dimmed, further symbolized God's presence. The magnitude of divine light became incorporated in Old Testament theology when the Psalmist wrote, "Your word is a lamp to my feet and a light to my path" (Psalm 119:105). This concept of light became reality with the birth of Jesus, who spoke of Himself as the "light of the world" (John 8:12), and then encouraged His disciples to reflect His glory to the world by also referring to them as the "light of the world" (Matt. 5:14).

What inspiring truth is found in Jesus' statement that after the days of tribulation, which the early Christian church certainly experienced, "the lightning will flash from the east to the west"? Historically, the Christian church spread in different directions at first, but centuries later evolved into eastern and western versions of the Christian faith. The westward movement of Christianity had the most profound impact on the world.

Roman persecution of Christians was intense and brutal and is historically well documented. But persecution only made the church thrive and grow. Despite this early antagonism toward the Christian faith, the church expanded and gained such widespread acceptance that in 323 A.D. Emperor Constantine declared Christianity to be the official religion of the Roman Empire. Any student of Western Civilization knows how Christianity thus became the religious and social bedrock of European culture and religion, and ultimately became the most influential religious concept in American history and culture.

Rather than struggling to find some literal meaning in Jesus's apocalyptic statement and arguing over a time chronology for which there is no certainty, one can find meaning in the historical evidence that the light of God's revealed truth in Christ indeed spread from the east to the west. This westward migration of the gospel of Jesus gave us not only Christianity as we know it today, but also the religious, political, and cultural basis of western life.

The New Testament clearly teaches that Jesus will return again in the future, but the date and time of are known only to God. This parable is not intended as a prophesy of the end times, but rather it is another admonition from Jesus for personal preparation for that life-transforming moment when it occurs. Consider the parable along with the theme of other parables: It is similar in meaning to the wise stewards who were watching and waiting for their Master's return, regardless of the time. Jesus emphasized the point of that parable by saying, "Therefore, you also be ready, for the Son of Man is coming at an hour you do not expect" (Luke 12:37-40). Likewise, it is akin to the wise virgins who had oil for their lamps and were personally ready for the Bridegroom's arrival, even if it occurred at midnight. Jesus concluded that parable by saying, "Watch, therefore, for you know neither the day nor the hour in which the son of Man is coming" (Matt. 25:1-13).

The parable of the fig tree encourages each Christian to look at unfolding events around us in a broader way. It is not for Christians to engage in fruitless predictions; rather, it is for us to personally and faithfully prepare. Explore the symbolism closely: When the fig tree of world events starts to put leaves on its branches, then the wise and watchful servant will be personally prepared for the glorious return of Jesus, regardless of the year, day, or hour that it may occur.

The Parable of the Sheep Gate

> *"Most assuredly, I say to you, he who does not enter the sheepfold by the door, but climbs up some other say, the same is a thief and a robber. But he who enters by the door is the shepherd of the sheep. To him the doorkeeper opens, and the sheep hear his voice; and he calls his own sheep by name and leads them out. And when he brings out his own sheep, he goes before them, and the sheep follow him, for they know his voice. Yet they will by no means follow a stranger, but will flee from him, for they do not know the voice of strangers... Most assuredly, I say to you, I am the door of the sheep. All who ever came before Me are thieves and robbers, but the sheep did not hear them. I am the door. If anyone enters by Me, he will be saved, and will go in and out and find pasture. The thief does not come except to steal, and to kill, and to destroy. I have come that they may have life, and that they may have it abundantly. I am the good shepherd. The good shepherd gives his life for the sheep. But he who is a hireling and not the shepherd, one who does not own the sheep, sees the wolf coming and leaves the sheep and flees; and the wolf catches the sheep and scatters them. The hireling flees because he is a hireling and does not care about the sheep. I am the good shepherd, and I know My sheep, and am known by them. As the Father knows Me, even as I know the Father, and I lay down My life for the sheep"* (John 10:1-15).

Religion has always been subject to manipulation by man. The word of God has at times been misinterpreted and misrepresented for both personal and political reasons, and even the merciful teachings of Jesus can become verbal missiles of malice when launched by a misguided malcontent. Jesus devoted Himself to inserting a new understanding of mercy and redeeming love into ancient religious principles that had been turned into callous, cold legalism. He was opposed at every turn by respected religious leaders who considered their interpretation of God's word as final.

Divine truth twisted by the mind of a religious zealot is seldom a good thing. Surprisingly, this is a parable about spiritual discernment and an individual's ability to distinguish between fact and fallacy, between true Christian doctrine and religious demagoguery, and between a true preacher and prophet of God and an opportunistic charlatan. Discernment between truth and error is not always easy, for the appearance of the sheep and the appearance of the wolf in sheep's clothing is nearly identical, and each offers a strong argument that he speaks for God. However, there are key differences: One is right and the other is wrong; one speaks divine truth and the other proclaims contrived falsehoods; and one's voice leads to Jesus and the other's voice often leads to himself.

Discernment of truth is a spiritual gift given to Jesus' faithful servants and disciples. Interestingly, this parable surprisingly sets forth an unusual challenge, because it essentially requires a faithful disciple to think like a sheep, and most Christians never give themselves that discipleship test. As one reads this parable, consider a fascinating truth: If the common sheepfold is visualized as the whole of contemporary Christianity, the central question of the parable is not how the various flocks of sheep got into the common sheepfold, but rather who will lead them out to pasture each day where they can be nourished and mature. Imagine a large flock of sheep in a common enclosure, and each morning the sheep hear the voices of different shepherds calling out to them and asking them to follow his leadership. Thus, you must place yourself in the midst of the bleating sheepfold and hear all the different voices enticingly calling out and offering to lead you along the path they have chosen for you.

In considering these verses, remember that a parable is a literary method of comparing two parallel truths—one physical and the other spiritual—in which the greater spiritual truth is derived from the facts of the physical truth. Thus, this parable's physical setting is a common sheepfold in which multiple flocks, led by different shepherds, are gathered together and protected at night. Each morning, the individual flocks are called out of the sheepfold by their shepherd through hearing and responding to their shepherd's voice.

But, if you learn to think like a sheep, you will know that in the midst of this cacophony of competing voices, only one is the voice of your Good Shepherd—the one you are willing to follow. The spiritual ability to think like a sheep and to hear His call, while ignoring all the rest, will change the thoughts of your heart about your Christian commitment and your individual discipleship.

We live in a common sheepfold of religious beliefs and practices made up of multiple denominations, traditions, and historic beliefs about the interpretation of God's word. Just as the sheep in the sheepfold look the same, many of these beliefs are strikingly similar. Jesus described Himself as the door to the sheepfold, and there is a fascinating truth in that description. Just as all the sheep of various flocks recognize the entrance door to the sheepfold, so do various religious beliefs recognize Jesus as "the way, the truth, and the life." They enter into the common sheepfold of contemporary Christianity by recognition of Jesus as Lord, but their response to the voice of the shepherd they follow can profoundly impact their Christian life and their understanding of the truth of God's word.

Each day a variety of voices call out to Christians and beckon them to "follow me." A shocking cross-section of beliefs is amplified daily by media evangelists calling out to millions of Americans. There are traditional, mainline Christian leaders, but there are also a multitude of "shepherds" who proclaim a form of Christianity at variance with the true teaching of Jesus. Some stress adherence to a form of Old Testament legalism, some stress a "prosperity gospel" in which faith and finances are joint partners, and some would make Christianity a central plank of belief in a political platform, just to name a few.

Christians by the thousands respond to the calls of these various shepherds. But, if the physical sheepfold in the parable is a representation of contemporary Christianity, who are the "thieves and robbers" that Jesus described who would lead the sheep away from the true Shepherd, and how do they succeed? Jesus used the joint phrase "thieves and robbers" to warn His followers about those who would take away spiritual blessings, either covertly or overtly. Thus, He cautioned against laying up treasures on earth where thieves break in and steal, but instead He urged His disciples to lay up treasures in heaven that are beyond their reach.

Maybe that warning gives this parable some additional meaning. "Thieves and robbers" is the description Jesus chose to use to describe the impact on Christians by those who beguile believers into a false belief about Jesus' gospel message. Often this is done through misrepresentation, and it can be subtle and disarmingly effective. A robber uses more direct pressure, though not always physical, including intimidation, condemnation, or haranguing someone to the breaking point. So, if thieves and robbers can physically steal sheep from the sheepfold, then thieves and robbers can spiritually rob a Christian of a true understanding of the gospel of Jesus.

For example, an overtly legalistic view of the gospel will deprive one of a deeper understanding of mercy. Television evangelists who equate faith and personal fortune are misleading millions. Jesus specifically stated that "...one's life does not consist in the abundance of the things he possesses" (Luke 12:15). Nowhere in the gospels does Jesus say that a Christian will get wealthy through being His disciple. Yet, countless people are robbed everyday by these thieves that try to convince them otherwise.

There are robbers all around us that take the teachings of Jesus and attempt to politicize and legalize them, thus forcing others to believe as they do. If one leans in that direction, this truth should be considered: The devil offered Jesus the kingdoms of the world if Jesus would model Himself after Satan by telling lies, misleading innocent people, promising one thing and doing another, and intimidating, coercing, and overpowering those who do not follow, all while pretending to be a model Christian. Jesus totally refused to use those tactics, yet millions of Americans idolize and blindly follow so-called Christian political leaders who do. Be very cautious in believing anyone who proposes to enforce the love of Christ on others by the power of civil law. You may have a spiritual robber in your midst.

The last group—hirelings—are in a separate category. Hirelings are mentioned six times in the Old Testament, but they are described in the New Testament only in this parable. Although Jesus admirably mentions the work of faithful servants in other parables and passages, He places hirelings in a special class of workers for whom He has no respect.

A hireling indeed performs a task. However, it is important to understand that his only motive is money because he is a mercenary. In whatever work that is involved, the only goal is to make as much money as he can for the time and service provided. A hireling has no interest in or commitment to the work he does and is unconcerned about its ultimate success. He is not concerned with the people or property involved. His only focus is how much financial gain he can reap from doing this job. When he has finished and is paid, the hireling moves to the next job without any further thought about what he has just done or who paid him. His only real master is money, and his only motive in life is making as much money as he can.

A hireling shepherd, though he walked like a shepherd, dressed like a shepherd, and talked like a shepherd, had one major personality flaw essential to a shepherd—he did not have a shepherd's heart. He did not personally care one iota about the flock, only payday. He made no personal sacrifice for the flock's benefit, and always protected himself first at any sign of danger.

In truth, Judas is a good example. True, he was one of the disciples, but most of the gospel references to him refer to his obsession with how much money he could make serving Christ. He regularly stole offerings given to Jesus, he complained about Mary wastefully anointing Jesus' feet with fragrant and costly oil of spikenard that could have been sold instead (probably so he could have more funds to embezzle) (John 12:6), and when he finally realized that Jesus was proclaiming a spiritual kingdom, and not an earthly kingdom in which he could greatly profit, he decided to get as much wealth as he could from being a disciple, and he betrayed Jesus for thirty pieces of silver (Matt. 26:15).

Christianity in America is plagued with hirelings who have little or no thought about serving Christ at a personal sacrifice, and instead focus on every possible scheme to convert Christianity into cash. The unmitigated gall of those who get sinfully rich off of contributions they beg from ministry donors is shocking. What God-called servant minister of Christ needs a private jet for flying to different events? Why does a preacher who proclaims the lordship of the One who owned nothing and had no place to lay His head need to extravagantly live in a palatial mansion and drive an expensive luxury car? These false prophets could not care less about the souls of the people to whom they preach, as long as they can get their greedy fingers into their pocketbooks. They are modern-day hirelings...just cold, merciless, calculating hirelings!

If one is to better understand the negative impact of a hireling on Christian beliefs, it is helpful to consider the concept of money and riches, as described by Jesus in the gospels. Wealth was not only considered a divine blessing, but, more importantly, it was also viewed by Jewish society as an indication of righteous favor with God. Thus, earthly riches were eagerly sought, and the wealthy openly flaunted their riches through extravagant living, wearing apparel made from expensive purple linen, and enjoying a sumptuous diet and lifestyle.

This presumption of righteous favor with God led to a merciless condemnation of the poor by the wealthy upper class, who viewed the poor as sinners, because if they were righteous and in God's favor, they would not be poor. The parable of the rich man and the beggar, Lazarus, is a classic example (Luke 16:19-31). The merciless rich man so detested poor Lazarus that he would not give him the bread scraps from his table, and instead allowed Lazarus to starve to death at his front gate.

In openly parading their wealth as proof of God's favor, these false practitioners of religious perfection often stood on street corners to pray, or openly did charitable deeds, not to please God, but rather to earn the compliments and favor of admiring and envious onlookers. When Jesus commented that it was easier for a camel to pass through the eye of a needle than for one of these merciless, self-glorifying rich people to enter the kingdom of heaven, His shocked disciples exclaimed, "...who then can be saved?" (Matt. 19:25).

In stark contrast, Jesus set a standard diametrically opposite to the prevalent attitudes of His day. He owned nothing and He wanted no earthly wealth. Jesus completely changed the concept of riches and righteousness from stressing self-righteous greed to the opposite standard of selfless service to God and others without thought of personal benefit.

Jesus was so committed to such selflessness that He described Himself as a servant of all, and that description merits serious consideration. A servant was usually a household slave who owned nothing and had no rights or interests—and basically no life—other than that bestowed on him by his master. For Jesus, that flowed from His Father in heaven. Jesus emptied Himself of personal desires and became completely "self-less" in His service to God.

Therefore, His life became the eternal balance scale between a Christian life that is selfishly focused on one's own interests and desires versus a life that is totally selfless and is focused on service to God and others, without one thought of self-enrichment. When the scale tips to the side of selflessness, a devoted servant of Christ is found. When the scale tips to the other extreme of self-glorification and self-righteous boasting, a Christian hireling is weighed out. A hireling always looks first for a way to advance his own self-interests in his religious service. He is never "self-less" in his Christian work for Jesus.

Here is a simple three-pronged hireling test: As you carefully and thoughtfully listen to someone's description of their Christian service and ministry, slowly an image will form in your thoughts about them that is painted by their own words. Who does your mind's eye see—them or Jesus? Which personal pronoun rings most frequently in your spiritual ears—I or He? Place their testimony on the balance scale anchored to the gift of discernment given to you by the Holy Spirit. Which way does it tip—selfish or selfless?

If the individual fails one out of three, he may just be a good servant struggling with his ego. If he fails two out of three, listen to your own inner voice of reason and follow your spiritual instinct. If he fails all three, you most likely have a Christian hireling on your hands. Use caution in following him and allowing him to influence and shape your Christian beliefs and values.

Christianity in America is flooded with individuals, groups, and corporate entities whose primary purpose is to profit from our Christian faith. The talent of Christian artists is laudable; however, the Christian industry in America that annually makes hundreds of millions of dollars selling Jesus is troubling.

The selfless image of our Lord, who gave His life to share the gospel without any thought of personal benefit, seems to have been forgotten. The issue is pervasive. Reasonable compensation of Christian workers is expected, but today there are multiple pastors and denominational leaders with six-figure salaries and compensation packages that rival a Wall Street executive. That, too, is troubling.

In this parable, Jesus set forth the ultimate test between the love of the true Good Shepherd for His flock and the self-centered indifference of a hireling. The test is simply one of personal sacrifice for the flock. Consider Jesus' description: The Good Shepherd loves the flock and will lay down His life for them. He does not think about Himself, but His thoughts about and commitment to the welfare of His flock is unconditional and uninterrupted, regardless of the circumstances or the danger. The Good Shepherd's love for His sheep is the ultimate example of sacrificial, selfless love.

In contrast, the hireling has no personal concern for the flock, and he thinks only of his individual welfare, safety, and security. Because of his indifference and lack of sacrificial concern, he cannot be trusted to adequately care for any flock placed in his care. If his area of service becomes upsetting to him, he will leave the flock alone and move elsewhere, having no concern for their vulnerability to predators that would prey upon them. In truth, he could not care less, and he will make no personal sacrifice for them.

According to Jesus' description, when the hireling "sees the wolf coming," he will abandon the flock and flee. It does not matter how distant the wolf may be. Even the thought of the slightest danger or threat to his personal safety and security will make the hireling abandon his responsibility. Ultimately, the flock will become confused and scattered by the wolf, caused by the absence of a caring shepherd. It is heartbreaking how often this same scenario happens in a local congregation of believers.

The Good Shepherd's devotion to His flock is motivated by love and personal sacrifice, but the hireling has no idea what that means. That test was true in Jesus' day, and it remains true today. We are all in the sheepfold of contemporary Christianity. We must steadfastly recommit ourselves to listen for the voice of our Good Shepherd calling us out to His nourishing pasture each day and ignore the calls of thieves, robbers, and hirelings who will do nothing but rob us of our true Christian faith, lead us astray, and then abandon us.

Parable of the Sheep and Goats

> *"When the Son of Man comes in His glory, and all the holy angels with Him, then He will sit on the throne of His glory. All the nations will be gathered before Him, and He will separate them one from another, as a shepherd divides his sheep from the goats. And He will set the sheep on His right hand, but the goats on His left. Then the King will say to those on His right hand, 'Come, you blessed of My Father, inherit the kingdom prepared for you from the foundation of the world: for I was hungry, and you gave Me food; I was thirsty, and you gave Me drink; I was a stranger, and you took Me in; I was naked, and you clothed Me; I was sick and you visited Me; I was in prison and you came to Me.' Then the righteous will answer Him, saying, 'Lord, when did we see you hungry and feed You, or thirsty and give You drink? When did we see You a stranger and take You in, or naked and clothe you? Or when did we see You sick or in prison, and come to You?' And the King will answer and say to them, 'Assuredly, I say to you, inasmuch as you did it to one of the*

least of these My brethren, you did it to Me.' Then He will say to those on the left hand, 'Depart from Me, you cursed, into the everlasting fire prepared for the devil and his angels; for I was hungry, and you gave Me no food; I was thirsty, and you gave Me no drink; I was a stranger, and you did not take Me in, naked and you did not clothe Me, sick and in prison and you did not visit Me.' Then they also will answer Him, saying, 'Lord, when did we see You hungry or thirsty or a stranger or naked or sick or in prison, and did not minister to You' Then He will answer them, saying, 'Assuredly, I say to ou, inasmuch as you did not do it to one of the least of these, you did not do it to Me.' And these will go away into everlasting punishment, but the righteous into eternal life" (Matt. 25:31-46).

Perhaps more than any others, this parable has the capacity to continuously grow in meaning. Jesus' use of a shepherd separating his sheep and goats to demonstrate God's final judgment on mankind is powerfully symbolic; the meaning of those on his right hand and those on His left hand is profoundly deep; the promised inheritance of the righteous is captivating; the merciful basis on which the separation will be made is comforting; and the reality that the separation of the righteous and unrighteous will be done by "the Son of Man" in the fullness of His glory and in the presence of the holy angels is awe inspiring.

One is immediately confronted with the significance of the title "Son of Man." Throughout the gospels, the titles "Son of God" and "Son of Man" are used numerous times to describe Jesus, along with "Son of David." Ancient Jewish belief focused on the messiah being a divinely chosen figure vested with extraordinary power and righteousness. The messiah was expected to rid Israel of her enemies, restore her economic power, and re-create a political and military kingdom akin to that headed centuries earlier by King David. Thus, a popular messianic title was "Son of David," or one whose kingdom would be like King David's.

The phrase "son of" denoted not only a direct biological connection, such as a man's son, but it was also used to describe one whose characteristics and personality epitomized a certain trait, such as Judas being referred to as "the son of perdition."

Jewish messianic hopes did not envision the messiah as the actual son of God, and they certainly did not focus on the messiah being God in human form. In fact, Jesus' references to Himself as the "Son of God" were considered by religious leaders as blasphemous and worthy of death. The messiah was to be the ultimate human leader and figure, manifesting every quality of a divinely gifted person—strong, wise, courageous, righteous, and committed to fulfilling God's will for Israel. Thus, as the ultimate human embodiment of every characteristic of goodness and godliness, the messiah was to truly be "the Son of Man."

But Jesus was uniquely both. He was fully God, and God's only begotten Son, and He was also the ultimate example of a godly man. Thus, only Jesus was both Son of God and Son of Man. More than any other traits, Jesus was the embodiment of divine love and mercy for others, both of which were noticeably absent under the cold, methodical practice of religious law.

Why did not Jesus just say, "I will come in My glory and judge the nations"? Why did He use the Son of Man messianic title to describe His role in judgment? A close reading of the parable yields some clues that are underscored by other words and deeds of Jesus. For example, the gospels record how the suffering plight of the poor was ignored, sinners were unmercifully condemned, and the sick and needy were shunned. The most frequently recorded plea from people in the gospels was "Lord, have mercy on me."

If one is to better understand the basis of judgment between the sheep and goats, then one must focus on the Son of Man's capacity to show love and mercy to those shunned and rejected under the law. Jesus infuriated religious leaders by befriending sinners, and even dining with them. He openly broke the religious law by touching and healing lepers. He defied expectations by refusing to condemn a woman caught in the act of adultery, and instead showed her mercy and understanding. And He pointedly and powerfully used Samaritans—the most hated people in Israel—to make some of His most remarkable statements of divine truth.

The Son of Man title then describes the ultimate example of a truly compassionate, caring, merciful, and kind-hearted man who would love and show mercy to all he encountered, even the lowest in society and the least important person around him—traits that were noticeably absent in both religious and civic leaders under the judgmental law of Israel. Quite understandably, then, through His ministry among the hurting masses in Israel, Jesus gave final and true meaning to the title "Son of Man."

When the Son of Man separates the sheep from the goats, He will look for those in His flock who both experienced and shared the love and mercy of their Good Shepherd with others, even the least among them. It is our sinful human nature to be a goat; but it is our divine nature given to us by the mercy, love, and grace of Christ to be a sheep in His flock. The Son of Man knows which of the two we are.

The meaning of words can change over time according to their usage, especially when they are translated from an ancient language into modern English. As used in this parable, "glory" is a good example. Our concept of glory is not exactly the same as it was in the original Hebrew or the later Greek language. Thus, when we look back at its earlier usage, we can find gems of spiritual truth not readily apparent today.

Interestingly, glory in the Old Testament was used in different ways and had multiple meanings. It was derived from a concept describing weight. When applied to money, for example, it could mean riches, such as the abundance or weight of wealth, or when applied to one's character, it could mean exemplary or radiant. But, when applied to personal wisdom, it usually meant that one was noticeably wise or thoughtful in his judgments and decisions, as he pondered under the weight of the options being considered.

The Greek term for glory, *doxa*, has multiple meanings also, and one of them includes a similar idea of judgment, opinion, or personal honor derived from a good and godly reputation. In terms of rendering judgment, it is how one exemplifies and magnifies good and godly character under the weight of having to make a serious decision. We use a similar concept to describe the weight on someone's shoulders when they are vested with a serious responsibility and have to make major decisions that bring them personal honor and glory.

Thus, in the language of this parable, the phrase "when the Son of Man comes in His glory," denotes the weight of His godly character and the wise and thoughtful decision He will be making. His wisdom, goodness, and merciful consideration of the issue He judges radiates from Him. The matter that the Son of Man will decide is weighty and constitutes a heavy burden and responsibility. God has prepared a heavenly kingdom from the foundation of the world reserved for the redeemed, and the Son of Man must determine those who will inherit that kingdom.

One should consider the weight of this decision. The Apostle Paul stated that, through faith in Jesus, Christians become "joint heirs" with Christ in all of the riches of the heavenly kingdom (Rom. 8:17). Determining who will inherit those eternal blessings and who will not is a heavy decision not easily made.

Jesus stated that He did not come to judge the world, but rather that the world through Him might be saved. His divine purpose was not to condemn, but rather to redeem. However, it is the responsibility of the Son of Man to make a final and fateful decision regarding those who believed in Him and those who did not, and thus Jesus said, "For judgment I have come into this world" (John 9:39). In other words, this fateful moment of judgment was inevitably destined by the demands of His teaching and preaching. Therefore, His greatest and most important decision will be determining and judging between those redeemed through faith in Him and those who have rejected Him, or, in the imagery of the parable, to separate the sheep of His flock from the goats.

There is no other person in human history more qualified to make this judgment. As the Son of God, Jesus will use all of His divine characteristics of love, mercy, and grace in making His decision. Equally, as the Son of Man, He will embody the wisdom and judicious insight granted to Him by God as the ultimate personification of human goodness. Our fate rests in the hands of the only One who was fully God and fully man. In making this judgment, the Son of Man will execute righteousness on the Earth, and He will radiate the holiness and goodness of God's redemptive purpose for mankind. God will be glorified in the final judgment made by the Son of Man.

The parable begins with a perplexing comment about the Son of Man bringing multitudes of angels to assist in separating the redeemed from the unrepentant, or the sheep from the goats. What will be their role in the judgment process? The answer is not specified in the parable, but a general understanding of the role of angels sheds some interesting insights. Angels are special spiritual creatures with specific functions within the heavenly realm. In general, they maintain a continuous atmosphere of praise and adoration. Some have served as herald angels and delivered divine announcements or proclamations on earth, such as the birth of Jesus. Legions of warrior angels would have come to Jesus' side had He beckoned them. And there are angels who serve as ministering spirits to assist us, just as those who ministered to Jesus after He was tempted by the devil.

Psalm 91:11 promises that God has given His angels charge concerning us so that they may guard and keep us in all our ways. Unseen angels care for us and provide protection in ways we do not always recognize, even though we refer to them as our Guardian Angel. But the most intriguing verse about angels, and one that may be at the heart of the angelic role in separating the sheep from the goats, is Hebrews 13:2, which states, "Do not forget to entertain strangers, for by so doing some have unwittingly entertained angels." That verse merits serious consideration and further comment.

The Bible also states in Hebrews 12:1, after describing the heroes of faith, that we are "surrounded by so great a cloud of witnesses...." The witnesses, however, are not specifically defined. They could include deceased faithful servants, but they could also include angels who are observing our actions and merciful attitudes toward others, including total strangers.

The judgment of who is a sheep and who is a goat focuses on acts of mercy either done or not done for those who are hungry, thirsty, and needy. What if some of those hungry, hurting souls were actually angels who will bear witness to the Son of Man about our words, deeds, and attitudes toward those in need of our love, compassion, and mercy? What if we unknowingly meet and relate to angels in our everyday walk of Christian life whose purpose is to test our level of discipleship and who will eventually testify as a witness to the Son of Man, either for us or against us, regarding our actions and attitude toward them, as the Son of Man judges whether we are a sheep or a goat? That thought should make every Christian read afresh the beatitude that states, "Blessed are the merciful, for they shall obtain mercy" (Matt. 5:7).

Goats are unlike sheep in many ways. They are independent minded, somewhat smelly, harder to control than sheep, prone to drift away from a pasture and forage on weeds, difficult to control and seemingly always looking for a means to escape confinement. Goats can quickly frustrate a shepherd far more than a sheep.

If this parable is to grow in meaning, one should visualize how many people act in a similar way toward God—defiant, headstrong, refusing any moral or spiritual restraint, looking for ways to escape His sovereignty and control, refusing to partake of the spiritual nourishment of His word and choosing instead to feast on the moral garbage of a worldly life.

From a shepherd's perspective, it is understandable that goats are used in this parable as the object of divine scorn. Interestingly, even though the devil is not described physically in scripture, early Christian art and writings often portrayed him as having goat-like characteristics.

Conversely, sheep tend to be more docile, and they trust their shepherd's care and leadership. Sheep desire the nourishment of the green pastures provided by their shepherd and remain together as a flock, while relying on him for protection. The sheep within a shepherd's flock seem to sense their shepherd's love for them and will follow the sound of his voice calling them. Thus, the Psalmist used the example of trusting sheep when he poetically declared, "The Lord is my shepherd; I shall not want. He makes me to lie down in green pastures; He leads me beside the still waters. He restores my soul; He leads me in the paths of righteousness for His name's sake..." (Psalm 23:1-3).

It is important to note the spiritual basis in the parable on which the separation is made. Throughout Jesus' ministry, He demonstrated mercy and compassion toward those hurt and scorned by the rigid coldness of religious law. When the Son of Man separated the sheep from the goats in the parable, it was because the goats on His left hand had shown no interest in following His merciful leadership. Rather than following their shepherd to green pastures and still waters of faith, they rebelled and chose instead to eat the briars, brambles, and bitter weeds of sin. And if there was a vineyard nearby, the goats probably found a way into the vineyard and destroyed all the grapevines.

Why did the Son of Man place the goats at His left hand and the sheep at His right hand? Interestingly, the left hand has historically been viewed differently than the right hand. Probably because most people are right-handed, the right hand is used as a metaphorical description for a variety of relationships and situations. For example, an indispensable assistant worker is often referred to as one's "right hand man." Viewed as an extension of one's trustworthy character, the right hand is raised when taking an oath. Friendship, loyalty, and commitment to an agreement are expressed by a right-handed handshake with another.

The Son of Man reflects these attitudes in the parable when He places the sheep at His right hand and the goats at His left hand. This involves far more than just placement in a position. In fact, for Christians, it is one of the most amazing aspects of this parable and one of the greatest promises of spiritual blessings in the gospels.

An ancient concept held that the right hand is a total extension of an individual's personality and power. Therefore, when the Son of Man places the obedient sheep, which hear His voice and follow Him, at His right hand, He is strategically placing them in a position to receive the fullness of His love, mercy, and grace into their lives.

By extending the parable's truth to our Christian life, the redeemed of Christ sit at His right hand and receive unto themselves the fullness of the life of Jesus. Every Christian life becomes an extension of Jesus' life in the world.

But there's more. The Bible states in Mark 16:19 that "...after the Lord had spoken to them, He was received up into heaven, and sat down at the right hand of God." Pause for a moment and consider the incredible depth and meaning of that verse as it relates to this parable and to one's Christian life. Every sheep of His flock is at the right hand of Jesus, and Jesus is at the right hand of God, and all the power and might of God flows through Jesus into those redeemed by faith who sit at Jesus' right hand.

However, that's not the limit of the blessings bestowed on His redeemed flock. Romans 8:34 states that Jesus sits at the right hand of God and makes intercession for us. What an amazing promise of love and grace! Not only is Jesus our merciful Lord and Savior, but He is our eternal advocate who assures our salvation, defends our faith in Him, and secures the fullness of the riches of heaven for us, because those at His right hand are a joint heir with Him, and the riches of the heavenly kingdom that belong to Jesus flow through His right hand into us!

That is the power and promise of the resurrection of Jesus expressed through His new covenant with believers. A covenant is the basis of an unbreakable relationship between two individuals who so totally give their life to each other that they become one—one mind, one spirit, one body, and one love. Each lives through the other. That is what Christianity is all about. We live a dynamic Christian life because God fully placed His life in Jesus and Jesus fully places His life in those blessed sheep of His flock that are placed at His right hand.

Sadly, there is no such relationship for the defiant, hard-headed goats that are placed at His left hand.

The New Testament clearly teaches that salvation is by faith and belief in Jesus as Lord and Savior. The Apostle Paul expressed it very simply in Romans 10:9, "...if you confess with your mouth the Lord Jesus and believe in your heart that God raised Him from the dead, you will be saved." But with faith comes the responsibility of discipleship and service to God and our fellowman. It is not salvation by works, but rather a demonstration of our faith through our work for Christ. But what type of spiritual conduct best demonstrates one's commitment to Jesus? The gospels provide an answer in two different places.

When John the Baptist was in prison and facing execution, he sent messengers to Jesus asking, "Are You the Coming One, or do we look for another?" Jesus replied to the question, "Go and tell John the things you have seen and heard that the blind see, the lame walk, the lepers are cleansed, the deaf hear, the dead are raised, the poor have the gospel preached to them" (Matt. 11:3-5). Rather than simply saying, "Yes," Jesus' answer to John affirmed a level of mercy so unheard of in Israel that only the Messiah would do it.

Thus, when the Son of Man separated the sheep and goats, He applied a similar test to their individual work and spiritual service. Why? Why wouldn't He just look at their level of faith? Jesus' words give us the answer. As He journeyed through Israel teaching and preaching, Jesus was asked which of the commandments was the greatest, and He replied, "You shall love the Lord your God with all your heart, with all your soul, and with all your mind. That is the first and great commandment. And the second is like it: You shall love your neighbor as yourself. On these two commandments hang all the Law and the Prophets" (Matt. 22:35-40). The word "hang" denotes a peg driven into a wall on which weighty items are hung. If the peg fails, all that it supports crashes down.

One should carefully consider the depth of Jesus' answer. At that time, there was not a New Testament, and the only concept of religion was contained in the religious law and the writings of the prophets, what we today call the Old Testament. Jesus declared a shocking and almost unbelievable new religious standard: If people did not love God supremely, and if they did not love and care for others—even the least among them—with a level of mercy and compassion they desired for their own self, then the whole idea of a covenant with God would fail and come crashing down. That is why Jesus established a new covenant with God based on redeeming love and not religious law.

Jesus came to fulfill the spiritual and merciful meaning of the law and the prophets, and not to destroy them. Therefore, the peg standard still holds true today. Without an overriding love for God and a merciful love for others, our whole concept of Christianity, our concept of America as a Christian nation, and even our concept of ourselves comes crashing down, if the peg breaks. Through His life and ministry, Jesus provided an example of how to keep the peg from breaking, and that was the basis of His response to John the Baptist.

What happened when that standard of merciful love for others was applied to the sheep and goats? In the New Testament, the ancient Greek word for mercy is derived from the name of the Greek god (or goddess) Eleos, who was believed to be the ultimate personification of compassion, pity, and mercy. In the mythology of the day, Eleos bestowed compassion on all who came to her, she provided care and succor to the needy, and her sense of mercy was shown to all without condition or qualification.

Understandably, when the ancient Hebrew concept of God's compassion, benevolence, longsuffering, and mercy was translated into the Greek language, the word *eleos* was used to describe divine mercy. It essentially means the highest level of compassion, pity, and charity shown by one person to another. *Eleos* conveys the idea of a god-like capacity of mercy so basic to one's personality that it comes naturally to them. It is neither pretentious nor a hypocritical religious display.

One may think of it in this manner: Mercy is the deepest characteristic of God, as He broods over the plight of man. When God's nature is vested in a Christian through covenant faith in Jesus, mercy likewise becomes the deepest characteristic of a Christian's character as he broods over the plight of his fellowman. Mercy flows unabated from the heart and soul of a Christian. It is who he is and what he does. He cannot help it. It is done because of his relationship with his merciful God, and not for self-glorification.

When the Son of Man separated the sheep from the goats, it was based on the level of mercy that naturally flowed from them toward others. The Son of Man specifically described the opportunities both had to feed the hungry, provide drink to the thirsty, assist a stranger, provide clothing to those in rags and virtually naked, assist those who were sick, and visit and help those hopelessly confined in prison.

The response from those on His right hand and those on His left hand was diametrically opposite. Those at the right hand of the Son of Man—those into whom all the mercy of God naturally flowed—had no recollection of helping anyone in either of those categories in order to gain the Son of Man's blessing. Why? Because divine mercy for others came naturally to them without even thinking about their actions.

"When did we do this?" they asked, and the Son of Man replied, "inasmuch as you did it unto one of the least of these My brethren, you did it to Me." That phrase can be more meaningfully understood as "the least and most insignificant thing you did to help one of My brethren." But, because it was such a part of their merciful personality, they had forgotten all about it.

In contrast, those on the left hand were stumped at the Son of Man's statement. "When did we not do this?" they asked. The Son of Man pointedly summarized their uncaring and unmerciful actions, in effect saying to them, "You saw hungry, hurting, sick people all around you every day. You saw people homeless, desperate, wearing nothing but rags, strangers who had nowhere to go and no one to help them. Yet, in all of your religious pretense about being merciful, you never did even the smallest thing to help one of My brethren. Nothing. You saw the opportunities all around you, but you had no compassion on them whatsoever. You simply did not care."

Thus, the Son of Man placed the merciful sheep at His right hand and the unmerciful goats at His left hand. Because their actions toward others had been so totally opposite, how the Son of Man treated the sheep and goats was also totally opposite.

The greatest spiritual treasure of this parable is the kingdom inherited by those at the Son of Man's right hand. The magnitude of the inheritance is vast in size, eternal in nature, and incomprehensible in human understanding. It is the ultimate and final gift of God to those redeemed by faith in Jesus, yet a divine blessing that many Christians seldom fully consider.

Interestingly, an ancient practice in allocating an ownership interest in one's estate to his heirs was by the casting of lots. Whatever method was used, it was essentially a random drawing that determined each heir's inheritance. That gradually changed to specific designations of property to specified heirs, but the old terminology was retained somewhat. The portion given to an individual heir was his "allotment" of the estate.

Thus, when one considers the inheritance of those at the Son of Man's right hand, the nature of the estate must first be considered and, secondly, the portion of the estate being allotted to those redeemed by faith in Jesus. The Bible describes the estate as a heavenly kingdom without a specified beginning and having no end. It is as old as God and will exist forever, even as God will. The writer of Proverbs, which is a book of divine wisdom, personifies wisdom by saying, "I have been established from everlasting. From the beginning, before there was ever an earth" (Prov. 8:23). The Gospel of John refers to the nature of Jesus as "the Word," and states that "In the beginning was the Word, and the Word was with God and the Word was God... All things were made through Him, and without Him nothing was made that was made...and the Word became flesh and dwelt among us, and we beheld His glory..." (John 1:1,3,14). Thus, the Son of Man promises those faithful followers at His right hand, whom He refers to as "you blessed of My Father," that they will inherit a kingdom prepared for them "from the foundation of the world."

What will be the size of the portion allotted to them as their inheritance? It will not be just a portion; it will be all of it. The Apostle Paul stated in his letter to the Christians in Rome that we are a "joint heir" with Jesus to all the blessings of the heavenly realm.

To better understand our inheritance, one must realize two great truths about Christianity: God reveals Himself in the Bible as Creator God and Redeemer God. His ultimate purpose as creator was the creation of a perfect, pure, heavenly paradise inhabited by the angels and by those redeemed by Jesus, our blessed Redeemer. As the Son of God and the Son of Man (fully God and fully Man) this kingdom belongs to Jesus—and to those to whom He gives His kingdom as their allotted inheritance and as a gift of grace.

The concepts of Christianity, such as spiritual rebirth, redemption, and sanctification, are not just religious phraseology. Considered in personal terms, they are the essential steps in making each Christian an heir to the kingdom. If you are reborn spiritually and re-created in Jesus' image and likeness, and if you share His life jointly with Him through His new covenant, then you will also jointly share His kingdom with Him. His heavenly kingdom was made for Him and for those spiritually recreated in His image to be like Him. The writer of I John specifically states that, "...when He is revealed, we shall be like Him..." (I John 3:2). The most amazing truth that one can personally fathom is that God created the kingdom of heaven to be jointly shared by Jesus and you! How much of His kingdom does he then allocate as an inheritance to those at the Son of Man's right hand? All of it! A joint heir inherits all of the heavenly estate, as do other joint heirs.

Heaven is not a subdivision with each heir receiving a few square feet. Every redeemed heir sitting at the Son of Man's right hand is an eternal co-owner through inheritance, along with Jesus, to all of the heavenly kingdom that God specially created before He laid the foundation of the world. If you are sitting at the right hand of the Son of Man, you will not inherit just a little portion of heaven, you will inherit all of it, and it will be your guaranteed possession for all of eternity.

Just as the life and expression of merciful obedience by the goats at His left hand was different, so, too, will their eternal fate be different. They have no inheritance or reward. Instead, the goats are sent away into everlasting punishment. Suffice it to say, the fate of the rebellious goats will be exactly opposite to that of the sheep, and it can only be described as a nightmarish, hellish fate, one that any wise and prudent person would want to avoid.

Conclusion

Deeply held moral values and spiritual beliefs that shape one's character and provide a foundation for life are formed over time through commitment rather than compulsion. Law can prevent bad behavior, but neither religious nor social law can compel moral goodness. No amount of divine admonition can force one against his will to love God with all his heart, soul, and mind and his neighbor as himself, but when he seriously ponders and accepts these words of Jesus, "A new commandment I give to you, that you love one another; as I have loved you, that you also love one another. By this all will know that you are My disciples, if you have love for one another," then his attitude toward God and his fellowman will change because the thoughts of his heart will be permanently altered by divine truth.

A Christian chooses to be a Christian: He cannot be compelled by religious law to be a disciple of Christ. If one believes that he can be scared from the consequences of judgment and damnation through fear of God, then that is all that concerns him, and he will advance no further in his spiritual growth. He will seldom become a good and faithful servant of Christ through mature discipleship and true spiritual love and commitment.

The fundamental difference between the Old Testament and the New Testament is the transition from religious law to redeeming love. It is a personal spiritual change in worship and service to God from a binding obligation to a blissful opportunity. Under the old covenant, one was compelled to worship God and follow all of the established religious ritual. Righteousness was a matter of self-attainment through obedience and compliance. One's hands may have been ceremonially clean through daily religious washing, but the thoughts of his heart were never cleansed. The acts of clean hands do not translate into the attitudes of a clean heart, which Jesus said was the true source of spiritual defilement.

Under the new covenant, however, righteousness is a free gift of grace given by God to a Christian as a result of one's faith in Jesus. The words of Jeremiah, the prophet, have been fulfilled, "…I will put my law in their minds, and write it on their hearts; and I will be their God and they shall be My people" (Jer. 31:33). Through the new covenant of faith, religion has been transformed from meaningless, memorized ritual to dynamic discipleship inspired by the word of God living in one's heart and motivating both transformed attitudes and actions.

Jesus' parables powerfully impact a Christian's choice to serve Jesus as a good and faithful servant. The parables inspire unwavering commitment, personal humility, gratitude for the unmerited blessings of divine grace, a deeper love for God and one's fellowman, gratitude and praise for God's mercy, and a rational preparation for God's judgment.

The decision to become a Christian begins a life-long growth in discipleship. The thoughts of our heart fuel the work of our hands, and the parables of Jesus change the thoughts of our heart. Our work, as His devoted disciples who glorify Christ in all aspects of our life, then follows.

www.ingramcontent.com/pod-product-compliance
Lightning Source LLC
Chambersburg PA
CBHW071427070526
44578CB00001B/25